Pass the Sugar

Pass the Sugar

JOE HACHEM
with Peter Ralph

M
MELBOURNE BOOKS

Published by Melbourne Books
Level 9, 100 Collins Street,
Melbourne, VIC, 3000
Australia

www.melbournebooks.com.au
info@melbournebooks.com.au

Cover design: Design By Pidgeon
Printed in Australia by Trojan Press

National Library of Australia
Cataloguing-in-Publication entry
Author: Hachem, Joe.
Title: Pass the sugar / Joe Hachem with Peter Ralph.
ISBN: 9781877096730 (pbk.)
Subjects: Hachem, Joe.
Poker.
Poker players–Biography.
Poker players–Tournaments–Nevada–Las Vegas.
Other Authors/Contributors: Ralph, Peter.
Dewey Number: 795.412092

To my wife Jeanie, whose courage and faith
have been the backbone of our success.

To Anthony, Justine, Daniel and James, my
wonderful children, whom I cannot breathe without.
Thank you, thank you, thank you.

And in memory of Uncle Vince, I hope
I continue to make you proud.
You are the reason I am who I am.

Preface

Firstly, I would like to say it is an honor to be writing this piece for my good friend Joe.

I have been lucky in my life to have met some amazing people from all different walks of life, but sometimes, someone stands out and it can be for a range of reasons, some good and some bad.

Joe and I hit it off when we first met in early 2007 and have formed a great friendship and respect for each other. Our families and children have also become friends.

Joe's calmness and sense of family struck me straight away, and over time I have realized how strongly he holds to his values.

There is no hidden agenda with Joe — what you see is what you get — and I really respect that. Joe is also a very loyal and caring person who puts others first ... well, unless it's on the green felt with cards in his hand. Then, and only then, he is happy to eat you up and spit you out.

Don't be fooled by the laid-back, friendly, warm facade you get when it comes to the poker table; Joe is very, very competitive. Whether he's playing a home game or the World Series of Poker, he wants to win.

I think his determination, passion and never-give-up attitude is why he is a World Champion. Joe is always trying to improve and is never satisfied with just being good. He wants to be the best. This attitude is why he is a fierce competitor at the table.

Away from the table, Joe loves nothing better than a round of golf or a hit of the tennis ball with his friends. He also cooks up a mean barbecue.

This book is a wonderful read. It is a very open account of Joe's story and his honesty really shines through. I'm sure while reading this book you will ride the journey with him and it will keep you entertained the whole way — it may even surprise you, too, at times. It's a great story about a wonderful man who has reached the top and lived his dream with his feet firmly still stuck on the ground.

On top of his many accomplishments, Joe has also become the Australian patron of the Shane Warne Foundation, which supports seriously ill and underprivileged children — a great cause that Joe has generously donated a lot of his time towards. The Joe Hachem & Shane Warne Charity Poker Event is the biggest charity poker event in Australia and has been a huge success.

Since retiring from cricket and taking up tournament poker, I have been very lucky to have a mentor like Joe; he has been an awesome and very patient teacher. Let's keep it to that, hey!

To Joe, Jeanie, Anthony, Daniel, James and Justine, I wish you guys all the happiness in the world for now and in the future.

Keep spinning.
Shane Warne

Foreword

Although I didn't know his name, I first met Joe while we were both on the TV table on Day Five of the 2005 Main Event. I had been on the TV table all day, and when we busted the player in seat nine, this quiet, dark-haired man with a medium stack moved into the empty seat. Of course, if you want to be a top player, the first thing you do when facing a new opponent is to try and figure him out. Unfortunately, I couldn't figure out too much. The new guy wasn't playing many hands and was mostly folding pre-flop. When he did play a hand, he usually came in for a raise, but since he was coming in so rarely he was usually able to take down the blinds and antes uncontested. It's not the best thing to have an opponent you don't really know, but in this case I didn't mind, because his absence from most of my pots meant I didn't have to worry about him.

Finally, I play a hand against him where I raise his blind and he calls. I have a big pair but not aces. The flop comes with an ace and I make a continuation bet. He raises me, and after agonizing for a bit, I fold. My radar is telling me that I have the best hand, but my logical analysis says that this guy is tight and you have to give him credit for a big hand if he is only going to play a few of them. So, eventually, I fold and pretty much forget about the hand. Months later, after Joe and I have become good friends, he brings up this hand, and says he sensed I didn't like the ace on

9

the flop, and that he was bluffing when he raised me. My radar had been right, but it didn't matter because Joe still had the chips; he was able to take advantage of his tight image and steal that pot from me. When I heard he had bluffed me, this was the moment I knew that my friend Joe was a real player.

Since that time, we have all learned that Joe wasn't some lucky amateur who won the world's biggest poker event and the title of World Champion just because he came good at the right time. Of course he got lucky that week. So did I during my week in 2004. However, even though Joe was almost unknown before his big win, he was a skilled player who played great poker and got a little lucky in the most important week of his life. Since that big week, Joe has done extremely well playing the tournament circuit full-time. He has made several final tables in other big events, including World Series of Poker circuit events, WSOP bracelet events, and has even won another $2.2 million and the title of Doyle Brunson North American Poker Classic Champion. And in case you're not already jealous enough, he always does well in the cash games to boot.

Despite all his success and talent, what really makes Joe shine has nothing to do with poker. What matters most about Joe is his natural talent for being a good guy, a great friend and a family man. Although I first met Joe at that TV table, at that time he was just another opponent and not even one with whom I had had a real conversation. However, after Joe won at about 7am Las Vegas time on the morning after the final table began and finished up his immediate obligations with interviews, he got my phone number and called me up to ask if we could meet for lunch the next day. You see, Joe wanted to talk to me, as the outgoing Champion, and get my advice. And he wasn't looking for personal advice, such as which agent to hire or what to do with his newly acquired $7.5 million. Joe was looking for advice on how to be a great champion and how to be the best ambassador he could be for poker worldwide. I had just finished in 25th place a couple of days earlier, and was still stinging from the cruel river card that Aaron Kanter needed, which crippled my stack. Yet after meeting with Joe and his wonderful brother Tony, I was in a better mood. I learned that if I wasn't going to pull off a miracle and repeat as World Champion, at least we had a new champion, and one who cared about the game and about improving its reputation in the public eye.

That was when I first knew for certain that we had gotten the right guy to be the 2005 World Champion. Since then, Joe and I have become great friends. The only reason we don't hang out more often is because we're living halfway around the world from each other, and we are both so busy traveling that we seldom have time for anything other than our careers and our families. Yet every time we are at the same event we always look forward to having a meal together and, better yet, a round of golf.

Of course, you the reader probably aren't in a position to have a meal with Joe, or to play 18 holes with him. However, with this book you can at least get a sense of the man and learn some of his poker wisdom. I hope you enjoy the book as much as I have, and that it lets you better appreciate the quality of the author. If you get a chance to get to know him as I have, you are going to love him as a friend for life.

Regards,
Greg Raymer
WSOP Main Event Champion 2004

Introduction

In 1970 the colorful owner of the Horseshoe Casino, Benny Binion, created the World Series of Poker (WSOP) by inviting six of his mates to compete and then vote on who was the best player. So it was that Johnny Moss became the first World Champion of No-Limit Texas Hold 'em. The following year the present format was established, in which participants stumped up $10,000 and played until one person had all the chips. Johnny Moss repeated his earlier win, again defeating six opponents, this time collecting the princely sum of $30,000. At the time who could have imagined that there would be 5619 entrants in the 2005 Main Event and that the winner would walk away with the richest prize in world sport — US$7.5 million.

'The Horseshoe, of course, is gonzo enough on its own,' wrote James McManus in *Positively Fifth Street* about his journey to the final table of the Main Event in the 2000 WSOP. 'Lewd, gaudy, infamous — people get whacked around here when things don't go right at the tables. Killers have hosted and won the World Series; so have hipsters and cowboys, Vietnamese boat people and Irish carpet manufacturers. Benny's aura of violence still permeates the game his family has helped make respectable: No-Limit Texas Hold 'em, the game we're all out here to play.'

Perhaps the most famous winner was the legendary Stuey Ungar who, in 1980 as a 27-year-old, defeated the man who wrote the bible of poker, *Super/System*, Doyle Brunson, a living legend and two-time Main Event winner himself. Stuey would again win the title the following year and then, after battling drugs for 16 years, return to win a third championship in 1997. Sadly, in 1998, at the still relatively young age of 45, he was found dead in a hotel room, the official cause of death being coronary atherosclerosis. Despite this, drugs were found in his blood including percodan, cocaine and methadone in small amounts.

The most famous player not to win the Main Event is T. J. Cloutier who has twice been runner-up and has won more tournaments than any other player in the world. T. J. has been playing poker for over 40 years in every environment from dingy back rooms with known criminals and killers to the tournaments promoted by the plush Vegas casinos. While he is yet to win the Main Event, many winners have studied his books, particularly *Championship No-Limit & Pot-Limit Hold 'Em*, written with Tom McEvoy.

The winner of the 2005 Main Event would later say that he had read *Championship No-Limit & Pot-Limit Hold 'Em* more than a dozen times, virtually memorizing it. He's not a killer, hipster, cowboy, Vietnamese boat person or an Irish carpet manufacturer, but a Lebanese-born Aussie who had many of his mates travel the 8000 miles from Melbourne to Las Vegas just to support him. This is the story of Joe Hachem, his pilgrimage to Vegas and his ultimate victory.

This is not a tale of violence or cheating, but the story of a man who suffered adversity through no fault of his own and lost the professional practice that he'd devoted his life to. A really bad beat that would subsequently prove to be the ultimate good beat.

Like many of his predecessors, Joe is tough, a toughness built around becoming the family bread-winner at a very tender age, a toughness that came with having to deal with double tragedies early in his life, a toughness expressed by a fierce desire to win and succeed. Despite this, Joe is extremely generous with his family and friends, and his personality and ego have not been affected by his outstanding success on the green felt.

Joe Hachem, devoted husband, family man and all-round good guy was the epitome of grace, class and dignity in winning the last Main Event ever played at its birthplace, the Horseshoe Casino. In many ways, his victory reflected how far poker has come since the first Main Event was played at the Horseshoe 35 years earlier. He plays in the best intersts of the game and is a credit to himself and Poker in Australia and around the world.

Maurie Pears
Chairman, Australian Poker Hall of Fame

Glossary of Terms

Ace high A poker hand with no ranked cards (pair, flush, etc.) but with an ace as the high card. This hand beats all other unranked hands.

Action An opportunity to act. Betting, raising and calling are all called 'action'. A poker game with a lot of 'action' is a game in which there is a lot of money in play.

Aggressive 'Aggressive play' is a forceful, often intimidating style of play that incorporates a lot of betting and raising.

All-in In No-Limit Texas Hold 'em, a player may describe himself as 'all-in', which means that he has bet all of his chips into the pot.

Angle shooter A player attempting to win extra money with questionable or dishonest tactics.

Ante A small compulsory bet that all players must post before the hand starts. Usually comes into effect in the later stages of a Hold 'em tournament.

APPT Asia Pacific Poker Tour

Bad beat A bad beat is a loss in which the losing player had the better odds on the winning player earlier in the hand. In general, the term is used when all the chips go into the pot when the losing player had the best odds to win the pot. To take a bad beat means to be on the losing end of a bad beat; to lay a bad beat means to be on the winning end of a bad beat.

Bankroll The money that a person has specifically set aside for playing poker.

Belly buster straight draw Straight draw in which you need one specific card and only one card. For example, if you have J-Q and the flop comes 8-9-4, you need a ten and only a ten to make your straight. Also called a gut-shot draw or inside straight draw.

Bet To put chips into the pot. Other players must call your bet, raise your bet, or fold.

Big blind The larger of two forced pre-flop bets. The player to the left of the small blind posts the big blind. Blinds ensure there is always money in the pot and action occurs on every hand.

Blank A community card that doesn't affect the standing of any player's hand.

Blinds In Hold 'em, these are the forced bets that take the place of an ante. The player on the left of the dealer must pay the small blind and the person after him must pay the big blind.

Bluff To make a bet when you know you have a weak hand. When you have a weak hand and bet, you're hoping that you won't be called by your opponents. The aim of a bluff is to 'buy' a pot because everyone else folds.

Board The community cards in a Hold 'em game — the flop, turn and river cards together.

Boat A full house, also known as a 'full boat'.

Bubble The critical point in a tournament where only one more player must bust out before all the remaining players become entitled to win a share of the prize pool.

Burn To discard the top card from the deck, face down.

Button The seat occupied by the dealer marked by a small disc to indicate the nominal dealer. After the flop, the 'button' is the last person to act in a round of betting.

Buy-in The amount of money you must pay to enter a tournament.

Call To put an amount of money into the pot equal to the last bet or raise in order to stay in the action.

Calling station A player with a tendency to call too many bets.

Chat Conversation you have with other players online.

Check To opt not to bet in that round while retaining the option to call or raise later in the round.

Check-raise To check and then follow with a raise after a player bets from a position behind you.

Chop the pot To split, if at the showdown two players have the same hand the pot is chopped, or split between them. In poker games where blinds are posted, everyone may fold around to the big and small blinds, who might agree to 'chop', which means they simply take their blinds back and move onto a fresh hand.

Connectors Two consecutive hole cards such as 9-10, J-Q, etc.

Continuation bet A bet that continues your pre-flop aggression. It is designed to knock out your opponents who would normally check and see the turn, but it costs you little enough so you can get away from it if someone raises and you estimate they're ahead of you.

Cutoff The table position to the right of the button.

Dead money Money contributed to a pot by a player who has folded out of the pot by the end of the action.

Double belly buster straight draw A run of five cards such as 7-9-10-J-K with two gaps, either of which can be filled to make a straight. Gives you the same eight outs as an open-ended straight draw.

Draw To play hole cards that could win if the right cards are hit.

EPT European Poker Tour

Fade To avoid a card. If your opponent goes all-in after the flop and needs, say, a ten to make his hand, you need to fade it.

Fifth street Also known as the 'river', it is the fifth and final community card.

Fish A weak player or beginner who throws his money all over the table.

Flat call To call when one would be expected to raise or re-raise.

Flop The first three community cards dealt simultaneously in Texas Hold 'em.

Fourth street Also known as the 'turn', it is the fourth of the community cards.

Freeroll Also used to describe a tournament with no entry fee. Many internet poker sites have freeroll tournaments, although most of them require a certain number of points to play. Online venues often offer seats in casino tournaments as the main prize, so instead of paying the buy-in for the casino tournament, you are freerolled the entry fee to the tournament online.

Freerolling When two players have tied hands, for example J-J versus J-J, but a flush draw on the board gives the freerolling player with the jack of that suit a chance to win the pot. Otherwise, the pot will be split.

Gut-shot straight draw When you need one specific card to make your straight. Say you have J-Q and the flop comes 8-9-4, you need a ten and only a ten to make your straight. Also called a belly-buster or inside straight draw.

Heads-up A pot that is contested by only two players.

Hole cards The two 'hidden' pocket cards dealt face down to players at the beginning of each hand.

H.O.R.S.E. Is a mix of five different games. No-Limit Hold 'em, Omaha Hi-Lo, Razz, 7 Card Stud and 7 Card Stud Hi-Lo.

Levels There are different levels of increasing blinds in tournaments. For instance, the blinds might increase from $25/$50 to $50/$100 after two hours.

Limp A player 'limps in' if he only calls the big blind.

Loose Someone who plays a lot of hands and is willing to see the flop more often than folding.

No-Limit A variation of poker in which players may bet any number of chips whenever it's their action.

Nuts The best possible hand given the board.

Off-suit A starting hand where each card is a different suit. These hands are weaker than suited hands because there is less chance of making a flush.

Out A card that needs to appear to make your hand win. Normally referred to as the outs needed to make a hand. If you hold four hearts, for example, the other nine hearts give you nine outs to a flush.

Overbet In No-Limit games, the act of firing a large bet into the pot to win only a relatively small pot; often an intimidating betting action.

Overcall To call a bet after one of your opponents has already called.

Overcard A card higher than any card on the board. This can be dealt to the community or can be one of the hole cards.

Overpair A pocket pair higher than any card on the flop.

Pair A pair is two cards of the same rank. If you make a pair with your hole cards, it's called a pocket pair.

Pocket pair In Hold 'em, if you're dealt two hole cards of the same rank it's a pocket pair.

Pocket rockets The Hold 'em starting hand of A-A.

Position Your seating position at the poker table is referred to as 'position'. The player on the 'button' has the best position because he acts last in the betting round and sees all other players' moves before deciding how to play the hand.

Pot-committed A point in a given poker hand where you're virtually forced to call because of the amount of money you've already bet into the pot.

Pot odds The amount of money already in the pot relative to the amount you must put into the pot to continue the action.

Pre-flop The stage of Hold 'em when you have two hole cards in your hand and there are no cards on the board yet.

Rabbit A weak player.

Rags Useless cards.

Rank The numerical value of a card.

Read To study your opponents — their body language, mannerisms, eyes and betting patterns — to help you ascertain the strength of their hands.

Re-buy The option to buy back into a tournament or cash game after you've lost all your chips. Cash games offer unlimited re-buys but only some tournaments offer re-buys.

Represent To play as though holding a certain hand.

River Also known as 'fifth street', the river is the fifth and final community card.

Semi-bluff A bet or raise that you hope will not be called, but if it is you have a few outs.

Set Three of a kind that you make with one or more community cards.

Short stack A small quantity of chips in front of you that is not large when compared to your opponents' stacks.

Sit-and-go Most sit-and-gos are single-table tournaments and are found online. Instead of having a scheduled start time, a sit-and-go begins as soon as there are enough people interested in playing to begin. So, as soon as ten people sit down at the table, it goes.

Slow play To play a strong hand weakly so more players will stay in the hand.

Small blind The smaller of the two forced or blind bets used in Hold 'em.

Smooth call To call when a raise is expected. See *slow play*.

Suck out To complete a lucky draw on the river, especially with a hand you should have folded earlier.

Suited Refers to a Hold 'em starting hand with two cards of the same suit. Suited hands are slightly better than unsuited hands because there is a chance of a flush.

Table image The image one projects at the poker table and the way a player is perceived by his opponents at the table.

Tell An unconscious hint that a player unknowingly gives about the strength of his hand.

Tilt To play loosely, recklessly and wildly without restraint. A player goes 'on tilt' if he is playing poorly or reacts angrily to a bad beat.

Top pair The best pair using either the hole cards or community cards.

Tourist Someone who doesn't reside in Las Vegas and is presumed to be at a disadvantage in the poker games, as opposed to the locals, who live in poker games, and who presume that the only purpose in life for tourists is to supply them with a living.

Trips Three of a kind.

Turn Also known as 'fourth street', the turn is the fourth community card.

Under the gun The player forced to act first; the one sitting to the left of the big blind before the flop, to the left of the dealer thereafter.

Value To bet for value, you bet small in the hope that your opponents call your bet. A player will place a value bet because he has the best hand and wishes to draw more money into the pot.

WPT World Poker Tour

WSOP World Series of Poker

Part One

The Main Event

♠

1

Raise or Call

Just after 5.00am in the Bullpen, two shot gun wielding suits step off the escalators followed by a team of more than a dozen guys toting cardboard boxes. They tip the contents onto an adjoining table and I'm looking at a $7.5 million pile of neatly packaged bundles of $100 bills. An announcement echoes around the room: 'Everyone without a shotgun, please back away from the money.'

I take a deep breath and try to contemplate how I'd got to this point — the final three players of the 2005 World Series of Poker Main Event. It seems like a dream; it *was* a dream — that strange, vivid dream I had on the plane to Vegas. Is this my dream turning into reality?

I snap out of my reverie and focus on the here and now. After all, a dream's just a dream; everyone has to make their own fate. Our 15-minute break is up and when we return the blinds are $150,000/$300,000 and the antes $50,000. Steve Dannemann raises from the button, and I look into the hole and see J-J. I give no consideration to folding, my only options being to raise or call …

2

July 2005
Vegas Virgins

I t's 7am on a bitterly cold July winter's morning and my breath is turning to mist as I walk from the car park to international departures at Melbourne's Tullamarine Airport. I've arrived early so I can avoid being stuck at the back of the long economy check-in lines, and it's still three hours before my flight departs for Los Angeles on the first stage of my trip to Las Vegas. My beautiful wife, Jeanie, and my fantastic kids, Anthony, Justine, Daniel and James, have braved the weather to come out to farewell me. I feel exhilarated and can't wait to get to Vegas, but my excitement is tinged with sadness that my family won't be joining me.

My 'support crew' and I board our flight just after 10am, and I'm finally on the way to fulfilling my dream of competing in the Main Event of the 2005 World Series of Poker (WSOP). I use the term 'support crew' lightly as the guys with me are great mates — my younger brother, Tony; my cousin, Billy Sukkar; and my close friend, Ian Schoots. This is only my second international flight since coming to Australia from Lebanon as a young boy 33 years earlier.

For some unknown reason the cabin crew have the plane on US time so the shades are pulled down and the lights are turned off — this at 10.30 in the morning. I also learn very quickly that there has to be better ways of traveling than cattle-class, but I'm on a budget that doesn't extend to sitting at the pointy end of the plane. It's a 15-hour flight from Melbourne to LA, the seats are cramped, it's difficult to sleep, and the food is hard to describe and even harder to eat. Like everyone else, I'd love to be sitting in one of those big comfy recliners up front.

After supper we're given thinly filled goody bags containing a tiny bag of peanuts, an apple and a bottle of mineral water — this is meant to keep us going until breakfast! Sleep doesn't come easily in these confined conditions, and my restlessness is exacerbated by the adrenalin I can feel pumping through my veins in anticipation of Las Vegas. I eventually manage to fall asleep for a few hours and experience a strange and vivid dream. The early morning light coming through the plane's windows coupled with my acute hunger awakens me. I know we're over the Pacific as I glance out the window, but all I can see are white clouds and the rays of a weak early morning sun.

Ian Schoots, who's sitting next to me, is not surprisingly already awake — he's tall, gangly, and had to squish himself up far more than me to try and sleep. His thin blonde hair is slightly mussed up and he's a little paler than usual.

I turn to him. 'Ian, I've just had the strangest dream.'

'Go on,' he yawns.

'I was on the David Letterman show making my acceptance speech after winning the Main Event, but I was watching it and at the same time taking the piss out of myself. What do you make of that?'

'You were on the Letterman show and watching it at the same time?'

'Yeah, that's right.'

'Aw, shut up, Joe,' Ian grins. 'Anyhow, what's Letterman got to do with the World Series of Poker?'

'I don't know. Nothing, I suppose.'

Tony's voice comes from the seat behind. 'What are you guys talking about?'

Before I can respond, Ian, who's normally quiet, but also a very funny guy, relates my dream with some of his own embellishments. 'Joe, you're watching too much American television,' Tony laughs.

'Go back to sleep, Joe,' Billy chimes in.

Fortunately this exchange is interrupted by the flight attendants serving an eagerly awaited breakfast, but after looking at it I drink the orange juice and pass on the rest. I'm really hungry but I can wait until we land in LA.

LA Airport is bustling with activity at 7am and the queues to clear security are long and slow moving. We finally arrive at the counter and are finger-printed by two huge intimidating African-American security personnel. I've never seen two bigger men in all my life; watching American football on television at home obviously doesn't do justice to the size of the players. We clear security but now have a five-hour wait before our flight departs for Las Vegas. What would any passionate poker player do when placed in this situation? You've got it — find the nearest game.

In direct contrast to Melbourne, LA is hot and steamy. It's a 20-minute cab ride to The Bicycle Casino and our cabby assures us that we'll be able to get a good hearty breakfast there. We head straight to one of the three dining areas, The Bicycle Deli, where our orders for eggs and bacon are taken by a waitress who struggles with our accents and mistakenly takes us for being

English — a common occurrence during the rest of the trip. Ten minutes later I look down at the biggest breakfast plate I've seen in my 39 years on this planet. On second thoughts, I can't really see any of the plate as it's covered in bacon, hash browns, cheese, eggs, and a sweet bread that I've never tasted before. What's on my plate represents at least four breakfasts, and although I'm very hungry, I leave more than I eat. For the second time in less than an hour I find myself taken aback by size.

Our stomachs are now more than full and we soon find ourselves in the Players Room, which houses more than 100 poker tables. The casinos back home in Melbourne and Sydney are larger, where every game from craps to keno is played, but in my 26 years of playing poker I've never been in a room with more than 30 poker tables. Despite this, there's very little action at this early hour, but we do manage to find a table where a gregarious, overweight punter sporting a large gold ring and matching watch invites us to join in. He's in his late 30s, with a chubby, cherubic face and receding hairline. The other players at the table look drawn and haggard and I guess they're losers from the previous night trying to get even. Our new-found friend takes us for being English, but Billy tells him we're Aussies, and then leads him on, telling him that I'm the Australasian No-Limit Hold 'em champion. My brother, Tony, is a fun-loving young man and with some help from Ian, he bolsters Billy's tale. The punter is really eager to know my name and when he asks me, the first name that comes to mind is *Michael Goodman*, but Billy's not about to let me get away with this and spells out my name. 'Joe, Joe Hachem,' the punter says using his cell phone to call a mate to get my name Googled — needless to say, it doesn't bring up any hits. Despite this he repeatedly asks me if I'm here to win the WSOP — as opposed to competing in it. I like to think I'm not superstitious; however, I can't help wondering if his words might be a good omen. I accept his invitation and sit down for a brief session of No-Limit Hold 'em. A few hours later we're on our way back to LA Airport. I've just won a tidy sum, but more importantly, I've played very well and I'm feeling confident.

❧

In late afternoon the plane banks towards McCarran Airport and I'm staring at the strip, totally mesmerized. The all-black Luxor, the largest pyramid in the world, shines in the sun, and the largest hotel in the world, the glistening emerald-green MGM Grand, blends in perfectly with the other monoliths surrounding it. This is not surprising as Las Vegas boasts 15 of the largest 20 hotels in the world. I look down at the gold Mandalay Bay where we'll be staying, and I'm pleased with our choice. There must be a zillion globes lighting the moving kaleidoscope of color that is Las Vegas. I've watched James Caan in *Vegas* on numerous occasions, the *Ocean's Eleven* and *Ocean's Twelve* movies, and travel documentaries on Las Vegas on the Australian travel show, *Getaway*, but nothing could have prepared me for what I'm now looking at. Breathtakingly magnificent!

The airport's throbbing, seemingly with a life of its own, and as we head to the baggage carousel I'm fascinated by the slot machines scattered throughout the terminal. It seems like there's a punter on every one of them, and I'm not sure if it's an airport passing itself off as a casino or a casino passing itself off as an airport.

It's stinking hot as we drag our suitcases out of the terminal, and I can actually feel the bitumen shifting under my feet. Despite the heat everyone seems to be in a hurry, and there's a rush to join the queue at the taxi rank. It's all new to us and we're looking around, taking everything in; I wonder if it'll be obvious to the natives that we're Vegas virgins. We hire a large black limousine and ask the friendly, overweight driver to take us on a tour of the strip. Nothing's too much trouble, he's eager to please and we're soon getting a guided tour complete with commentary. We're crawling along the strip and I'm looking at places I'd only ever seen on television — the Mediterranean themed Monte Carlo complete with towering palm trees; roller coasters on the roof of New York, New York; the fountains of the Bellagio; and the red and white striped flashing lights of the Flamingo, where the gangster Bugsy Siegel inspired the creation of the Vegas strip. The driver is talkative and affable but by the time we reach the Venetian we're fatigued and have heard more than enough about Bugsy, Wayne Newton, Steve Wynn and the other legends of Vegas. It's been a hectic 24 hours since we left Melbourne and we're too tired to enjoy the tour so we ask the driver to take us to the Mandalay Bay. He looks really pleased knowing he's had a nice win because we've already paid for the full tour.

We trudge across the glistening marble floor of the lobby of the Mandalay Bay, which with its surrounding palm trees makes me think that I might well be at a seaside location. Within ten minutes we're in our rooms. They're newly remodeled, large, comfortable and well-furnished with two double beds, a desk, lounge, plasma TV, high-speed internet access and a well-stocked bar. Ian and I are sharing a room on the 15th floor with views overlooking the 11-acre sand-and-surf beach; Tony and

Billy are on the 13th floor. Unbeknown to us, the Mandalay Bay has a reputation for attracting swingers, something we'll later experience first hand. I jump onto my bed, put my head on the pillow and I'm out like a light, but half an hour later I'm awake again, as are my companions. We're just too hyped to sleep, but the brief power nap has provided us with a fresh store of energy.

One of my closest friends, Dusan Stoevski, has been in Vegas for two weeks already. I phone him on his cell phone and find that he's over at the Rio, the venue for the preliminary tournaments of the WSOP. He's a very good player in his own right. A few years back he was going down the escalators at the Crown Casino in Melbourne and saw that there was a No-Limit Hold 'em tournament on, and although he'd never played the game before, he entered and won. Now he prefers grinding out a living online rather than playing 'live', but he's my most emphatic supporter, always encouraging and cheering me on at all the tournaments I compete in back home. He's about six feet tall, very skinny, and as a result of suffering from enzyme intolerance he can't eat any foods containing sugar. In spite of this he's a fine athlete, a very good tennis player and loves playing cricket. He's a great mate and has an essential quality that I look for in all my friends — unconditional loyalty. I'm anxious to catch up with him so we decide to head over to the Rio. It's too hot and too far to walk so we grab a cab, which becomes our standard mode of travel for the remainder of the trip.

The last remnants of dusk are slipping away as the cab moves slowly down the dazzling Las Vegas Boulevard. The Rio's situated off the main strip, to the west of and about a mile from the more palatial Caesar's Palace. We enter the enormous foyer of the Rio and ask one of the doormen where the venue for the

WSOP is. 'It's the Amazon Room; through the slots,' he says, pointing. 'Then just keep walking along the hallways for about five minutes.' We laugh, presuming he's taking the mickey out of us, but it truly takes all of five minutes before we run across a sign saying 'Welcome to the 2005 World Series of Poker'. Even after this, it's another three minutes of solid walking before we reach a massive convention room in which the First Annual Poker Lifestyle Show, a trade show for poker vendors, is being held. It's cleverly set up, as you have to walk through it to get to the Amazon Room. Dusan is waiting just inside the double doors to the entrance and we shake hands warmly.

I'm astounded by the vastness of the room, which in size is a mirror of the adjoining convention center. It holds 200 tables, and I'm momentarily lost for words, which is rare for me, before Ian asks, 'Are you going to play tonight, Joe?'

I shake my head, partly in response to the question but more in awe of the room. 'No, Ian, I think I'll give it a miss tonight, but maybe tomorrow after a good night's sleep.'

'If you're not playing, can we get something to eat?' asks Billy. 'I'm starving.'

The last solid feed we had was at the Bicycle Club nearly 12 hours earlier, and we've been running on hype and adrenalin ever since we arrived in Vegas. 'Yeah, good idea,' I say. 'We shouldn't have any trouble finding somewhere to eat in a place this size.'

Five minutes later we stumble across the All-American Bar & Grill, which never closes, and which will become our regular hangout while I'm playing at the Rio. We order rib-eye steaks and 15 minutes later the waiter returns with what might as well have been the carcasses. My steak must weigh more than a pound and it's about one-and-a-half inches thick (perhaps they should change the description on the menu from 'rib-eye' to 'Brontosaurus'). This is topped off with a heap of fries that completely covers the rest of the oversized plate. Man, if I become accustomed to the American diet I'm going to go home weighing at least 250 pounds.

Back at the hotel, I sleep fitfully before eventually crashing in the early hours of the morning, and I don't wake up until noon. This is partly jet lag and the intensity of the previous day, but it has more to do with the buzz and thrill of being in Vegas. I'm normally an early riser, very disciplined, and I know that I'll have my routine down pat before the tournament starts — it most certainly won't include midday sleep-ins. I make a mental note to pick up some sleeping tablets from a drugstore; once the hype of the tournament kicks in, getting a good night's sleep will become nearly impossible. The others have also slept in and we eventually make our way to Raffles Café, which becomes my permanent breakfast venue.

'Did you check out that $1,000 re-buy tournament that starts tomorrow, Joe?' Tony asks.

'Yeah,' I reply, 'looks okay and it's a good opportunity for me to spend some serious time at the tables, before the big one. I think I'm gonna enter it.'

'How's it work?' Billy chips in.

'You know,' Tony responds, 'you start off with $1,000 in chips and anytime you drop below your starting stack during the first three levels of play you can top up for another $1,000. That's right isn't it, Joe?'

'Wow, if you don't win any hands you could be in for $20,000 before the third level even starts,' Billy interrupts.

'That's right,' I laugh, 'but there's no way I'm going to let it cost me that much.'

I know the lines for registration in the WSOP will be longer later in the day so after eating I grab a cab to the Rio, part with my $10,000 entry fee to the Main Event, and also enter the $1,000 re-buy tournament. I'm relaxed and content knowing that my organizational tasks are now complete and I make my way to the Amazon Room looking for a cash game.

I don't stop in the Lifestyle Show but I walk slowly, looking at the multitude of booths and the enormous variety of products on display. The presentations are sensational; there's nothing that you can't buy. There are poker books, card protectors, poker tables, videos, DVDs, and even bobbleheads of famous players. Little did I know that I'd be part of the circus within 12 months and I'd even have a bobblehead of my own. When I ask someone what the long queues are for, I'm told they're fans queuing to have books and photographs signed by their favorite pros. Amazing! Oh, and I almost forgot to mention the beautiful, almost-dressed girls who seem to have become a feature at all trade shows, irrespective of the product.

Once in the Amazon Room it doesn't take long to find a table playing $25/$50 Hold 'em and I buy $5,000 of chips and settle in. Five hours later I cash in my chips after having won about $9,000, my second winning day in a row, which is a further boost to my confidence. I've been in good form lately. In fact, before I left for the US my hometown casino in Melbourne, Crown, put on three $500 tournaments in April, May and June, and I won or had a piece of the win in all of them.

The following day I'm back at the Rio for the $1,000 re-buy No-Limit Hold 'em tournament. The Amazon Room is humming and I'm caught up in the vibe of nearly 900 hyped-up poker players all charging in different directions in search of their tables.

My initial chip stake drops below $1,000 so I buy another $1,000 and then top up with another $1,000. Late on the first day, 840 entrants have been eliminated but I'm still alive. This is when for the first time I witness the enforcement of the f-bomb rule where players are penalized with a time suspension for dropping the F word.

It's the last hand of the day. Howard Lederer is on my right and a young American professional, David Wells, who I later become good friends with, is on my left. Everyone else folds pre-flop, and Howard and David go heads-up before they split the pot, both turning over K-J after the river. 'Jeez Howard, you play that f***ing shit!' David says jokingly. In a flash, one of the floormen is at our table telling David that he's suspended for the first ten minutes of play the following day. David protests and tells the guy he knows Howard and that he was only joking, but it's to no avail and the suspension stands.

Next day, play starts at 2pm with 54 players still remaining. My good form continues and I become the first and only Aussie on this trip to make the final table of a WSOP event. The final table also includes two well-known players, Barry Greenstein and Freddy Deeb, but despite my great respect for them I'm in no way over-awed or intimidated by their presence. I don't get flustered by anybody and I just get on with the job of playing my game irrespective of who's at the table.

I can be fiery and volatile, but in the past few years I've become a far more controlled and patient player. Once I learned how to control my temper I noticed an immediate improvement in my game. I used to be very excitable and, possibly because of my Lebanese heritage, my blood seemed to hover around boiling point. When I took a bad beat, I used to berate and belittle my unfortunate opponents. However, after a long time and a lot of soul searching, I came to the realization that I had it all wrong. I knew that I was a better player than these guys and if I wanted them to continue playing badly then the best thing to do when they got lucky would be to grin and bear it, because — and this is a big because — in the long run, I would end up with all their money. Mike 'The Mad Genius' Caro sums it up perfectly when he says, 'You want weak players in your game. They may even enjoy going up against the odds. When you insult them for their bad plays you're making them uncomfortable and motivating them to play better in the future. Don't do that.' Patience in poker can take many different forms. You need to be patient with your opponents when you suffer a bad beat; you need to be patient, not reckless, when you're card dead; and you need to be patient during the course of play.

This last form of patience is reinforced in spades for me when I watch Freddy Deeb play one particular hand. There's a guy at the table who clearly can't play but who keeps going all-in after the first two cards are dealt to steal the blinds. He gets away with it a few times and then goes all-in again, and Freddy asks him to count his chips. The guy doesn't respond and just sits in his chair like a stunned mullet. His earlier bravado has disappeared; minutes go by and still he remains motionless, but Freddy's not going anywhere. The guy looks sulky and upset and finally the dealer asks him to count his chips, but it's to no avail. The table becomes quiet and the tension is magnified, but Freddy's as cool as a cucumber and not in any rush. Eventually, the pressure gets to the guy and he reaches down and starts counting his chips, but his hands are trembling so badly he can barely pick them up. This is not a tell, it's a public broadcast and Freddy's patience is about

35

to pay off big time as he calls the 'all-in'. The guy turns over A-7 and Freddy flicks over A-Q, clearly dominating him, and a few minutes later the perpetual 'all-inner' is eliminated.

There are 200 spectators around the final table, including 20 noisy Aussies supporting me. I've been playing the short stack all day, battling to survive, and I resolve to go all-in if I get half an opportunity.

Shortly after Barry Greenstein raises to $50,000 from early position, another guy pushes all-in from middle position and I call the all-in with the last of my chips. Barry gets out of the way, and my opponent shows me 8c-8s, against my Ad-10d. The flop comes 7s-9d-7d and my opponent has two pair, but I have a flush draw and two overcards. The turn is the seven of clubs. I'm now up against a full house, but I can still suck out and win the hand by hitting an ace or a ten to make a bigger full house, or even a miraculous seven which will give me four of a kind and a higher overcard, and I can chop the pot with a nine — I have ten outs. My supporters appear to be collectively holding their breath. Perhaps it's my imagination but the dealer seems to take an eternity to burn a card before flipping over the two of diamonds, and, seeing that I've hit a flush, my raucous supporters go delirious. They haven't noticed my opponent's full house on the turn and now, much to their disappointment, they realize my hand is just not good enough. Although I didn't win, I've beaten 885 players and cashed in for over $26,000.

After I get busted, I head to the cage with Tony to pick up my winnings, thinking that there are a lot of good players in Australia but there's far more depth in the US. 'Jeez, Tony,' I say, 'I'd love to play against these guys for six months and then I'd back myself to match it with any of them.'

'Joe, you've won nearly $40,000 in the last three days. Just keep doing what you're doing and there's no telling how far you'll go in the big one.'

3

The Main Event — Day One
A Pair of Nines

At 10.30am on the first day of the Main Event my taxi drops me off at the entrance to the twin gleaming blue and red towers of the Rio All-Suite Las Vegas Hotel & Casino. I'm dressed for comfort in a black shirt, blue jeans, black shoes and sunglasses, and I'm listening to 50 Cent on my iPod. The mercury's nudging 100 degrees (38°C) as I enter the foyer through the large glass revolving door. It's bloody cold inside, and there's a buzz of excitement and anticipation in the crowded room. I head through the blackjack and roulette tables and the countless poker machines, and I'm caught up in a throng of humanity of all types, sizes and nationalities moving along the vast smoke-filled hallways toward the cavernous Amazon Room. There are nearly 2000 first-day entrants, and another 2000 spectators, relatives and friends milling around the room. I'm momentarily over-awed. *What have I done? It's gonna be so hard.* I give myself a quick mental slapping and steel myself not to worry about what's going on around me and to just concentrate on the action to come at my table. By the end of the day about 1400 players will have been eliminated and I sure don't intend to be one of them.

Even at this late stage, registrations are still being accepted, and the final count is unknown. But ultimately, 5619 players will contest the Main Event — more than double the number that participated in 2004. This will make it the biggest tournament in the history of poker and first prize will be the largest of any contested sport or games event in the world — larger than Wimbledon, the Masters at Augusta, the Kentucky Derby and the Melbourne Cup. It's so big that there are three consecutive first days, numbered 1A, 1B and 1C, and after they're completed only 1900 players will still be alive to continue playing on the fourth day. I've been lucky enough to draw day 1A, and I would've been equally happy with 1B, but I'm sure glad I didn't cop 1C, as those who did will have to front up again on the following day, without any rest. This may sound soft, but it's incredibly taxing playing poker for 14 hours and then having to front up fewer than 12 hours later to do it all again. If I make it through the first day I'll have a two-day break before Day Two.

The night before, I had shared a drink with my good friend Emad Tahtouh and swapped ten percent with him. This means that I'll get ten percent of his winnings and he'll get ten percent of mine, so it's a form of poker insurance. If I'm knocked out early and receive no prize money, I'll still have an interest in Emad for the remainder of the tournament. These trades are all done on a handshake, and your word is your bond. We have another mutual friend, Arul Thillai, and Emad asked me if I was going to swap with him as well. I'm more than happy to, but doubt I'll see him before the tournament begins. Somehow the word gets back to Arul and before I sit down at the table a friend of mine, Chris 'The Barracuda' Newton, who is a poker player, reporter and photographer, passes the message to me that Arul wants to swap five percent, which I readily agree to.

The enormous room is normally used for conventions and trade fairs, and has been broken up into four quadrants, each containing 50 tables. The tables are roped off but already spectators are four and five deep around them, and even though my table's at the front of the room, I have to push my way through the crush just to get to it. I take my seat and glance around the table but I know no one, which is not surprising given that this is my first trip to the US and I've only been in Vegas for five days. Despite this, I've watched a lot of poker on television back home in Melbourne and know that neither Doyle Brunson nor T. J. Cloutier is at my table. Equally unsurprising is the fact that I'm sure no one at the table knows me, even though I did make the final table of the one preliminary event I entered. I cast my eyes around the all-male table again, taking in my opponents' clothing, their watches, their rings and other jewelry, their mannerisms and I even listen to their small talk as I try to get some type of early read on them.

Johnny Grooms, the Tournament Director, makes an announcement that covers the do's and don'ts of the tournament. He stresses that any player who drops the f-bomb will be suspended for ten minutes, a rule that is frequently enforced thereafter. Later in the day, one unfortunate loose-lipped player is hit with 20 minutes for using it twice in one sentence! I think it's a funny rule given the everyday use of that word, but rules are rules, and I resolve to say it under my breath if I have to — very, very softly. A few minutes later, Johnny gets the tournament underway with his announcement: 'Ladies and gentlemen, poker players from around the world, shuffle up and deal.'

The starting blinds are $25/$50 and we're scheduled to get through seven levels today. The blind levels are periodic monetary increases and in two hours we'll move to the next level of $50/$100. Initially, there's a lot of slow cautious play at my table; everyone appears to be trying to preserve their initial $10,000 in chips and avoid the ignominy of being the first player eliminated. Eight minutes into the tournament there is loud shouting from the back of the room as the first of the 5619 starters bites the dust. A collective sigh of relief travels around the room as a lot of players think, *Thank God that's not me.*

Shortly after the first elimination, a pasty-faced, beady-eyed young guy, sporting a short-trimmed beard and decked out in the standard internet attire of a PokerStars cap, T-shirt and cargo pants, limps in from middle position. I've mucked a number of earlier hands but now I'm on the button and have a hand I can play, a pair of nines, and I raise five times the big blind, outlaying $250. The small blind and big blind fold and now it's me, heads-up against Mr Beady. He looks at his cards for a long time before calling and there's now $575 in the pot. I don't put him on anything really strong, and surmise that he has two picture cards, a small pair or ace rag. However, I've only been playing 15 minutes, I don't know him, and he may well be slow playing a pair of aces — though I seriously doubt he has the finesse to use this strategy.

The flop is A-K-5 rainbow (three different suits), which is obviously not a good flop for me, but Mr Beady seems to have ants in his pants, and is continually twitching and blinking incessantly. The odds are that he's now got the best hand, but he reminds me of a deer trapped in headlights as he bets $500 and I flat call, representing that I have a big hand with the aim of taking it away from him on the turn — of course with a pair of nines I still leave myself outs. Intuitively I sense his uncertainty, his nervousness and because my initial pre-flop raise represented strength he's probably thinking that I've flopped two pair or a set and am now slow-playing him.

But this doesn't seem to deter him and he fires $1,000 at me when the turn card is a queen. I continue to show strength and raise him to $3,000. My elbows are on the green felt and I make fists of my hands, resting my chin in them, all the time maintaining my composure and table presence. Mr Beady picks up his cards and studies them carefully; his squinty little eyes are darting everywhere as he nervously plays with his chips — the minutes tick by and he tries to stare me down but can't hold my gaze. The room is air-conditioned but I can see beads of sweat on his forehead, and the overhead lights accentuate his blotchy complexion. The noise of 2000 players echoes around the room, but I block it out completely as I contemplate his next move. Eventually he calls my raise, which better defines his hand for me, and I now know for sure that he has a hand that he likes — it's unlikely to be J-10 to have the nuts, but it's probably two pair and he may even be holding A-J or K-J, which in either case is better than my nines. Shit! I expected him to fold on the turn. Now I have a decision to make on the river. Do I continue with the same aggressive line and try and bluff him out of the hand or do I shut down knowing that there's an 80 percent probability that he'll call me regardless? It briefly crosses my mind that the flying time from Melbourne to Vegas was 17 hours and maybe I'm going to be saying *hasta la vista* just 17 minutes into the Main Event, or if not, I'm going to be fatally short-stacked. I get rid of these negative thoughts but I know for certain that Mr Beady has a hand, or that he's just too inexperienced to be bluffed. I'll be proven right on both counts as he's an internet player, this is his first live tournament, and the flop and the turn have been very kind to him.

My journey flashes before my eyes as the dealer burns a card and flips over the river.

4

Vegas With the Boys?

I first met Emad Tahtouh when he was playing Limit Hold 'em in the Vegas room of Crown Casino about five years ago. Even then he seemed to have a table presence — tall, dark-haired, brash, young, topped off with an arrogant *I can take you* smile.

Emad recalls: 'Joe came in and was getting ready to play his first hand — I was already at the table — and for some reason as soon as he sat down I thought, "I'm going to try and bluff this guy out of the pot on the first hand." He was talking it up and I just wanted to show him who was boss. So I re-raised his raise with 6-9 and he re-raised again — there was a lot of action before the flop. Then on the flop I decided I was going to make it look like I had a big hand. I checked, he bet, I check-raised him, he called. The board was 8-5-2. The turn was a ten and I led in, and he called. I got lucky on the river with a seven for a straight and led into him again. He gives me the filthiest look and calls, and I turn my cards over — he's flopped a set of eights and he's not happy. He stormed out of there and a bit later I run into a mutual friend, Tony TC, but I didn't know that at the time. I'm talking to him when Joe walks past and Tony says, "Hey Joe, have you met Emad?" He just looks at me with daggers but a week later we both happen to be at a friend's birthday party and we get to talking. I apologize for playing such an awful hand and sucking out. After that we became really good mates.'

Little did I realize, though, that meeting Emad would one day change my life. I used to organize tournaments in my garage with the cream of Melbourne's poker crop and as he became a regular at those games his play improved immeasurably. He loves poker just as much as I do. Emad recollects: 'Well, Joe always managed to get the best players around Melbourne to play in his tournaments, and yeah, I credit that for helping me a lot, but I guess the most I learned wasn't so much playing, but talking with Joe about different hands and how we would play them. It was basically talking crap for two or three hours, but I'd walk away having learned a lot from him.'

It's a Saturday night and I'm looking to celebrate my 39th birthday, so who better to invite over to have a few quiet drinks than Emad. He tells me that he'll have to take it easy because he's playing in one of Crown's regular Sunday tournaments the following day, so with the best of intents we resolve not to have a late night. Somehow, the alcohol takes hold and our best intentions are put to one side; we continue to talk poker and imbibe into the early hours of the morning. We're still sober enough to know we've drunk a little too much and realize that it wouldn't be safe for Emad to drive home, so he props at my place for the night.

The next morning, he sleeps in with a bit of a hangover and he's still feeling woozy when he realizes he's running late for the tournament. He splashes some water on his face, throws on his clothes and he's out the door and into his Alfa Romeo racing to Crown. Unfortunately his foot must have been a little too heavy on the accelerator and he blows up the differential. The good news is that he makes it to Crown on time, and the bad news is that a replacement differential for an Alfa costs a bloody fortune. Thankfully, he does very well in the tournament, picking up a nice cash prize that more than covers the cost of the car repairs, but as fate would have it, things are about to get even better.

He takes the following day off and puts the Alfa in for repairs, and while he's waiting at home he does the obvious — goes online and enters a $33 buy-in tournament on PokerStars.com, and wins a $12,000 package to the Main Event of the 2005 World Series.

Next thing I know, half a dozen of my mates decide to join him, and the cogs in my brain begin to work overtime. *How am I going to be able to convince Jeanie to let me go to Vegas with the boys?* I'd promised her that I wouldn't go unless I could take the whole family, and right now my bankroll isn't big enough to cover the expenses of six air fares, the accommodation, the $10,000 entry fee and what I know the girls will spend shopping. Anyhow, I summon up all my courage and call Jeanie into my office. 'Honey,' I say, 'I need to speak to you. Look, the boys are going to Vegas, and I'm not going to be able to take the family, but I really want to go. What do you think?'

'Get a life! You're not going anywhere. If I can't go, you can't go.' Jeanie turns on her heel and vacates my office post haste — end of conversation, end of negotiations. I gave up any hope of Vegas and got on with my regular life.

Jeanie and I had already planned to go on vacation to Queensland's beautiful Gold Coast a few weeks later. We're sitting on the white sands of Broadbeach one balmy afternoon, watching our kids swimming in the aqua-white capped breakers when Jeanie turns to me out of the blue and utters the most unexpected words. 'Honey, you know what, why don't you go to Vegas with the boys? I think it's your time and I know how desperate you are to join your mates. You can take us next time.' After I came around I gave her the biggest kiss, before running back to the hotel to phone my mates, screaming, 'Boys, book the tickets! We're going to Vegas.' I'd just flopped a monster hand and now I need to make the most of it.

Jeanie recalls that afternoon: 'I watched Joe just sitting there and saw it in his eyes. He didn't say anything but his eyes were saying, "Honey, please let me go," and I thought, "Nuh." But next thing I'm saying "Why don't you go with the boys?" and he's gone — he didn't waste a minute getting back to the hotel to book the flights.'

🐝

Unlike Emad and the two previous World Champions, Chris Moneymaker and Greg Raymer, I didn't qualify for the World Series Main Event through an internet satellite on PokerStars. Don't think I didn't try: I did, and it wasn't as if I didn't have any online experience. I made the final table of the $500 Pot-Limit Hold 'em event in the 2003 World Championship of Online Poker at PokerStars and although I was confident of winning, the cards didn't fall my way and I had to settle for $19,000, my biggest win up until that date. Unfortunately, in the time available before departing for Vegas I just couldn't win a satellite giving me direct entry into the 2005 Main Event, so I had to part with the full $10,000 entry fee from my poker bankroll. I felt I'd done the hard yards and for five years had been making the final tables of tournaments in every state of Australia, but disappointingly my best result was only a third. My mates kept telling me, 'Joe, the way you're playing it's only a matter of time before you break through in a big event.' I'd been playing well in the Crown Casino's recent tournaments and if I could repeat that form in Vegas, I knew I'd do well.

Fate deals many strange hands. But as in life and poker, it's not the cards you are dealt but how you play them that counts. In my case, had Emad not won that tournament on PokerStars I wouldn't have traveled to Las Vegas to play in the 2005 WSOP. That was fate. But even Emad's win wouldn't have had me playing in the Main Event had it not been for Jeanie's love and selflessness — that, too, was fate. These instances were in themselves remarkable, but there was one other event, the absolute bad beat that I would manage to turn into the best possible beat within a few short years — the ultimate act of fate.

5

The Main Event — Day One
Dodging a Bullet

The dealer flips over the river and I stare down at the table knowing that I couldn't have hoped for better — a beautiful nine to give me three nines. I know I have the best hand, but I remain impassive with hands folded in front of me. Now it's time to make Mr Beady pay. He checks and I ponder my cards carefully before betting $4,500. Without the slightest hesitation he calls, and before I can flip my cards over he proudly shows me K-Q. I turn my nines over and watch what little color he has in his face drain away as he comes to the realization that his two pair is not good enough. I drag in a very healthy pot of about $17,000 — a real bonus so early in the tournament. I'm on my way.

I'm normally conservative and play tight in the early rounds of a tournament when the blinds are small, looking to preserve my chips while stealing a few pots along the way and milking my big hands for all they're worth. However, there are times when you have to break your own rules and I was so confident of my read on Mr Beady that this was one such occasion. As it turned out, my read on him was perfect, and had I not hit the nine I would've definitely shut down on the river and let him take the pot, knowing that there was no way I could bluff him. Trying to bluff inexperienced players early in a tournament is a high risk strategy that more often than not is likely to see you behind the rail as a spectator. I definitely didn't play my hand against Mr Beady conservatively and was more than a little lucky to get away with the hand, but it was having the outs that saved me. Dan Harrington in *Harrington on Hold 'em* writes, 'In order to reach the final table of a big tournament, it's not enough to get paid off on your monster hands. At least once or twice during the event, you're going to have to come back from the dead. You're going to be all-in against someone who has you beat, and you're going to catch a card on fourth or fifth street that miraculously keeps you alive. I've been to a lot of final tables, but I've never been to one where I didn't hit a perfect card somewhere earlier in the tournament. That's a fact of life in all gaming tournaments and poker is no different.' Sure, I wasn't all-in against Mr Beady, but had I got beat I'd have had a very short stack that would've made getting through the first day a lot more difficult.

Late in the afternoon I receive the bad news that Emad has been knocked out of the tournament, which means my ten percent interest in him is down the drain.

At 1.41am, Johnny Grooms, who's looking the worse for wear, makes the announcement that we're down to 690 players but that play is going to continue until we've lost another 40. Thirty minutes later the day's play is finally over and we're congratulated and advised not to leave our positions until our chips have been counted. We're each given a large tamper-proof plastic bag in which to store our chips and registration cards. The bagging process takes about 30 minutes and as I look around the vast room I see a lot of almost-transfixed, bright, shiny eyes. We've been playing for nearly 14 hours, but there's still a lot of chatter and little sign of tiredness. What is most noticeable is how the room has thinned: there are only about a third of the players and spectators that we started with still remaining. Our last task is to give the dealer a card with our name and exact chip count on it. I end the day with $67,000 in chips, which is approximately double the average — a good first day!

A group of eight friends has watched the last hour of play and they're in mixed spirits as we head off to the All-American Bar & Grill for drinks, a snack and the mandatory post-mortems and bad beat stories. They're elated for me, but their enthusiasm is tempered by commiserations for Emad, who's still replaying the bad beat that saw his hopes of winning the big one crushed earlier in the day.

When I was in the rest rooms during the breaks, the two words I continually heard were 'bad beat'. It's the same walking along the corridors, and now as I try and relax in the restaurant those dreaded words seem to be coming from every table. I'm mentally exhausted but also exhilarated, not physically tired in the slightest, and I'm still replaying the day's hands in my mind. It's hard to describe the suspense, the pressure, the near misses, and the highs and lows that go with playing through nearly 14 hours of intense top-class poker. It taxes every ounce of concentration and resolve.

Tony asks me if I'm going to watch the following day's play. I tell him I have no reason to, and that I'll be putting some petrol back in my tank by spending the day floating around one of the Mandalay Bay's pools.

It's nearly 4am when I get back to my room and shortly after, Jeanie phones me from Melbourne, where it's 9pm. I'm lying on my bed in darkness as I let her know the good news that

I've survived the first day, and she's thrilled for me. I'm missing her and the kids even though we talk every day, and without fail she always says something to lift my spirits. We're trying to keep things as normal as we can on the family front, and Jeanie proudly tells me that our eldest son, Anthony, who plays Australian Rules football for the Victorian under-15 side, has been named best on ground in a match against South Australia. I'm excited to hear it but feel dejected that I missed out on seeing it myself. Up until now, I've watched every game he's played. I feel the tears welling up and I'm about to tell Jeanie I love her and say goodnight when she says, 'Honey, I know Vegas is for you. You're destined to win.'

'How do you work that out?' I say, half grinning, half sniffling.

'I just know.'

❧

I'm tired but I just can't fall asleep. I've heard a rumor that oxygen is continually pumped into the rooms of the major hotels in Vegas, which doesn't help in getting a good night's sleep; the story goes that the casinos would prefer you to be at their tables rather than in their beds. They certainly don't need the oxygen to keep me awake as I'm totally wired and continue replaying the day's hands over and over in my mind like a DVD on loop. I curse myself for not having bought sleeping tablets and know that I'll have to pick some up if I'm going to have any chance of progressing in the tournament. It's 9am when I last check the clock, and tiredness finally overwhelms me. I wake just after noon but I'm listless and still tired. I'm annoyed that I'm wasting time sleeping through the day, and I resolve to get into a routine that will provide me with the mental alertness and stamina that I'll need if I'm to make it to the final table.

It's another sizzling day as we make our way down to the incredible pool complex named 'The Beach', which the Mandalay Bay proudly claims is a replica of a Caribbean resort. This is no idle claim as there is a wave pool, three swimming pools, a river, a huge amount of sand, hundreds of sun lounges surrounded by numerous cabanas, and a variety of tropical palms and vegetation — all this in the middle of what was once a parched desert. Sun lounges around the pools are at a premium and there are two ways of getting one: get down to the pool at 7am or tip. We choose the latter, after which we loll around the river pool drinking ice-cold Coronas and kicking back. The coolness of the pool under the hot sun helps me to relax and take my mind off poker, even if only for a few minutes. I could get used to this lifestyle.

$$\clubsuit$$

After dinner and a few more drinks no one is even remotely tired and Ian and I decide that a little poker action might be what's needed to help us sleep. Billy and Tony join us as we head up to our room to get some cash from the safe. As we enter the elevator we're joined by this cool dude — imagine a tall, heavily tanned, dark-haired Don Johnson in *Miami Vice* — who is looking very smooth in a tight-fitting suit that seems to have been hand tailored, an unbuttoned open necked shirt, gold chains around his neck and the mandatory sunglasses. He has a stunning 20-something brunette under one arm and an equally attractive blonde under the other. He starts talking to us while at the same time slipping his arm further around the brunette so he can fondle her breast. She's smiling and certainly not complaining about what her boyfriend's doing in front of us. When he finds we're from Australia, he invites us to a party in his suite upstairs. I'm the only married guy in our group so I decline but I whisper to Ian, 'Hey, here's your chance to sample some hot Vegas action, and who knows, you might get lucky.'

'Umm, I don't think so,' he replies.

'The cards will always be here tomorrow,' I say, 'but the chance you've got to party won't.'

'Nah, I just feel like playing cards tonight.'

I suspect Ian's a little nervous about going upstairs to a party with people he's never met and confides in me that he's just not into casual flings. But Billy has no such reservations, and he lets the guy know he's up for anything and heads off with him and the two foxes.

We find a $500 buy-in table with $2/$5 blinds and we've barely sat down before Ian goes on a huge rush and is hauling in chips hand after hand. *Maybe he made the right decision choosing the cards instead of the party.* An hour and a half goes by and Billy calls the poker room and tells me that he's in a room full of beautiful girls, there's plenty to eat and drink, and that he's having an absolute ball. I look over at Ian, whose rush has come to an end. He has virtually no chips left. 'Jeez, Ian,' I laugh, 'you're a double loser. You've lost your money and you've lost your chance to score. Why didn't you go upstairs?'

'Aw, shut up, Joe,' he says, and grins sheepishly.

I'm continuing my good form and have dragged in some very big pots. As the morning wears on I'm busting player after player. I have almost every chip and the piles in front of me take nearly a quarter of the table. At 9am there are only two other players left and both have small stacks. I'm still running hot, and they look at me, then look at each other as if to say, *we're not taking you on anymore*, and pick up their few remaining chips. I thank them for the game but they look spent and unhappy.

Ian remembers the night well: 'We sat down next to each other on the table. After a few hands it becomes obvious these guys all know each other and have played No-Limit here together many times before. We're the intruders at the table and you can see them looking at each other and thinking, "We'll take some money off these tourists." But this is a very rash thought, as they don't know us, nor do they know how well Joe can play. He's an aggressive player who enjoys talking, and even as we're sitting down he starts, and you can tell they're thinking, "We're gonna enjoy this." Joe's not insulting but loves to make over-the-top comments designed to put his opponents on tilt as well as giving him a read on them. Because of this they play over-aggressively, intent on busting us, and do a good job on me, but Joe's another matter. When they call or raise him, he's got big hands, and turns them over with great relish. When he bluffs, he rubs it in and shows them his cards, and he's sure not shy when he drags in the pots. I can see they're getting really pissed off; he's damaged a few stacks when he gets Q-9 in late position. There's a raise and a call before the flop and Joe calls as well. The flop is Q-9-4; one of them raises, the other calls and Joe bets. When they both call you've immediately gotta know these guys have got a queen in their hand. The turn card is an ace, which might be really ugly for Joe, and one guy bets, while the other goes all-in. I can see Joe's hole cards and think to myself that he's gotta get out of this hand, he has to fold because he's almost certainly up against trips or a higher two pair. Without the slightest pause he goes all-in as well and I almost fall off my chair, but that's Joe. The dealer flips over the river and it's a nine! Joe jumps out of his chair, slams his cards down on the table and shouts, "Pass the sugar!" They both have A-Q and immediately start bleating about how lucky Joe was. I jump to his defense and say, "Hang on, you guys called a raise when you were miles behind on the flop, and then got lucky spiking a two outer on the turn." Joe agrees with a convincing "Yeah," but he's not worried about what they think as he drags in a huge pot. For the rest of the night he busts one after another, until he's got nearly every chip on the table, and there are only two of them remaining. They decide to cash in what they've got left, at least walking away from the table with a few chips — very few, in fact. Joe, who's always the gentleman, thanks them for the game, but they're not happy about losing to a tourist.'

I've had a good night's work, and I'm relaxed and at ease when I put my head on my pillow. For once, sleep comes easily, but four hours later I'm awake and kick myself again for not having bought sleeping tablets. Perhaps it's just as well as I might have overslept and missed seeing Arul playing his first day. I'm anxious to get to the Rio to support him, and of course, to see how my five percent is faring.

❧

I get to the Rio just before 1pm hoping Arul hasn't been unlucky enough to be knocked out in the first two hours. I have no reason to be concerned as when I locate his table I see he has a very healthy stack in front of him. I met him a few years ago playing at Crown Casino where he has won a number of tournaments. He's a young electrical engineer born in Sri Lanka, who happens to be an excellent poker player.

This is one of the great things about our game — it transcends all professions and nationalities and is one of the few sports or games where men and women compete on an equal basis. In what other sport or game can a builder's laborer compete with doctors, professionals and the greatest players in the world? Can you imagine entering a tennis tournament and getting to play against Roger Federer? Never! Yet for the cost of the entry fee into a poker tournament you may find yourself on a table doing battle with Johnny Chan or Greg Raymer.

Arul is in his late 20s but appears to be younger; perhaps it's because he's so skinny and looks more like a boy than a man. Anyhow, his boyish looks do not detract from his card-playing skills and at the table he is chilled and totally focused. Despite his demeanor, he plays in a very forceful manner, continually pressuring his opponents to make hard and uncomfortable decisions. If he has one fault it's that he's just too aggressive and keeps pounding all the time — he finds it extremely hard to take his foot off the accelerator.

At the dinner break we have a bite to eat at the All-American Bar & Grill, and Arul informs me that he has about $70,000 in chips. My five percent is looking safe and I'm really pleased for him as it looks like he'll be joining me to play the second day of the tournament tomorrow.

Much to my disappointment, all of Arul's hard work and fine play is undone in the ten minutes after the dinner break and he's knocked out of the tournament. He's so good and yet so reckless at the same time, and all of the chips he's accumulated over seven long hours disappear in the blink of an eye. I commiserate with him but know all too well that when you're playing No-Limit Hold 'em, there's always the possibility of a momentary lapse or an overly impetuous play that can bring your tournament life to a sudden end. Sadly I'm the only surviving member of the trio and will carry Arul's and Emad's hopes for the remainder of the tournament.

On the way back to the Mandalay Bay I ask the cabby to stop at a drugstore and make one of my most important buys of the trip, a bottle of sleeping tablets. I take two at around midnight and set the alarm for 9am. I'm determined to sleep well so that I'll be sharp and focused on Day Two of the tournament.

6

Pocket Aces

In the property markets we all know about location, location, location, while in the money markets, as in poker, it's all about timing, timing, timing. In 1972 I was far too young to understand how lucky I was and how opportune the timing of my parents' decision to move to Australia. I would only gain an appreciation of this as I grew older and learned more about the history of my beautiful ancestral Lebanon.

In June, 1967, the Six-Day War between Israel and its neighbors Egypt, Jordan and Syria erupted just 15 months after I was born in Beirut. When it ended, Israel had control of the Sinai Peninsula, the Gaza Strip, the West Bank, East Jerusalem and the Golan Heights. Palestinian refugees under Yassar Arafat poured into Southern Lebanon, making it their base. This resulted in numerous Israeli bombings of more than 150 towns and villages in South Lebanon from 1967 to 1974. Lebanon, through no fault of its people, was a very unstable place in which to live after 1967.

My mother loved her parents dearly and could never have left Lebanon while they were still alive, despite the country's instability, and it was only after they passed away that she and my father chose to move to Australia. My uncles and cousins were already living there so my family had a 'heads-up' regarding Australia; that it was clean, safe, well governed and jobs were plentiful for those who wanted to work. My parents' decision had absolutely nothing to do with the war, but as fate would have it conditions in Lebanon would soon escalate to dangerous, and in hindsight their timing could not have been better. We left in 1972, and three years later a vicious and bloody civil war broke out between the Christians and the Muslims; this war would rage on until 1990 and totally devastate the country. I would learn that Beirut was once known as the Paris of the Middle East but sadly the only vision I would see on Australian television was that of bombed-out rubble.

I love and am proud of my Lebanese heritage, but I was dealt pocket aces when I was lucky enough to land in Melbourne. Make no mistake: I'm an Aussie through and through. It's a wonderful country in which to raise a family, a place where anyone who's prepared to roll up their sleeves and work hard can be successful. We Aussies also have a healthy irreverence for authority and those who look down on us from lofty towers.

Up until we immigrated to Australia I spent winters in Beirut and summers in the mountains of North Lebanon in my mother's birthplace, the warrior village of Bescharre, also known as 'the town next to Heaven'. I still remember the winter snows, often to a depth of three meters, and the glorious summer days where 90-degree (32°C) temperatures were cushioned by soft mountain breezes. Bescharre sits 75 miles from Beirut, nestled high in the mountains beneath 1500-year-old Cedars. The Cedar tree, noble and immortal, is the emblem of Lebanon and adorns its flag. In spring, it's one of the few places in the world where you can swim on the coast in the morning and ski in the mountains in the afternoon.

A medieval mentality pervaded the village and to survive you had to learn to look after yourself. One of my mother's brothers, Bescharra, was named after the village (a name meaning 'sparkling star in the night'), but his family and the villagers knew him as Bill. He was the toughest man in the village, but Mum was also very strong and she needed to be. Often she would be at Uncle Bill's shoulder when he was involved in altercations. This was very much a community that settled disputes by applying the Biblical 'an eye for an eye and a tooth for a tooth' to the letter. My father ran a car service, not unlike being a chauffeur today, and my mother looked after the house, my two brothers and me.

My maternal grandfather doted on me and I loved him dearly. I was his favorite, perhaps because I was his first-born grandchild. No one in my family had ever had a complete education and my grandfather was determined to live long enough to send me to university, even if it meant selling his land. He used to carry me around the village on his shoulders telling anyone who would listen that one day I would make something out of myself. He spoiled me rotten but instilled in me his vision of my success. Sadly, he passed away when I was only six, but he had already imbued me with a sense of responsibility and a desire to achieve. I still have these qualities today and they are the priceless legacy that my grandfather left to me.

As an aside, my mother's maiden name was Sukkar, which means sugar, and I wonder if it was prophetic given that 'Pass the Sugar' is now one of the most famous catch cries in poker.

So it was that in February 1972 my Mum, Dad, brothers, Elei (four years old), Tony (one year old), and I boarded a plane for a new life on the other side of the world. I was just six. My emotions encompassed an overwhelming excitement coupled with a fear of leaving behind the familiar and everything else in between. I was sad, happy, excited, apprehensive and curious. It would have been virtually impossible for my parents to borrow the money to get us to Australia from a bank, as they were poor, and the cost of the air fares would have been a small fortune to them. Fortunately, the Catholic Church was helping families to emigrate, and my father met with our local priest and the church loaned him the money. After arriving in Australia it must have taken my parents years of toil before they could repay the loan. I'm so glad and grateful that my parents borrowed that money and gambled it on our emigration to Australia.

In the early 1970s, Australia had a growing motor vehicle industry, and Ford and General Motors were always looking for workers at their plants. Almost before the planes had landed, immigrants were being signed up to work on the production lines. My father was employed by Ford and my mother by General Motors. Shortly after our arrival, Australia would enter into a severe recession which would not end until 1975, and now as I reflect I know my parents must have worked very hard just to retain their jobs in the face of cut-backs and retrenchments across the country.

Our first home was a small one-bedroom bungalow at the back of my Uncle Bill's house in the suburb of Northcote, about four miles from Melbourne. My uncle worked as a contract welder doing high pressure maintenance work in factory shut-down periods. A factory would close for a specified period of time and a team of welders, up to 20 in number, would work 12 to 14 hours a day for two to three weeks straight with no weekends off. My uncle made a very good living, earning up to six times the average weekly wage at the time.

Life was tough, and cramming a family of five into a small bungalow was no mean feat. We slept in one double bed with Mum, Dad and Tony up one end, and Elei and me up the other. No one in the family spoke English, so life must have been very difficult for my parents.

I was shuffled off to Helen Street Primary School in Northcote where one of my enduring memories is sitting next to a young boy while we were drawing pictures. It was just before knock-off time and the teacher said, 'Please write your name in the top left hand corner of your drawing.' That meant nothing to me, but I did watch the young boy sitting next to me write his name, and copied it perfectly — using his name on my drawing! One of the great advantages of childhood is the enormous capacity to learn quickly, and I would hear words at school and mimic them at home almost creating my own language. I soon became proficient in English.

My parents rented our first real home at 528 Rathdowne Street in North Carlton, another inner-city suburb, about a year after we landed in Australia. It was one of six tiny old terrace houses, and the toilet and bathroom were located in separate sheds out in the backyard. There was no spin dryer and after Mum had washed our clothes she used an old set of rollers to get rid of the excess water — it was nothing flash, but it was home.

On the day we were due to move out of the bungalow my parents told me that they'd pick me up from school, but midday came and went with no sign of them, and I began to panic. I thought that maybe they were doing a runner and leaving me behind. I could no longer stand it and I ran all the way home, tears pouring down my cheeks, only to find them still packing. They whisked me back to school as quickly as I'd come from it, but I breathed a big sigh of relief knowing they hadn't deserted me.

By the time I turned seven I was looking for my first casual job, but when I asked the local chemist in Rathdowne Street, Carlton if I could deliver prescriptions for him, he knocked me back. He thought I was too small and too young to be riding a bike around the streets, but all was not lost. He led me out to the back of his shop to a storage room with 20-foot high ceilings littered with empty cardboard boxes that his stock had been delivered in, and offered me the job of flattening and tying them in bundles. I couldn't say 'yes' fast enough and I had my first paying job, earning $2 an hour. It doesn't sound like much, but in 1973 it was enough to buy fish and chips to feed a family. I felt responsible and proud that I was making a contribution to my family.

The man in charge of maintenance on the terrace houses, Joe Askar, was in his 60s, tall and skinny, and I never saw him dressed in anything other than overalls and work boots — but this isn't why I remember him. He was a kind, friendly man who taught me about Australian Rules football and a type of kick called the 'stab-pass' which was no longer used by modern-day players at that time. You dropped the ball to the ground, lace up, and kicked it with a short jabbing motion just as it was starting its upward bounce, causing it to spin through the air with great velocity while barely getting off the ground. (It was also known as a 'daisy cutter'.) Joe taught me the kick and I practiced it for hours, stab-passing into lampposts even though I would never use it in a game.

The Victorian Football League was the premier football body in Australia in 1973, made up of 12 Victorian Clubs (it's now a national competition with teams from all mainland states participating). It's almost mandatory for Victorians to follow one of these teams, and Joe Askar lived, breathed and ate the Carlton Football Club, who were also known as 'The Blues'. He regaled my brothers and me with tales of their great players, like Alex 'Jezza' Jesaulenko, Bruce 'The Flying Doormat' Doull and Robert 'Wallsy' Walls, and the closely fought games that they won. Jezza was born in Austria to a Ukrainian father and a Russian mother, and many still consider him to be the greatest Australian Rules footballer to have ever played.

Joe's enthusiasm was infectious, and this coupled with living in Carlton soon had us converted into ardent, dyed-in-the-wool Blues supporters. As kids we collected footy cards with pictures of the star players along with their personal details such as age, height and weight — precious currency. With these cards we played a game where we flicked them up against the wall, and the kid with the closest card to the wall won them all. Tony became the most passionate of Carlton fans from a very early age, and remains so today.

Crowds in excess of 100,000 attended football finals, particularly when the two most famous clubs and bitter inner-suburban rivals, Carlton and Collingwood (the 'Magpies') played each other. Their matches were often spiteful and violent, and I grew to dislike Collingwood with the same passion as the players who played for my beloved Carlton. How ironic that I would end up marrying a Collingwood supporter.

After we shifted to North Carlton I was sent to St George's Catholic Primary school, which was run by the adjacent Sacred Heart Church. I had an inquiring mind, enjoyed learning, and excelled in my studies. I loved sport and in my last year of primary school I was captain of the football team. Four years earlier I'd been living in a village in the mountains of North Lebanon, and now I was leading my school's Australian Rules team. What a transformation! At that young age I had thoughts that maybe I might be another Jezza and go on to star with my revered Carlton, but it was not to be.

Mum got a job as a part-time cleaner with Clegg's, a fabric shop in Melbourne. Every second Sunday we'd catch a bus to the city and she would take us to a movie, and afterwards we'd share a pizza. It was a very special treat, and my brothers and I used to count down the days to those fantastic Sundays.

When I was in sixth grade Mum saved up $100 and took us to the Royal Melbourne Show, an annual, week-long event held at Flemington Showgrounds in inner-city Melbourne. Every little boy and girl wants to go to the show. More than 50 acres are crammed with pavilions, fairground rides, side shows, a variety of foods, farm animal displays, dog shows, equestrian show jumping, and every kid's favorite — showbags. It has its own aroma and the first smell that hit me was of straw and cows' droppings, but it wasn't at all unpleasant. Soon I was taking in the aromas of hot dogs, freshly cooked chickens, donuts, fairy floss and meat pies. For kids, there's a magic about the show, a fascination, an excitement, and even though the festive crowd is shoulder to shoulder, you don't seem to notice it. For three young boys finding something new every ten steps it was immense and we walked for what seemed like miles. We were captivated by the roller coasters, the side show spruikers and the games of chance that looked so easy but were really very hard, like knocking over six cans with two throws of a ball. There was a huge variety of brightly decorated showbags to choose from — Cadbury's Chocolate, Action Heroes, Licorice, Batman, Spiderman and Coca Cola, to name just a few. But they're not cheap, and choosing creates its own dilemma. We had a wonderful day racing from one attraction to another, far too excited to slow down, but when it came time to go home Mum realized that she'd spent all of her money, leaving nothing for our bus fares. Like us, she'd got caught up in the excitement. We were tired, our feet were sore, and our voices hoarse, and now we were faced with a four-mile walk home— and of course we were all carrying our treasured showbags. Tony was only five years old, but he handled the walk like a trooper; in fact, there wasn't one word of complaint from any of us on the two-hour walk to Carlton. None of us had ever experienced a day like it before. We were far too happy to even think of moaning.

Mum also made sure that our birthdays were celebrated every year, and while we were poor, the saying 'Love conquers all' could have easily been created for the Hachem family.

In January 1978 I started at the Marist Brothers secondary school, St Josephs, and went through what most kids undertaking the Australian education system do, which is to go from being a big kid in primary school to being a small kid in secondary school. I was 12 but many of the older boys were 18 or 19 and, while they were in no way threatening, their sheer size was quite intimidating.

Sadly, my mother and father separated when I was 13, after which my maternal uncle, Vince, visited us more regularly and became like a father to me. He was generous, kind and scrupulously honest — and these were the values that he passed on to me and my brothers. We were poor but we never went hungry, and my mother and Uncle Vince made sure we never wanted for love. While he wasn't big in stature, he had the heart of a lion; he was a true warrior of Bescharre. He had a badly impaired eye, the result of being too curious as a young boy when, after finding a cartridge, he smashed it with a hammer, causing it to explode. The force of the explosion was such that it blew the tops off his right thumb, middle and index fingers, and splattered into his face and eye. Because of his vision problems he never took driving lessons, and his main method of travel was walking.

Uncle Vince moved in with us a few months after my parents' separation, and he and Mum started talking about buying a house in partnership. One Saturday when he was reading the newspaper, he found a house in Northcote that he wanted to inspect. We set off on the three-mile walk (walking was his favourite mode of transport, and I had no choice) at about 10.30am and to this day I can't remember inspecting the house, but that morning will forever be indelibly etched in my mind. He took me to a Just Jeans store, where he had me try on jeans, boots and shirts, and when I'd made my selections he asked me to choose a belt. The floral shirt I chose was outrageous, but at the time I thought it was the coolest shirt in the world. I left the shop wearing my new clothes and carrying my old ones in a plastic bag. I was on top of the world — most of my clothes had come from St Vincent de Paul's second-hand stores, but now as I bounced down the street everything I was wearing was brand new. I can never repay Uncle Vince for his love, kindness and being my ultimate life mentor. He made me the person I am today.

7

The Main Event — Day Two
From Their Lips to God's Ears

I've slept well, showered and shaved, and by 11am I'm sitting in Raffles Café having breakfast with the boys. I have two eggs sunny side up on toast, coffee, and finish with jam and more toast. I like order in my life, I'm a good planner, and I resolve that this will become my morning schedule for the rest of the tournament. The midday sleep-ins, with a little help from my sleeping pills, will be consigned to the past. It's only Day Two and Tony is waffling on about me winning — he is irrepressible and his enthusiasm is infectious, but I just have to slow him down. Billy is almost as optimistic and is already talking about Day Three, while Ian is more measured and thoughtful, and tells me not to get too far ahead of myself. I ask him to keep an eye on me during the tournament, and to let me know when I'm making bad plays.

'Let me get it clear, Joe,' Ian says. 'Just exactly what do you want me to look for?'

'I want you to tell me when I'm playing like a dickhead,' I respond. 'You know, when I start to lose concentration and make loose plays, and when I talk myself up and big note. I want you to tell me to pull my head in.'

Ian mulls over what I've said before responding. 'It's a big responsibility. You're really asking me to keep you focused and to make sure you stay on the rails.'

'Yeah, that's right,' I say, grinning. 'Jeez, Ian, how hard can it be to tell me I'm a dickhead when I deserve it?'

'Well, when you put it that way, Joe, I might even get to like it.'

'Just don't put him on tilt,' Tony chips in.

Ian knows what I'm looking for; really, what I'm asking him to do is to make sure I keep my feet on the ground. It's a long, grueling tournament and to make it to the end I'll need all of my stamina and wits about me. I know if I goof off, Ian won't hold back on me, but by the same token he won't harp or drag out my mistakes. I've seen far too many poker players dwell on bad beats and mistakes they've made to the detriment of their game, and that's not what I'm looking for. If need be, a short, sharp verbal clip under the ear from Ian will get my mind back on the job.

I know my crew are busting for me to do well and I can feel the goodwill they're imparting; it's a great feeling knowing you have mates as fantastic as these. I'm excited about what the day might hold and I jump in my cab oozing with confidence.

❧

Of the original 5619 starters, 1884 remain to contest Day Two, and their names, chip counts, and table and seat numbers are posted on one of the doors to the Amazon Room. If anything, it's more crowded than the first day and I have to wade through the milling mass to locate my table. I don't know and haven't heard of Haakon Waerstad, who leads the field with $169,200 in chips. I do wonder, though, whether he's aware of the 'curse of the Day One leader':

in the history of the tournament, no first day leader has ever gone on to win. From the conversations around me, I find that former champions, Doyle 'Texas Dolly' Brunson, Phil 'The Poker Brat' Hellmuth and Chris 'Jesus' Ferguson have already been knocked out. I know that between 900 and 1400 players will be eliminated today, and my primary goal, as it was on the first day, is to ensure that I'm not one of them.

I take my seat just after midday, and again, don't know anyone. I smile facetiously, thinking that perhaps all the famous players have been knocked out in the first round. Unfortunately, my table is in the middle of the room and my supporters, who have to remain behind the ropes, are too far away to see the action.

I have one of those days that all poker players have at one time or another in which I just can't get any playable hole cards, and even when I get dealt a pocket pair or suited connectors, I'm out of position or up against a huge early raise. I play really tightly, stealing a few pots from late position when I have nothing in my hand.

It's an amazing day. The overhead monitors are continually flashing and eliminations are taking place at a rate of more than one a minute. Sometimes it appears too slow and then there's five or six combatants busted out in a short burst. On the tables around me there are guys leaping up on chairs and yelling when they have a good hand; others are standing and hurling their cards on the table face up to celebrate a win. And then there are those who are holding their heads and bemoaning their bad luck. It's organized bedlam where the inmates seem to be running the asylum, and I again resolve not to get distracted by what's going on around me. But that's far easier said than done.

Around mid-session, my chip count is stagnating at around $65,000. But I'm not unhappy as I've had very few hands that I can play, and it's only my ability to pick good spots to take down uncontested pots that's saved me from a deteriorating position. The blinds are now $400/$800 and the antes are $100. I'm playing three to the left of the big blind, who I've observed to be a really tight player who isn't prepared to defend his blind without a decent hand. I'm dealt ten and four of clubs and I raise to $2,200. While I wouldn't normally condone raising with this hand, I'm playing the player, and based on my observations the likelihood of taking down the pot is high because he's going to fold most of the time. The table folds around to him, and when he calls, alarm bells start to ring. He has $80,000 in chips and for most of the morning has only played when he's had a pair of aces or kings. I steal a glance at him. He's in his mid to late 20s, has a strong face, a powerfully jutting jaw, and a deadpan expression that I'm struggling to get a read on. He's wearing a tight PokerStars T-shirt that accentuates his bulging muscles and I guess he might have been a college or pro footballer. What I know for sure is that he must have a real hand or he would have folded. I'm also aware that he doesn't have the slightest idea of what I have, as I've played very few hands, and haven't had to turn my bluffs over.

The dealer spreads the flop and I'm staring at 8-4-4, which I surmise has given him two pair at best, but I now have trips and am a clear favorite to win the hand. There is nearly $5,000 in the pot and I gaze across the table, refusing to make eye contact with him, but I can feel him looking at me intently. He's very cautious but I'm sure he must feel he has the best hand, and I sense that by taking so long he's trying to figure out whether to check or bet, as there's no way that he can put me on a four. He eventually checks, conveying weakness, while giving me the chance to hang myself. But I'm one step ahead of him and know precisely what he's trying to do, so I bet $3,500 and in textbook fashion he raises to $10,000. I take my time before smooth calling him.

The turn is a three; he checks, and I immediately bet $15,000. This time I glance to the right and he looks tentative and unsure. I know what he's doing — he's replaying the hand and trying to figure out whether I'm bluffing and what my two hole cards are. 'I call,' he says confidently, but by calling he's signaling that he's uncertain and doesn't want to make the pot bigger than it already is.

The river is an eight, giving me a full house, and he checks again. I spend about 30 seconds considering what the possibility of him having an eight in his hand is, and decide it's negligible as he plays far too tightly for that. Now I'm confident that he has an overpair and that my full house is going to be good enough. I'm not going to get beaten but I ponder whether he'll call me if I go all-in. I put him on a big pair, probably aces or kings, and after a lot of consideration I'm convinced he'll have to call, so I go all-in. He looks at his cards again, stares at me, and riffles his chips. He's racking his brain about what I might have and his gut is churning — I know because I've been in his shoes many, many times before. Five minutes goes by and some of the other players on the table are starting to get impatient. I can feel him staring at me but I don't move my head and continue to look across the table, hands together in front of my face, in my normal position.

Dusan, who has been watching the standoff, has seen me push all my chips in. He can no longer stand the suspense of not being able to see what's going on from behind the ropes, so he breaks all the spectator rules by charging down the aisle and standing behind me just as my opponent calls and I turn my hand over. 'Yes!' Dusan shouts, 'Yes!' pumping the air with one fist, so relieved that I haven't been knocked out. He starts to say something to me and then looks up to see the Tournament Director making a beeline for him, and before he can finish what he's saying, he's racing back down the aisle, fearing that he's about to be kicked out. Luckily for him, the tournament officials have been kept busy, threatening and warning the mainstream media, who have been jamming up the aisles for most of the day, and he's allowed to escape his small misdemeanor.

The big blind, who's a real gentleman, shows me a pair of kings and congratulates me on the way I've played my hand, but the deadpan expression is gone, replaced by abject disappointment. I have more than $130,000 in chips, which is just as well, as my hole cards don't improve, and I continue to bleed chips for the rest of the day.

During the day an enormous burst of applause erupts from the rear of the room when an Englishman, Barry Paskin, nicknamed 'Mr Stinky' by the other players, is eliminated. This guy hasn't showered for days, has long dirty hair, is a show pony, and shouts and screams at every opportunity in the hope that ESPN will film him. On day 1B of the tournament he drops the f-bomb twice and is suspended for 20 minutes. When he returns to the table he has Band-Aids pasted over his mouth. What a joke. Today, officials force him to change out of his favorite David Beckham jersey because it's giving off a vile odor. He moans, 'Tell me where it says in the rules that you're not allowed to wear smelly clothes.' Shortly afterwards, he comes back to the table having dispensed with the Beckham jersey and is knocked out. Funnily enough I had spoken to him during the $1,000 re-buy and he seemed like a nice guy. I wonder whether he was just putting on a show for the cameras.

At midnight there are still 630 players alive and another 61 will be eliminated before the Tournament Director calls an end to play at 1.15am. It has been an incredible day with 1315 players eliminated, leaving only 569 from the original 5619 that fronted up on the three first days. When another nine players are knocked out, the rest of the field will be in the money to the extent of $12,500. I've hardly had a hand all day and I've had to grind to finish with $95,900 in chips, which is a little less than the average of $99,000. In a marathon seven-day tournament everyone who gets to the final table will have at least one day like I've had today and I'm glad to get through such a tough time in comparatively good shape.

I have a view that if a poker player's head is not pounding after a long session he hasn't been working hard enough. In this game, one or two loose hands can see you eliminated and back in your room packing, wondering what went wrong. As we head to the All-American Bar & Grill the boys are jubilant, but my head is aching. I order a rib-eye steak, which is my standard fare, but I'm still replaying hands in my head and it's too early to start winding down. Tony and Billy tell me I'm certain to make the final table, and I pray that what comes from their lips goes directly to God's ears.

❧

I get back to my room just after 3am, prop myself up on the bed and phone Jeanie. She's ecstatic about how well I'm doing, and says in the most serious of tones, 'Joe, I know that you're either going to win or finish third.'

'Hey, you were only telling me a few nights ago that I was destined to win. What's changed?' I laugh.

'Joe, I'm being serious.'

'I know you are, honey. Love you.'

8

Everyone Starts Somewhere

Like all poker players, I had to begin somewhere. I had been watching my parents and uncles get together at Christmases and Easters for years to play poker. These festive occasions involved far more than cards and there was much eating and drinking, but what I remember most was the noise, the talking, the sound of laughter and an overwhelming feeling of warmth and goodwill. I loved these times when the whole family celebrated together in a raucous and spontaneous manner. I didn't get too close or appear to watch the cards too carefully, though, as the harmony and festive season wouldn't have saved me from getting a good clip under the ear. The adults playing poker was fine, but God help us if they found us kids doing the same.

Despite this I didn't miss a trick, and my cousins and I started playing penny ante poker just for fun. We played Manila, a basic form of poker in which you're dealt two cards from a short deck made up of 32 cards, with the smallest value card a 7. One card is open, then there's a round of betting after each card, until there are five cards open. Using your two cards and three from the board, players try and make the best five-card poker hand, with a flush beating a full house. We always played in a bedroom behind closed doors, just to make sure the adults didn't catch us. I grew up on card games and loved playing them.

However, I was well aware that life didn't revolve around playing cards and in my early teenage years I was getting up at 2am during the school holidays to work in a bakery. The early hours didn't worry me; I enjoyed the work and I loved the aroma of freshly baked bread wafting through the air — something that has stayed with me all my life. Uncle Vince was living with us, so I wasn't the sole bread-winner (forgive the pun), but I was making a contribution and saw myself as the head of our house. The seeds of leadership my grandfather had sown within me when I was barely more than an infant had blossomed, and responsibility was something I thrived on.

I was 15 when I first met Jeanie at a newly formed local youth club, she was only 11. During one of our first meetings I was teaching another girl how to play cards when Jeanie suddenly started running rings around us chanting, 'Joe loves Morna, Joe loves Morna!' I used to think of her as my kid sister and certainly didn't have any romantic inclinations toward her, even though I later found out that she had a crush on me. My Mum and Vince were friendly with Jeanie's parents and I got to know them all quite well in the following years; nevertheless, while I was very fond of her, I never saw her as a future girlfriend, let alone my wife — she was just too young. A four-year age difference then seemed enormous.

It was at this time that my uncles offered me the chance to work with them over the holidays performing welding maintenance on factory equipment. I was so thin that they couldn't find a pair of overalls to fit me, so I wore three layers of clothes just to fit into the smallest pair they could find. It was my job to ensure the welding and electrical leads didn't become tangled, and to remove obstacles so that the welders and their machines could work unimpeded. I worked very hard, putting in 12 hours a day, seven days a week over the holiday period, for which my uncles paid me the huge sum of $100 per day. Looking back, there was probably some nepotism involved regarding the size of my pay packet, as I'm sure they could have employed a part-time laborer for a lesser sum who would have been stronger and more experienced than me. I was grateful to my uncles; I loved working with them and the sense of belonging that went with it. When school resumed I quit working at the bakery and took a part-time position at Coles in the delicatessen department. It was better paying and I got to work at more reasonable times, after school. It was about this time that I started to have an appreciation of my value as a hard-working, conscientious employee.

My next foray into the labor market saw me working in the early morning hours again, this time at the more civilized starting time of 5am, but the work itself was tougher and more menial: packing, stacking, and hanging produce in a meat factory. Sometimes I'd get to ride on one of the trucks doing the first run of deliveries to butchers. Even though I'd grown taller and stronger, the carcasses were huge and far heavier than me; however, the drivers soon showed me how to balance them on my shoulder, and after a few weeks I could carry them without difficulty.

I learned to bluff at a very early age, but sometimes it got me into trouble. I was successful in securing a job selling new and used motor vehicles, where I was expected to take potential customers out on test drives. Employees were allowed to use one of the cars in stock for personal use, but I guessed they wouldn't let this happen unless you had a license, and seeing I was still underage this presented me with a problem. There was no option but to fold my hand and phone the dealer, saying that something had come up and I couldn't accept his offer.

I was never afraid of hard work and I took something away from every job I had, all the time developing my business knowledge and acumen.

I had a lot of friends at school but my two best mates were Joe Fruci and Dominic Russo. We became thick as thieves. They were good kids, loved music, and were not part of the bully group that tried to run the school. By the time we reached Year 12 they were DJ'ing at parties and gigs all over Melbourne. I became their roadie, in title only — I can't ever remember loading or setting up their gear. There were always plenty of girls at the places they DJ'd, which made it a lot of fun, but my career as a roadie was cut prematurely short by the demands of university and money-making pursuits.

In 1983 I finished my six years of secondary education. I had enjoyed my time at Marist Brothers and had avoided becoming involved with the ruling groups, but I wasn't someone who was picked on or bullied. The 'nerds' liked me because I was cordial to them and didn't put them down, and the hooligans had a begrudging hard-earned respect for me. I wasn't a thug but had meted out a few painful experiences to those who misinterpreted my courteous manner as weakness, and I soon acquired a reputation as a guy who couldn't be messed with. After that I was left alone. I attained my Higher School Certificate with a B+ average and, while this was a good result, I'd expected at least an A. Perhaps my obsession with work and making a monetary contribution to my family had impacted on my studies.

I wasn't sure what career or tertiary studies I should pursue, but one of my best friends at the time, Robert Belia, a gentle, softly spoken kid of gigantic proportions, had been reading articles on natural healing, and had made an appointment to visit a chiropractor practicing at Preston Market. Robert invited me to tag along with him and we fired off numerous questions to the chiropractor, who was very generous with his time and advice. He was a proponent of natural healing without the use of drugs, and this had great appeal to me. I followed up the interview with quite a bit of reading on chiropractic, and the more I read about this form of healing, the more appealing it became. Robert and I applied to do a five-year Bachelor of Applied Science degree at the Royal Melbourne Institute of Technology. I was accepted, but unfortunately Robert wasn't, and his father, who was extremely domineering, banned me from ever visiting their house again. Robert was severely chastized, something he'd suffered all his life. Shortly after this, Robert turned his back on his family and broke the bonds that had been strangling him by shaving his head and joining the Hare Krishnas. Sadly, I too lost contact with him, but even now I often find myself wondering if the choice that he made in life enabled him to achieve the peace and happiness he'd missed growing up.

9

The Main Event — Day Three
Life on the Line

My mate, the poker reporter Chris Newton, phones me at 10am and he's in a complete flap. 'Joe,' he groans, as if it's the end of the world, 'you're on Mike Matusow's table today.' I know of Matusow's reputation as a tough, aggressive player who likes talking trash and needling his opponents at the table, hence his nickname, 'The Mouth'. He boasts two WSOP bracelets and a sixth place in the Main Event in 2001, and more recently was released from prison after doing six months for being in possession of cocaine. Chris is worried that he may get to me and cause me to go on tilt. I tell him not to worry and that I've played against plenty of tough guys before, but I know Chris is far from convinced. I order a coffee to go, grab a cab and head to the battleground for another day's warfare at the tables. It's my intention to fly under the radar and build my chip stack virtually unnoticed.

Even though we're down to only 569 players, the Amazon Room is packed with spectators, many of whom are eliminated players and members of the media, whose access has been restricted as a result of the disputes with tournament officials the day before. Day Three kicks off at 1pm with blinds of $1,000/$2,000 and antes of $300.

Roger Pardey Jr, a resident of Las Vegas who I've not heard of, leads the field with a chip count of $464,000. At the other end of the spectrum there are 33 players holding chips of $20,000 or less with the shortest stack being only $3,200. We start the day playing hand for hand, with nine players to be eliminated before we get to the money. Hand for hand is designed to stop short-stacked players playing slowly in the hope that someone from another table will be eliminated. When a hand at a table is concluded the dealer stands up, signifying completion. When all dealers at the 57 active tables have stood up the next hand is dealt and the process repeated. This is painfully slow and the players with tiny stacks know they can only survive by successfully going all-in, while a number of those around the $20,000 chip mark play tight, hoping to hang on until they reach the money, which starts at $12,500 for 560th place and culminates with $7.5m for the winner.

Three to my right is Minh Ly, a Vietnamese-born American professional poker player with some very good results behind him, including a ninth place finish in the Main Event in 2002. Three to my left is Mike Matusow, who has about $120,000 in chips, and even as he's taking his seat his mouth's going full bore, although his vitriol isn't directed at anyone in particular. Earlier in the tournament a dealer has called one of the floormen and told him that Mike had dropped the f-bomb. The floorman agrees with the dealer and suspends Mike for ten minutes, to which Mike responds, 'F*** that.'

'That's another ten minutes.'

'F***ing joke.'

'Make that 30 minutes.'

'F*** you too.'

'Forty minutes,' says the floorman, and Mike finally shuts up and leaves the table to start serving his penalty.

The clear chip leader at the table is a young Scottish internet player, Graeme Harrison, sitting two to the right of me, who has about $300,000 in chips in front of him. Small, red-haired and baby-faced, he looks as though butter wouldn't melt in his mouth. He's wearing the standard PokerStars cap and gear — it seems half the field has qualified on PokerStars, but it turns out that it's only one in every five. Only! He looks over at Mike and says something like, 'Okay, bigmouth, we've heard enough from you. Let's play cards.' You could hear a pin drop at our table; obviously someone telling Mike to zip it isn't a common occurrence.

'How the stuff did you get so many chips?' Mike snarls, and Graeme retaliates, asking Mike if he loves flapping his gums. 'All those chips are gonna be mine before the day's out,' Mike growls, 'and then you can go back to playing your kiddy games on the net.' I haven't said a word while this exchange has gone on but I know that Mike's attention is going to be focused on Graeme — and that's exactly how the day pans out. I later find out that Graeme has quite a checkered history, having been banned from nearly every casino in Britain for card counting. Forced out of blackjack, he turned to spread betting and then about two years ago took up poker. What was I saying about butter not melting in his mouth?

The young American guy sitting directly to the left of me plays a few early hands but now he's folding hand after hand. He doesn't look 21, but he must be, because Harrah's are far too thorough to let an underage player into the tournament. He has started the day with a healthy $97,000 in chips, and is playing very solidly, but after getting rolled in the few hands he plays he completely shuts up shop and is now folding hand after hand. I ask him why he's mucking every hand and he tells me that he's a college student on a freeroll and that $12,500 is a lot of money to him. He's going to make sure he hangs on until the bubble is eliminated.

ESPN have positioned cameras all around the room, ensuring they'll capture the agony embossed on the bubble's face as he or she is eliminated. The downside to the cameras is that all the nutters see them as a golden opportunity to get on television, and if anything there's even more screaming, yahooing and jumping up on chairs than there was yesterday. Our table agrees that we're not going to do anything stupid, and that we'll keep playing without adding to the drama going on around us. If something happens on our table that warrants coverage by ESPN, we'll embrace it, but we're not about to start screaming just to get on television. I don't know Mike Matusow, but from what I've heard about him, I'm surprised that's he not doing something to attract the cameras.

No one is throwing chips around and play is incredibly tight. Finally, after nearly an hour and 20 minutes, in which fewer than 20 hands have been played, the unluckiest player in the field, Carl Ygborn from Sweden, is eliminated in 561st position having started the day with $74,000 in chips, and misses the money by just one place. The cameras are there to catch his anguish, and applause and subdued cheers of relief reverberate around the massive room. I feel a little sorry for him; being the bubble is undoubtedly even worse than being the first player eliminated. As I'm pondering this, an announcement comes across the PA system that he has won a seat in the 2006 Main Event courtesy of the benevolence of Harrah's, and this time the cheers are spontaneous and generous in spirit. I silently thank Harrah's for their fine gesture.

The hour and 20 minutes lost is added back on the clock, making the $1,000/$2,000/$300 level the longest of the tournament. The young college player sitting next to me goes all-in within 15 minutes of the bubble being eliminated and is knocked out. He's a nice young kid and gives us a big friendly smile before heading to the cage to pick up his $12,500. In the next two hours we lose another 142 players at an average of more than one a minute, compared with an average of one every ten minutes when everyone was fighting to make it to the money. The monitors above us, which update blinds and antes, how much time is left in the level, blinds and antes at the next level and the number of players remaining and the average stack, are in perpetual motion as the eliminations gather momentum. Many players who are now in the money start to gamble loosely with the intent of either adding to their chips or getting out.

Graeme Harrison is a wild player who takes his chip stack from $300,000 to $40,000 and then back to $280,000. He's a loose cannon and I have little respect for the way he plays and hope that I can go heads-up against him. Mike Matusow has settled down and is playing controlled poker. He is now only occasionally jibing Graeme, and I seem to be getting on okay with Mike; he's certainly not focusing on me, which is just fine.

Unfortunately, I'm about to make my first major mistake in three days. The table folds around to me in late position and I limp in with A-2 of clubs. *What am I doing limping in when I should be raising?* The small blind makes it up, and the big blind, Bryant King, an American about my age, checks. By failing to raise, I haven't qualified their hands and have no idea what they're holding. I am, however, acutely aware that Bryant is a tight solid player and I haven't seen him play a hand all day in which he hasn't had the goods. The flop comes A-K-10 and I'm in a self-induced quandary. *What have they got?* It could be K-Q, Q-J, A-K

— I just don't know! I do know that Bryant's short-stacked, with about $50,000 in chips, and that he's not going to risk his chips without having a real hand. I've got top pair with no kicker and when he leads out with $7,000, I raise to $21,000 and the small blind folds. Without so much as a pause, Bryant shoves all his chips into the pot, and I call. *What am I doing calling? What am I doing throwing my chips away? I should've folded knowing he had to have at least two pair.* He hasn't had a cent in play all day without having the nuts, and I shouldn't have called his all-in. This hand has gone from mistake to mistake, and when he turns over Q-J, giving him an ace high straight, I lose $65,000. I silently beat up on myself before trying to put this debacle out of my mind; I'm not going to go on tilt as a result of one poorly played hand.

Just before dinner Minh Ly and Mike Matusow start exchanging banter about how many players will still be 'alive' at the end of the day's play. Minh thinks there'll be more than 200 and Mike thinks he is wrong, so they decide to resolve the issue with a $10,000 cash bet.

By the time dinner is taken at 7pm, another 68 players have gone and we're down to 351. I have a steak with Ian and for the first time he calls me a dickhead over the way I played that hand against Bryant King. I snap, 'I know, I know,' before I settle down and thank him. After all, that's what I asked him to do when I stuff up or get too cocky. On the first two days' play, he'd been in bed when I'd got back to the room, and when I bounded in all hyped up and said, 'I'm still in and playing really well,' he responded with, 'That's great Joe, but there's a long, long way to go yet.' He's making sure that I keep my feet on the ground, and that's exactly what I want him to do.

Straight after dinner the blinds are $1,500/$3,000, the antes are $500 and I'm in the small blind. The table folds around to Graeme Harrison on the button, who has about $240,000 in chips, and he raises to $8,000. I have $140,000 in chips and I call with As-9h. The big blind folds and the flop is A-7-3 with two spades and I check with the intent of check-raising. Graeme bets $10,000 and I raise to $30,000. He ponders his position for about two minutes before taking me by surprise and going all-in. I feel that I have a good read on him and am fairly certain that I have him beat, but do I have the gumption to go with my read? I'm absolutely petrified that I might be wrong. I glance over at him and sense weakness. I just know that he doesn't want me to call. It's 7.30pm and I'm faced with my first really dangerous encounter in three days of playing.

I take a deep breath and push all my chips into the pot, knowing that my tournament life is now on the line. I turn over my A-9 and the look on his face is priceless as he realizes that I have his A-6 totally dominated. Only a six or running straight cards can defeat me. I know that the next two cards will determine my future in the tournament. My table is right next to the rail and I look over and see Tony and the rest of the posse concentrating intently, the strain written all over their faces. I can't watch the turn or the river so I get up and walk over to them with my back to the table. It's less than 30 seconds, but it feels like minutes, and then they burst into applause and start shouting. I've just doubled my stack.

At around 10.30pm, Haakon Waerstad, the chip leader after the completion of all the first days, is eliminated in 314th place and takes home $21,070. The curse of the first day leader remains intact.

The next few hours I'm card dead and lose two pots when my bluffs are called. As a result I'm down to $120,000 in chips and revert to playing tightly. Just after midnight the blinds are $2,500/$5,000 with $500 antes and we're down to 209 players. A few minutes later, Graeme Harrison, who has provided us with so much entertainment, is knocked out, collecting $33,197 for his efforts. As he departs he grins and wishes us well for the rest of the tournament. Surprisingly, Mike Matusow is quite gracious and says, 'Well played, kid.' Maybe he's not the ogre Chris Newton painted him as.

During the course of the day a number of new players have joined our table, and the latest replacement sits down in the seat to the left of me and can't stop grinning when he looks around the table and sees he has by far the biggest stack — about $400,000. He's in his late 20s, clean shaven with cropped short brown hair, and noticeably is not wearing the regulation poker players' cap and gear. His most obvious features are his smirk, an in-your-face cockiness and a very aggressive attitude. With less than an hour of play to complete the day, I'm dealt two kings under the gun and raise to $15,000; Mr Cocky raises to $40,000 and everyone else folds. I'm getting short-stacked and haven't had anything I can play for the past two hours, but now I have the second best pair. He has me covered three to one in chips, and I need to double up or get out, preferably the former. I know that if I go all-in he'll almost certainly call in the realization that a loss won't hurt him, and we'll end up playing for a big pot which could double me up. Alternatively he could get lucky and eliminate me.

As I'm contemplating my decision I catch Emad's eye and give him a cheeky wink, letting him know my hole cards are strong. I gather up my chips and push them into the pot — I'm all-in. He takes only a few seconds to call, turning over A-Q and feigns nonchalance when he sees my kings, but try as he might he can't hide his disappointment. I can feel the ESPN cameras on me as I get up and go for a walk for the second time today, knowing my tournament life is once more on the line. I return to the table and see the flop, 2-6-3, and breathe a sigh of relief. Two cards to go and I can't stand still so I head over to my supporters on the rail. I can't stay at the table but I can't stay away either and I get back to see a ten on the turn. One card to go, one card to determine my future, and I grimace as the dealer flips over the river — a beautiful five, and the weight of the world is lifted from my shoulders. I've doubled up again and have $240,000 in chips.

With less than half an hour to go to complete the day, Greg Raymer, the 2004 World Champion, and Tim Phan, a well-known professional, are shifted to my table. Their stacks are massive and they need the help of the floor staff to carry their chips. I do a quick count and squirm when I realize that Greg has more than a million in chips, and Tim has about $800,000. Fortunately, I don't get into any standoffs with either of them in the short amount of time remaining to complete the day.

At 1.30am the day is over. There are 185 survivors, and Mike Matusow has won his $10,000 bet with Minh Ly. I have $231,000 in chips, against an average of $304,000.

10

Vale

It takes only a few days at the Royal Melbourne Institute of
Technology for me to realize that 12 years of having teachers
chasing me to submit assignments and essays are gone forever.
I'm doing a six-year degree compressed to five years, and for me
university turns out be an almost ideal learning environment. I've
always been a good planner and I soon work out the exact number
of hours I need to spend attending lectures, doing research and
submitting assignments. Then I get to the important part of my
scheduling, which is to work out how much time I have left in the
week to work on a casual basis and to pursue my entrepreneurial
interests, which are only limited by my bankroll. I'll trade
virtually anything I think I can sell at a profit. I like the good life
— going out, nice clothes, fine restaurants — plus I want to go on
contributing to my family, and I can only do this thanks to my
business ventures. Things are also looking up on the work front:
I'm no longer lugging carcasses but pulling what I think are the
finest beers in Melbourne at the Croxton Park Hotel. I have hardly
any free time but that's the way I like living my life — something
that's never changed.

Midway through my second year of university I'm approached

to do some modeling work, parading some of the latest fashions from Melbourne designers. It seems to me that, as I'm about to leave my teen years, the work I'm doing is becoming more lucrative and less taxing. From talking to the other models I find they don't like planning or organizing bookings — they want someone to do it all for them and to tell them when and where their appointments are. With this in mind I decide to form my own troupe from the young female and male models who I've worked with on the basis that it will be more profitable for them and me. I organize rates and bookings and take a percentage of the fee earned by each model. It's a win-win for everybody and I'm making more than double the money I was from modeling. For the next 18 months business booms and my ever-expanding troupe is booked out at nightclubs and shopping centers most weekends. This is great as I can continue providing for my family while still having enough to go out with my buddies and have a good time. Unfortunately, my university studies are becoming more difficult and I'm faced with a tough decision. Do I continue to manage and grow the modeling business or opt to complete my degree and pursue my ambition of becoming a chiropractor? I choose the latter, but know that I'll have to replace my business income with something else that's less demanding on my time.

I'm still busy over the weekends in 1986 and can't get to the Grand Final to see my team, the Carlton Footy Club play Hawthorn (the 'Hawks'). Much to my disappointment, the Blues just can't cut it on the day, and are comfortably beaten.

On the last day of September 1987 the same two sides meet again in the Grand Final and to my sheer delight, before a crowd of nearly 93,000, the Blues avenge their 1986 defeat and crush the Hawks. I'm in Sydney visiting my uncle and cousins, but as expected a jubilant Tony is at the game screaming for the Blues. The following day is the worst of my life.

My middle brother, Elei, was born with a slightly deformed rib cage which would sometimes pinch his breathing. As a result, he missed a lot of school. When he was 13 he had an operation to correct the misaligned rib, but it was unsuccessful and made the condition even worse. Because of his chest problem, the time spent with doctors, and the lack of school, he also developed a speech impediment. He didn't like or excel at school, and perhaps I should have spent more time trying to teach him, but I was only two years older, and leading a very hectic life. Because of the pain and discomfort Elei suffered, Mum was very protective of him and he was her favorite. She certainly didn't love Tony or me any less but it's a natural maternal instinct to pay greater attention to the child who's in most need. By year ten, he'd become something of a rebel, and dropped out of school to become a laborer.

My cousins had driven down from Sydney to visit us, and on the Friday before the 1987 Grand Final, I joined them on the return trip so that I could visit my Uncle Anthony and his family. Before leaving, I'd said to Elei that I'd be gone for a week and that I wanted him to take my place to sell sheepskin covers at the stall that my business partner and I had set up at the Coburg Market on Sundays. I didn't want to let my partner down while I was away so Elei agreed to man the stall on Sunday morning in my place. On Grand Final night, Elei and two of his mates went out nightclubbing and having a good time. One of his mates had a Statesman Caprice, and after a night on the town, they decided to drive down the coast and spend Sunday at Frankston beach near Melbourne. Elei went home at about 5am, and while his friends waited in the car out the front, he woke Mum up, either by accident or intentionally, and gave her a big hug and a kiss.

The boys hadn't slept all night. On the way to the beach they fell asleep and the car crashed head-on into a bus traveling along the Nepean Highway in Seaford. Elei and the driver, Harry (I never knew his surname), were killed instantly. They were only five minutes from their destination when the crash occurred. The boy in the back, Joe Afif, was in a bad way and was rushed to hospital, but with time he eventually pulled through. Joe was a friend of the family, and while it wasn't his fault, I couldn't bring myself to face him for a long time. Elei was only 19 years old, with all his life in front of him.

I'd been out in Sydney, but when I return to Uncle Anthony's home it's quiet, and he and his sons are grim-faced and red-eyed. They tell me the dreadful news and the shock is something like being hit with a sledge-hammer. I'm devastated, distraught and desperate to get home. These days, jets travel between Sydney and Melbourne every half hour for the one-hour flight, but that was not the case in 1987. I'm forced to travel to Melbourne via Albury and with the stopover the trip takes over four hours.

Elei's death is a major tragedy for Melbourne's Lebanese community and the reaction is overwhelming. When I finally reach home there are over four hundred friends and relatives there. I find Mum, Tony and Uncle Vince and we try to comfort each other but we're numb with grief.

In Lebanon, when a family experiences a dreadful loss, their friends and relatives visit them day after day, trying to take the minds of the immediate family off the terrible tragedy they've experienced by surrounding them with kindness, and this can go on for months. We had those who loved and cared for us visit daily for three months as they tried to alleviate the unbearable pain and dreadful suffering we were going through.

Jeanie's parents visited almost every day. By that time, Jeanie had grown into a beautiful young lady. During this period of commiseration I grew very fond of her and we developed an unspoken bond — there was no need for words. The connection was strong and we both felt it.

Jeanie's brother, Joe, would tragically lose his life in a car accident just five months after Elei's death. He, too, was only 19, and he and Elei had been very close friends. My family and I did everything we could to assist Jeanie and her family in much the same way as they'd helped us. This was a terrible period for Jeanie and me, and our respective families, and it is difficult to describe our agony. We felt angry, miserable and helpless but adversity drew Jeanie and me closer together and we found ourselves simultaneously courting and mourning. Amidst all the terrible pain and grief, I was falling deeply in love.

After Elei's passing, Mum could no longer live in the house that she'd bought in Northcote with Uncle Vince — the memories were just too raw and painful — so they sold it and bought a house in Cameron Street, Reservoir, which became our new home.

11

The Main Event — Day Four
Gazing into Space

The first three days of play and the early morning finishes catch up with me, and even with the sleeping pills I toss and turn most of the night. It's a late start today and I've treated myself to a sleep-in and set my alarm for 11am. I'm finally in a deep sleep when I feel someone shaking me, and I hear Ian's voice, 'Joe, Joe, you've slept in. You're missing the tournament.' In a complete panic, I jump out of bed in one bound, babbling, 'What? What? How? How?' I look at the clock; it's 10.30am and Ian's laughing. I want to kill him as he says something like, 'Jeez, Joe, I've never seen you move that fast before.' That's what you get when you room with a practical joker. He'll keep for another time, but at least there's no way I'll be late for today's play.

When I get to the Amazon Room, quite a few tables have been removed. One-third of the room has been roped off and a meter-wide track runs around the whole area for use by the media and photographers. ESPN have blanketed the room with cameras and they'll catch any exciting or outrageous performances on all tables rather than just the TV table. Play kicks off at 12.20pm with blinds of $3,000/$6,000 and antes of $1,000. There's a rumor circulating that the organizers are looking to reduce the 185 starters to 100 by the end of the day. The room is peaceful on the surface but the undercurrent is menacing.

As I take my seat I look at the faces around the table and again I know no one. I'm pleased that the table-talk centers on how long my opponents are going to have to survive to make it to the next level. Seven players have the list of prize money levels in front of them, which show payouts increasing the longer each one remains alive. The first 15 players eliminated today will receive $39,075, the next 30, $46,245, the next 30, $54,965, and so on. Everyone is talking about hanging on and minimizing risk. I add my support, but secretly I'm licking my chops knowing how easy this is going to make stealing pots and playing aggressively. I'm not interested in the prize money list as there's only one prize I'm after, and everyone knows its value. There's also some conversation amongst the players about the possibility of lasting long enough to have the chance of getting on the TV table, but that doesn't concern me and will have no impact on the way I play. I start the day feeling very comfortable.

After about an hour we're down to 164 and Jason Lester, a resident of Miami who finished fourth in the Main Event in 2003, is moved to our table. He's highly respected and has the reputation of being a very good cash player. I discreetly check him out. He handles himself like a true professional, playing tightly while getting a read on players he has not encountered before.

Play goes as I expected and while I have no big hands up until dinner, I accumulate chips all day, bluffing and stealing pots with impunity as my opponents fold around me, anxious to get to the next level. In the few hands I get called, I'm able to show down good hands and this helps when I need to bluff. I knew the prize money list would help me, but it's even better than I thought.

Mum, Elei, Tony and I before coming to Australia. Mum always found a way to dress us nicely.

I was an angel at school, just look at that smile.

Strike a pose. I was so young.

My best friend, Pierre Kairouz. Always has been, always will be.

Elei and me.

Sneaking a kiss while the priest wasn't looking. The wedding party was strictly Jeanie, Tony, Denise and me. The priest, Monsignor Paul, God rest his Soul, was part of the deal.

The boys huddle around me for some serious post-hand discussion.

You can't see it but I am mortified at the prospect of taking my little chip stack up against Ivey's monster stack.

Steve, me, and the money. And of course the shotgun wielding security guard.

Tony and Billy were so excited, they nearly threw me into outer space.

Emad, showing off my bracelet.

At the Wynn, celebrating with the boys.

Hachems never do anything by halves; look you can even see Collette (Cookie) right at the back.

Dusan congratulating me and presenting me with a trophy.

Jeanie and the kids surround me as we are about to cut the cake.

We return from dinner down to 102. We have a new player on our table, Scott Lazar, a Californian who has a fair-sized stack of about $650,000. He's a big guy in his early 40s, with a rugged, friendly face and dark, brushed-back hair. He's wearing sunglasses with transparent lenses and you can clearly see his eyes. His nickname is 'Magic' — not as a result of his adroitness in handling a pack of cards, but rather because he was a professional magician before he turned to his first love and became a professional poker player. We're sitting opposite each other and I have a similar sized stack to his, making us joint chip leaders at the table. I decide to play cautiously while I work him out and he plays tightly and sensibly. He is clearly not an erratic player.

Our first clash comes about 30 minutes after Scott sits down when the blinds are $5,000/$10,000 and the antes $1,000. He raises to $30,000 in late position, and the table folds around to me in the big blind and I call with A-Q. The flop is Q-Q-8 with two clubs. I take plenty of time before checking to him, and he bets $50,000. I smooth call him. The turn card is a blank and I check again, looking to trap him by check-raising, but Scott foils my strategy by checking back. The river is another blank. I bet $100,000 and he instantly folds showing me J-9 of clubs. I drag in a nice pot which could've been larger, but I take the table lead. I'm happy to have won the pot, but feel a little disappointed as I didn't win anywhere near the chips I'd expected. It's then that I realize a club or a ten would've destroyed me, and that maybe I got lucky.

It would be remiss of me at this point if I did not relate two of the most remarkable hands of the tournament, both featuring the young American player of Korean heritage, Bernard Lee. He is dealt K-K in early position and raises to $35,000. Kevin McCarthy, the guy to the left of him, re-raises to $60,000, and everyone else folds. Bernard, almost without hesitation, says, 'I know you have aces, Kevin, so I'm going to lay this down,' and he flips his kings over. Kevin looks shattered as he turns over a pair of aces, and Bernard leaps from his chair and yells, 'Yes!' Jason Lester and I both congratulate Bernard, saying it's the best lay-down we've ever seen and I'm glad I'm not in Kevin's shoes. To this day I don't know how Bernard knew that Kevin had aces.

In the second hand, Bernard is dealt Q-Q and raises to $35,000 from mid-position. Kevin McCarthy calls and I raise to $125,000 and everyone else folds. Bernard instantly mucks his queens, Kevin shows 3-3, and I turn over a pair of kings. Now I know exactly what it's like to be in Kevin's shoes. Bernard's two lay-downs are the highlights of the session. He seems like a nice guy and a real gentleman, and we become quite friendly.

Late in the night I'm in the big blind when Ayhan Alsancak, a Swedish guy who's short-stacked, goes all-in in late position. Jason Lester, who's on the button, looks over at me. I look down at J-J and feel him staring at me, his eyes shifting from the small blind back to me and then back to the small blind. These cat-and-mouse tactics go on for minutes and I can see Jason wrestling with himself — he obviously has a hand that he thinks can beat Ayhan. It seems that he's more concerned about what the small blind and I might do if he calls or raises. Jason looks like someone who's been in this position before and suffered a very bad beat. He reminds me of a little boy waiting to cross the road who won't step off the curb even when there's a break in the traffic. Finally, Jason goes all-in and, much to his relief, the small blind folds and I muck my jacks. Jason has K-K, and is elated when Ayhan turns over K-8, confirming his earlier thoughts that he had him beat. Sometimes the poker gods can be very cruel and when the flop comes 8-8-6,

Jason's in big trouble. The turn card and the river don't help him, and despite doing everything right, he's now seriously short-stacked and a few hands later he busts out.

As he leaves the table he puts his hand on my shoulder and whispers, 'I think you're the best player left here, kid. Now go on and win it.' This is a massive boost to my confidence, especially coming from such a respected player.

I play my last big hand of the day when Ayhan Alsancak in middle position raises to $45,000. The table folds around to the small blind who calls, and I'm in the big blind with K-8 of hearts and also call. The dealer spreads the flop, which is A-9-7 including two hearts, the small blind checks, and I bet $85,000. Ayhan calls and the small blind folds. The turn is an irrelevant six and I bet $240,000 and Ayhan calls again. I cross my fingers for a heart on the river but it's to no avail and the dealer flips over another blank. I have absolutely nothing but I don't hesitate for a moment before going all-in. I have Ayhan covered by about $200,000 chips, and I put him on A-J, and rationalize that he can't risk his tournament life by calling. I gaze out into space but feel him watching me, and then he checks his cards in one hand while riffling his chips with the other. He says something like, 'I know I have you beat,' but I ignore him and continue to stare out into nothingness. Five minutes elapse and the other players on the table are starting to get agitated, with one impatiently asking Ayhan what he's doing. I feel his eyes on me and know he's still searching for a tell, but he can't find one, and he folds, showing me A-J. For the first time in the tournament I show my bluff, and the tension around the table lifts as my opponents, in disbelief, burst into spontaneous applause. I see the pain and remorse in Ayhan's face and he moans, 'I was so close to calling. You have no idea how close I was to calling. I knew

I should have called.' He is visibly hurting and will probably carry this hand around in his head for the remainder of the tournament — perhaps even longer.

I hear that the other remaining Aussie in the field, Sarah Bilney, has just been knocked out in 63rd place. She's played very well and had a great tournament, finishing with prize money of $145,875.

Play finishes at 1.30am and the field is down to 58 with an average chip count of $969,000. I've had my best day, increasing my chips from $231,000 to $814,000 without having once put my tournament life at risk.

There are a lot of Aussies in Las Vegas and word of my progress has spread so that when we get to the All-American Bar & Grill there's more than a dozen of us and we're becoming quite well-known to the waiters and bar staff. As I get deeper into the tournament, no one wants to miss the finish of each day's play, and the boys are elated that I'm now only one step away from the final three tables. I stick to my routine and order a steak but tonight I also treat myself to a Corona — a couple of Coronas, in fact. Ian and I replay a few hands and he tells me that I haven't made any dickhead plays today — a high compliment coming from him. However, in usual Ian style, he finishes with, 'But just remember, Joe, there's still a long, long way to go.' In contrast, Tony and Billy already have me at the final table, and I reflect on how lucky I am to have a balance among my supporters between those who are totally over the top, and Ian and Dusan who are more conservative and careful in the way they're assessing the hands I've played today and what the future might hold. The Coronas slip down nicely and I'd like to say that I begin to relax, but that would be a lie. The pressure during the day is relentless and you're never further than one hand away from being out the door. This goes on for 12 straight hours and by the end of the day you're wound up as tight as a spring; I know I'd need a dozen Coronas before I could even get close to unwinding. But that's not even a consideration as I know I'm going to have to be clear-headed if I'm going to make it to the Horseshoe. Once back in my room I'll pop a few sleeping tablets and hope they'll be strong enough to shut down my hyped-up brain for a few hours.

12

Jeanie

After five hectic years of study, work, business ventures and courting Jeanie, I put university behind me by completing my Bachelor of Applied Science. I then look to find a busy chiropractic practice in which to do my internship. Although I could work in the city, I opt to work for Angela and Wayne Todd in the Todd Chiropractic Clinic, a very active practice in Sale, a large country town about 150 miles to the east of Melbourne with a population of approximately 10,000. It's a beautiful location close to the Gippsland Lakes, the Ninety Mile Beach and the mountains — a long way from the hustle and bustle of city life. In terms of practical experience I couldn't have chosen better and I see up to 200 patients a week; in fact, some weeks I'm so busy that I think I've seen every person in Sale. I'm made to feel very welcome, and it crosses my mind that the country could be a very good place to raise a family. I rent the caravan out the back of Angela's parents home and on weekends I drive back to Melbourne to see my family, and of course to be with Jeanie.

By this time, the bond we've built over a period stretching back eight years is incredibly strong, and we do things as if we're one, without the need for long dialogue. That's how it is when we decide to get married. I don't propose and nor does Jeanie, but we both know we've found our life-long partner. We book the church and the reception but then there's a hiccup. The invitation list becomes complicated, and what we thought would be simple becomes long and drawn out. I'm young, impetuous and becoming impatient so one day I just come out with, 'Jeanie, do you really want a white wedding with all the bells and whistles?'

'I just want to be with you,' she responds, giving me a beautiful smile.

'Great. Let's elope then,' I say, grinning and thinking how lucky I am to have Jeanie as my partner in crime.

We immediately start shopping for furniture, and I begin looking for an apartment in Sale so that when we make the big move we'll at least have somewhere comfortable to stay.

Early in the morning of 8 October 1989 I drive to Melbourne from Sale with an enclosed steel furniture trailer in tow. As I cruise along the country roads I give a silent prayer of thanks for what is a beautiful spring day. As soon as I arrive I start visiting the many stores where we've bought furniture, and before long the trailer is packed to the seams, ready for the trip back to Sale later that night. I drop it off out the front of a friend's house, pick Jeanie up and we're off to celebrate the most exciting day of our lives.

We're married in the Sacred Heart Church in Rathdowne Street, Carlton, which adjoins my old school, St George's Primary. It's a beautiful old church and a wonderfully spiritual and romantic setting for our marriage.

Jeanie looks stunning in a white gown, and I'm wearing a smart double-breasted navy-blue suit. Our witnesses are Jeanie's sister, Denise and my brother Tony, who've both been sworn to secrecy. Even as Father Paul, our parish priest, is conducting the marriage ceremony, Jeanie's Mum, who loves to help out at the church, is cooking a barbecue at a function in the surrounding grounds for our parish youth club, blissfully unaware that I'm only meters away being married to her daughter. After the ceremony, we go to back to our friends' house where they bring out some nibblies, open a bottle of champagne and toast a long and happy marriage. Over the years we have drifted apart from these friends, but we'll always be grateful for their help and kindness.

Eloping is no big deal in the tribal villages of Lebanon; in fact, it's almost traditional and many couples do it, without fear of any backlash or ill feeling from their parents. When Jeanie's parents had recovered from the initial shock, and her mother got over her disbelief that she was so close to us while we were getting married, they grabbed a couple of bottles of wine and visited Mum and Vince to celebrate.

Jeanie doesn't like Sale. She misses the city life, her family and her friends, so after nine months we pack up and head back to Melbourne. We've never scrimped and have little money when I find a great little chiropractic practice for sale with huge potential in mid-market Ivanhoe. I bargain the owner down to $50,000, but there's one major problem — I don't have any cash. Mum and Vince's house is still mortgaged but they have a lot of equity in it, so I ask them to put it up as security on a $50,000 loan for me. They're anxious to see me do well and readily agree, and I commit to not only repaying the loan, but their mortgage payments as well. They never asked me to do this and would have done anything to help me, but quite simply it's the least I can do for them.

I trial the practice for two weeks and it confirms everything I first thought — it's a good little business with great potential for growth. I settle the practice and assume full ownership two weeks after completing the trial. Jeanie is eager to help me as my receptionist and personal assistant; however, almost immediately after settlement, she is suddenly struck by horrific vomiting attacks in the morning — the Hachems have an unexpected but very welcome surprise on the way. Jeanie holds on in the office for as long as she can before the sickness completely overcomes her. I don't believe there's any such thing as typical morning sickness but it's difficult to believe that Jeanie's suffering could've been worse, and there's little I can do to ease the pain and nausea. In the end it's so bad that she's admitted to hospital and put on a drip.

We're now living in a unit in Station Street, Fairfield, and Jeanie spends many uncomfortable days and nights lying on the couch. Anthony arrives on a glorious autumn day at 3.45pm on 20 March 1991 at the Royal Women's Hospital in Melbourne. I'm standing by the bed holding Jeanie's hand. Every time she has a contraction I start talking about painting the living room, changing the curtains and anything else I can think of to take her mind off the pain, but she mustn't think I'm being very helpful because she screams at me to shut up. After the birth, I pick Anthony up, walk over to the window cradling him in my arms, and I become teary-eyed. Words can't describe the love I feel for my wife and newly born son. A nurse takes him from me to be weighed and the emotions I'm feeling well up inside me — cases of babies being mixed up in hospitals have been reported in the media and I'm taking no chances. I'm feeling panicky and I just don't want to be one of those people unlucky enough to have his baby mixed up with someone else's. I say, 'See ya, Jeanie,' who has her legs still up in the air, and I'm out the door trailing after the nurse, never taking my eyes off Anthony.

I'm happily married and have the most wonderful son, but Uncle Vince, who's looked after Tony and me all these years, is still single. Later in 1991 he travels back to Lebanon to visit Bescharre, and Jeanie and Anthony, who is only five months old, go with him. A week later Jeanie phones me and says that it was a mistake for her to go, that she can't stand being away from me and that she wants to return home. I tell her she should stay and enjoy herself, but after a few weeks she can't stay away any longer, misses home too much and returns to be with me.

It's Uncle Vince's first trip to Lebanon since 1973 and it totally revitalizes him. He's had so much bad luck: first, the cartridge exploded in his face and then later, when he's in his early 20s, he falls in love with a married woman and she breaks his heart — something he's never really gotten over. Now, back in his birthplace, he's on top of the world and for the first time in years he can feel the blood flowing through his veins. His cousins say to him, 'Cousin, what have you achieved? You've lived in this wonderfully prosperous country for 20 years and now you are back in Bescharre and what do you have to show for it? Have you achieved anything?' He proudly responds, 'Yes, I made a doctor,' referring to me becoming a chiropractor.

But now we're in for a surprise. Uncle Vince phones and tells us he's fallen deeply in love with a lady named Amne, who lives in Beirut. They embark on a whirlwind romance and six weeks later they're married. It's the most wonderful news and back in Australia we are overjoyed. I couldn't believe that my uncle, who was in his early 40s, had got married. After he returns to Australia, he and Amne move back in with Mum and Tony, and I know he won't leave because he'll think that he's letting them down. Two months go by and I say to him, 'Look, Uncle, you don't need to live with Tony and Mum anymore. They can look after themselves. You have a wife. You two should be together in your own home.' They buy a house and settle in Reservoir, eager to start a family. Unfortunately, nothing happens and we send them off to countless fertility specialists. After spending a small fortune and waiting for an eternity, it finally happens and Amne falls pregnant. In 1996 they have a son, and name him Dib after Uncle Vince's elder brother.

Despite the morning sickness suffered with Anthony, Jeanie is keen to add to our family. We soon find that every time we even talk about it, Jeanie becomes pregnant. We want to have our kids born close in age so they can grow up together and become great friends, and we can enjoy them while we're still in our youth. While we always planned to have six children, we decide instead that four is a lovely number. Justine, Daniel and James are born in the next four years, and our family is complete.

I continue to grow my now-flourishing practice, but I also have overheads, including a replacement for Jeanie, modern office equipment and of course the loan repayments, all of which are conspiring to hold me back from building a healthy bank balance. I'm also living very well and paying little attention to my personal expenses. I'm not worried; I've trebled the practice's fees and I know with time my bank account will grow healthily. I'm doing well, but Australia is in the grip of an economic downturn. Our Federal Treasurer declares that 'This is the recession that Australia has to have,' which receives enormous derogatory coverage in the newspapers. Economic activity severely contracts, unemployment numbers rise significantly and interest rates are as high as 22 percent. Just as I'm thanking my lucky stars that I have limited debt, my landlord asks me out of the blue if I'd like to buy the freehold for $215,000. I respond with an instant yes, the only problem being that I don't have a cent to bless myself with, and I'll have to borrow. What was I saying about being thankful that I only had limited debt?

I march into the Commonwealth Bank of Australia's branch in Upper Heidelberg Road, Ivanhoe, and ask to see the manager, a lovely gentleman I know quite well. He's getting close to retirement age and at this stage of his business life it'd be far easier for him to say no rather than yes. I tell him that I'd like to buy the building I'm practicing in, and he smiles benevolently and asks me what I can put up by way of cash or collateral. I have nothing other than a piece of foolscap paper on which is printed my weekly fees for the past five weeks, which are still trending up strongly. With nothing other than a summary of my fees and the fact that he knows me, he offers me 80 percent of the purchase price as a housing loan at an interest rate of 18 percent and the remaining 20 percent as a business loan at an interest rate of 22 percent. I accept, knowing that all I have to find before settlement are the legal fees and stamp duty. I sell the practice after five years but retain ownership of the building to this day.

Soon after this, I set up a practice amongst the corporate elite in Collins Street, Melbourne, specializing in helping those with headaches. I've moved too soon: it's too early for chiropractors to specialize in one area, and the practice isn't successful. Like a bad hand, I quickly muck the practice and minimize my losses.

In 1996 I acquire a large successful practice in the up-market suburb of Armadale. I then divide it into segments and sell them off, after which I'm left with about half of what I acquired, but because of my sales I'm on a freeroll. I'm looking for a masseur to help my patients and to contribute to the rent, so I interview a number of applicants before meeting Peter Eves, a friendly, very impressive guy in his mid-30s who seems to really know his stuff. He's wearing one item of jewelry that I'm not all that keen on, so I say, 'I'll see you on Monday morning, Peter — without the earring!' We still laugh about that little incident today. He rents a room from me at the rear of the practice and, as I anticipated, he is very good at what he does. About this time I also employ Remy Rudegeair as my receptionist/assistant and I couldn't have chosen better — she's vibrant, gregarious and always optimistic. Along with Peter, we become the A-team. We get to know our patients very well, and we're so efficient that the results we achieve are outstanding, but we're also having so much fun that it never seems like work. I worked with these two fantastic people for about five years and the three of us have remained close friends ever since.

I have a good practice in an area where the people are friendly and affluent, but I'm spending everything I make, and therefore cash is still tight. I also have four young children and need to find a house that's large enough to meet their growing needs. The property market is incredibly hot and large crowds are attending the weekend auctions, relentlessly driving up prices. If you missed out on buying a house and go back to the same street four weeks later you find similar houses selling for $10,000 more. I need to bite the bullet and buy, or I'll be chasing my tail forever.

I find a nice place in West Preston but I'm outbid at auction. However, the couple standing next to me say they have a house for sale in the next street, and that they've done a lot of work to it. It's in great condition, large, well built and meets nearly all my requirements except one — it's weatherboard and I've been looking to buy brick or brick veneer. We start haggling over price.

They say they won't accept one cent less than $300,000 and I say I won't pay one cent more than $280,000. Who would have thought one cent could exert so much influence? In the end they don't cave in and I walk away.

Two months later that same weatherboard house goes up for auction, and I attend without having made one inspection, aiming to catch the auctioneer by surprise. This is one of those times where I slow-played my hand on the turn and then got beaten on the river, and soon after I'm the proud owner of a very nice house at the bargain price of only $323,000. Ouch! I write out a cheque to the auctioneer for $32,300, knowing that I have only $5,300 in my bank account. I borrow enough to cover my deposit cheque from my sister-in-law Denise, but now have to find a way to come up with the funds to pay her back and settle the house. I have 120 days until settlement so I pull my head in and significantly cut back on my private expenditure. I pay Denise's loan back and set up bank finance for 90 percent of the value of the property plus costs, and by the time the day of settlement is upon me I'm coasting. I'm becoming very adept at purchasing businesses and property with no money of my own. I'll always be grateful to Denise for having the faith to lend me such a large sum, with only my word as security.

My training and passion is in natural healing so I've never had my kids vaccinated. I believe that the vaccine may be a poison itself, and I've not read any clinical evidence to suggest that it actually helps. There are many in the medical profession who would dispute this, and I'm not professing to give advice, but merely expressing my view. Having said this, I love my kids more than anything in the world and I'd never do anything to jeopardize their health or well-being.

When Dib is two years old, Uncle Vince asks me if I've had my kids vaccinated, and I say I haven't, but I tell him that he must do his own research, that it's his child and in the end it must be his decision. They decide to get Dib vaccinated, and after a month it's noticeable that he's not the same bright little boy anymore. A year later we learn that he's autistic, and no, I can't be certain that his autism was caused by the vaccine. Vince and Amne are shattered and their lives are now in turmoil. They start going to specialists, pediatricians and saying prayers in a vain effort to help Dib recover. I'm really hurting for them and am the only one in the family who realizes that the affliction Dib has is incurable. There are words of hope from everyone else but it's killing me because I know that for Dib there's no light at the end of this black tunnel. They take him to healers and churches all over Australia and Lebanon, and they leave no medical or spiritual stone unturned in their pursuit of a 'cure'. I was slowly watching my Uncle wither away; for someone so selfless he had the worst luck imaginable. He'd always told me, 'Look after your Mum; take good care of your family; don't go out too much,' but he never asked for anything for himself. He now blames himself for Dib's condition and says, 'I wish I had listened to you, I wish I had done what you did.' However, there's no sure way to know whether Dib would've been any better, had he not been vaccinated.

He's placed in special education and Vince's house now becomes the central focus of the whole family. We get together every Saturday for a barbecue, and if we can't turn up for any reason we're severely chastized. Amne would phone us and say, 'Where are you, where're the kids? We've got the chicken ready and the meat's cooking!'

13

The Main Event — Day Five
I Only Play Big Pairs

I sit in my cab on the way to the Rio thinking about some of the hands I'd played the day before and how great it had been for me. I'm very confident and can't wait for the action to start. My aim to win the tournament has never wavered, but there are 58 players left, and before I can win I have to ensure that I make it to the final 27 today. My practice of setting objectives each day of the tournament and treating them in my mind as stepping stones has worked well up until now and I'm not about to change as I get closer to achieving the ultimate goal.

For the first time in the tournament, I know some of the players I'm seated with, either because I've played with them before or I know them by reputation. Because we are down to 58, there are two nine-handed tables and four ten-handed. I'm on one of the latter. Tiffany Williamson, a London-based American lawyer, is the last woman remaining in the tournament. She is sitting four to my left, and with a daunting stack of chips in front of her, is table chip leader. My old adversary, Ayhan Alsancak, is sitting two to the right of me with $775,000 in chips, and I wonder what he thinks about me having position on him in most of the hands that we'll play today.

The day kicks off at 12.15pm, blinds are $8,000/$16,000 and the antes are $2,000. I drop about a third of my stack in the first hour. I play four or five pots and lose them all, missing everything — so much for my early morning confidence. Most of the hooligans and camera hogs who want to see themselves on television have been eliminated in the earlier rounds, but there's still a lot of raw emotion in the room; Bernard Lee and Andy Black have big wins on other tables, and leap to their feet with triumphant shouts of, 'Yes! Yes!'

During this time members of my crew are coming up to the table and feeding me running reports on the histories of my opponents. I already know that Lee Watkinson, an American from Tacoma, Washington, sitting opposite me can play; sometimes you only need a few hands to make this determination and the way Lee handles his cards tells a story in itself. He plays aggressively and I put him down as a professional, which is confirmed by my team. By the start of the second hour I'm one of the short stacks at the table when I pick up J-J under the gun and raise to $50,000. I'm called by Lee, and Johnny Howard — no, not the former Aussie Prime Minister but an American, resident of Maryland. I'm more than a little wary because I expect Lee, who has me covered, to raise pre-flop, but he doesn't, and now I wonder if he's slow-playing me, trying to trap me after the flop. The flop is 10-8-3 with two hearts, which, when you're holding jacks, is a good flop. I lead the betting with $100,000, and Lee calls instantly, while John Howard folds. Looking at the signs I proceed very carefully: I'm sure not planning to exit the tournament at this early stage. Fourth street brings another eight, so I check to Lee, who moves all-in in a heartbeat. Now I'm in a flurry and my brain goes into overdrive trying to fathom the different outcomes and the strategy Lee is using. *Am I still ahead, and if so, by how much? Or is he trying to double-bluff me, making me think he's trying to steal the pot? Should I call him? Does it warrant pushing all my chips in now, or should I wait for a better time?* My tournament life is on the line. My head is pounding and I can feel physical pain around my temples as I try to determine what I should do. I fold, deciding to live to fight another day, but I feel gutted and sick to the soles of my feet.

I'm on the verge of tilting but fortunately after that dismal hand we break for 15 minutes and I have some time to regain my composure. In the rest room one of the guys asks me what I was holding, and I respond, 'Jacks.' Right then Lee pops his head up from one of the wash basins, and says, 'Good fold. I had queens.' In that instant I go from being down to being elated, knowing I'd just made a great lay-down. I'm pumped. I've made a tough decision and folded at the right time. Lee's comments have restored my mental balance. I head back to the tables, all self-doubt having disappeared. I'm confident I'm going to build a big stack before the day is out.

I run across Lee a few months later and this time he tells me he was bluffing all along. I'm really glad he didn't tell me that in the rest room because who knows what the outcome might have been? Maybe I would've gone on tilt. Thanks, Lee. I'm happy to think you had queens for the rest of my life.

Within five minutes of getting back to the table my luck begins to change — or at least I think it does. I get dealt pocket aces in mid-position and immediately raise to $50,000; the table folds around to the big blind who calls. The dealer scoops up the muck and in doing so he picks up my two aces, and now I'm playing the big blind without any cards. He turns over 7-7 and I lose yet another hand, this time to the dealer. I'm angry with him, but know he's feeling terrible, so I don't go over the top berating him. We all make mistakes and it certainly wasn't intentional on his part, but when you're already short stacked it really hurts. So much for my luck changing …

By mid afternoon I'm on another table, right on the rail, sitting between Andy Black on my right who has $2 million in chips and Phil Ivey on my left who has $3 million. I'm still struggling and have only $350,000, but I'm not quite the short stack: John Juanda has only $320,000. Phil and John are talking and whispering, and knowing their reputations, I find this unnerving. On the plus side, my supporters, who have grown to number about 20, are virtually on top of the table.

I know that if I don't add to my chips within the next hour my tournament life may well be over, and I start going all-in pre-flop on virtually anything, and finally begin to add to my stack. In one hand the table folds around to Andy Black in the small blind who raises three times the big blind. I'm in the big blind and haven't picked up or looked at my cards, but I'm totally determined not to let Andy push me around, so I go all-in again. Andy spends a long time looking at his cards before turning them over. He has K-7, and I steal the blinds and antes once more. When I pick up my cards I see 4-7. Had Andy called, my tournament would have probably been over.

I've built my chips back up to $550,000 but I'm still short-stacked. I look down at my hole cards, see J-J, and go all-in. This time I'm not allowed to steal the blinds as Terence Burt, who is in late position sitting two to my left, calls, turning over A-K of spades. Now it's a classic race, where I have to fade an ace or a king. As has become my habit when I'm all-in, I stand up and walk over to my supporters, with my back to the table. I'm resigned to whatever happens but the faces of my friends are strained and tense, their eyes looking past me to the table. Suddenly they erupt into, 'Aussie, Aussie, Aussie, oi, oi, oi!' and I know my jacks have held up and I've just doubled my stack. I later find that the chant is the work of Tony and a mate from Crown Casino, Brian Hull. I've known Brian for years; he's one of the 'old school' who played at Crown, and over the years he's been a very successful tournament player. He's one of the 30 top Melbourne players who participated in the monthly tournaments at my home. He's 50-ish, very solid, with a white Charles Bronson moustache and a booming voice that resonates around the room — which is just as well as he assumes the role of chant leader for the rest of the tournament.

A few hands later I raise with pocket aces, and Roland Israelashvili, who's sitting two to the left of me with a short stack, goes all-in with pocket nines. I know what he's doing, because I've been doing the same all day, but he's chosen the wrong time to make a stand. I have him easily covered, and am fired up by the opportunity to make a sizeable increase in my stack. I immediately call, and when the flop comes Q-J-10 he now has an open-ended straight draw which increases his outs from two to ten. Fourth street is a three and I clench my hands a little tighter and pray that the river won't be an eight, nine or king. As always seems the case in these situations, the dealer appears to take ages before turning over a harmless four. Roland is knocked out in 37th position and takes home $235,390 for his troubles. My chip stack now exceeds $1.5 million.

Just after 7pm a strange incident occurs that graphically illustrates the stress and emotion of the tournament. I'm no longer on Andy Black's table, when the passionate Irishman becomes very upset because Bing Wang hasn't returned from a short break (he got it mixed up with the dinner break). Andy very sportingly asks the table to play slowly to give Bing a chance to get back. When this spirit of fair play is not shared and the table pushes on, Andy, being a Buddhist and genuinely nice guy, gets upset. When Bing returns to the table he's smiling and oblivious to what has occurred in his absence. Andy, on the other hand, is still teary and emotional and needs to go for a walk to regain his composure. The intense concentration of the past five days coupled with broken sleeps has obviously got to him. As it turns out, Andy's efforts are wasted as Bing only lasts a few more hands before being knocked out in 34th place, earning himself $274,090.

A little later, the floorman comes over to the table and says, 'Okay boys, pick up your chips, your table's breaking up,' and randomly drops nine cards face down in front of us. We each pick one up, and printed on the other side are our new table and seat numbers. Mine is the TV table, which is positioned at the rear of the Amazon Room on a small, elevated mini-stage, with dark blue curtains behind it. I immediately let the boys know and they start racing off to get a good position, only to find ESPN staff waiting for them with a specially allocated section. Clearly the boys' excited support for me is something ESPN want to catch on camera. I sit down and immediately notice the stacks in front of Greg Raymer and Tim Phan. Tim looks over at me and says, 'Welcome to the jungle.' I know I'm now playing against the best and toughest players in the world. I mentally adjust my seat belt and strap myself in, determined that, come hell or high water, I'm going to make it to the last 27. I adopt my normal style of play at a new table and am very careful for the first 30 minutes. Then, as if on some type of time cue, I'm dealt pocket aces. Shawn Sheikhan to my immediate right raises to $115,000, I re-raise to $415,000 and Karlo Lopez on my immediate left wrestles with himself for a long time before folding A-Q off-suit, and the action's back to Shawn. My hands are in front of my mouth and face, and I'm staring vacantly across the room, refusing to make eye contact with Shawn, who thinks about it and folds. I show my aces, representing to the table that I only play big pairs, and hope it will set up some nice bluffing opportunities. I glance over at Karlo. He looks relieved knowing he's made a good lay-down. He must have been so close to calling or raising. My supporters are screaming the house down and chanting 'Aussie, Aussie, Aussie, oi, oi, oi!' every time I take a pot down.

On the very next hand I get pocket aces again, which is a real rarity. The odds against it are staggering. Who said I wasn't lucky? One of the aces is a spade. The table folds around to me and I raise to $110,000. Karlo to the left of me, who's just laid down A-Q, finds pocket queens with a spade, and moves all-in. I call and he is distraught when he sees my aces. The flop is 2-6-4 — all spades. I stand up, face my supporters and say, 'A spade's all right, put a spade down.' The turn card is the seven of hearts, the river's the three of hearts and it's *hasta la vista* Karlo. My supporters erupt again with the chant that has become so associated with me, and ESPN's cameras lap it up, with one of their commentators saying, 'Did those guys clear customs?' Karlo finishes in 33rd place. Just five more to go and I've made it to the last 27.

I haven't been on the feature table before, and despite the storm of noise that my supporters are kicking up, I'm very quiet and respectful. After all, I'm on a table with the reigning World Champion, Greg Raymer, and top professional Tim Phan. As it turns out, I'm soon in my first and only battle with Greg, who raises two and half times the big blind in mid-position. The table folds around to me in the big blind, and I call with two rags. The flop comes ace high and I check it to see what Greg's going to do. He makes a continuation bet, but I sense uncertainty and immediately check-raise, even though I have nothing. I've been playing very tight poker and I'm guessing that Greg thinks that I've paired an ace. He agonizes for a short time before folding, and I scoop up the pot. I feel fantastic. I've just made a move on the World Champ, and I mark it down as a moment in the tournament to remember.

I started the day on the same table as Tiffany Williamson and she was on the TV table when I was moved to it. She'd won her seat by winning a satellite at the Gutshot Club, and her mode of play is slow, painfully slow. No one can read her. I summed her up on the basis that if she can't work out what she's doing I have no hope of knowing. She tortures all of us by agonizing over decisions that are relatively simple. An example of this came when she was playing against Shawn Sheikhan before I joined the table. Shawn raised $100,000 with pocket aces and Tiffany re-raised to $250,000; in a blink he's all-in. She stands up and walks around the table, talking all the time to Shawn, saying stuff like, 'I don't think you have the nuts.' He doesn't say a word but when she walks over near the cameras, he shouts, 'Hey, you can't walk over there.' She comes back to the table but still won't make a decision, and Shawn and the others on the table are getting really exasperated. Eventually, one of the floormen puts her on the clock and starts counting down from ten seconds. With two seconds to go and after 20 minutes she mucks her hand, and then says to Shawn, 'Can I at least see your cards?' He says no, which is exactly what he should've done. If you want to see what your opponent has in this game, you have to pay.

Mike Matusow knocks out Burt Rice at 9.48pm and we're down to the 27 who'll be off to Binion's tomorrow. It's been the shortest playing day and the earliest night I've had.

Mike is the chip leader with $5,140,000 and I'm in seventh place with $3,125,000. I'd been down to $350,000 earlier in the day and I'm totally ecstatic about having made the final 27. For the first time my team and I give the All-American Bar & Grill a miss and head for Buzio's Seafood Restaurant. As I'm leaving the Amazon Room this young kid, about 18, comes up and asks me for my autograph. I say to him, 'Are you talking to me? Are you sure you want my autograph?'

'Yeah, yeah,' he replies.

'But I haven't done anything yet.'

'I want your autograph,' he persists.

'Okay,' I say, and a friend takes a picture of me giving my first-ever autograph. *Wow*, I think. It's all so surreal, but it's a great way to cap off my last few minutes in the Amazon Room.

There are about 20 of us at Buzio's and the mood around our long table is euphoric when I phone Jeanie in Melbourne and tell her the good news. For the first and only time during the playing of the tournament I talk to her about money, and let her know that, no matter what happens, I've won enough to pay off our mortgage. I get emotional and teary. Perhaps it's the pressure of the tournament, the draining hours, the broken sleeps, or just the fact that most Australians take 20 to 30 years to get rid of their mortgages while mine has gone in just five days. I'm slumped in my chair when Jeanie says, 'It's alright, hon. Don't worry. I know you're either going to finish first or third,' a prediction she's never wavered from. I've heard her say it before, but this time she immediately snaps me out of my somber mood and back to reality.

Emad and Arul, the mates I swapped with, have been playing all my hands from behind the rail and I think they're more stressed than me. It's definitely not just about money; they're genuinely rooting for me out of friendship. I'm careful about what and how much I drink; nevertheless, a lot of alcohol's consumed and Emad, who normally wears his heart on his sleeve anyway, loosens up even more after his tonsils are lubricated. He and Arul are loudly calculating, 'How much will we get?' depending on where I finish, and the others sitting nearby join in. I tell them to shut up but it's to no avail. These are the nights when you wish you could bottle the atmosphere and take it home with you.

14

Pouring on the Pressure

I've been playing poker with a group of friends once or twice a week for years, and the completion of the luxurious Crown Casino on the banks of Melbourne's Yarra River in the mid-1990s provides us with a safe, well-run venue where we can play regularly. In 1998 I watch the classic movie *Rounders* and I discover the game known as the 'Cadillac of Poker', No-Limit Texas Hold 'em. In the film, Mike McDermott (played by Matt Damon), is forced to return to high-stakes poker to help his friend Lester 'Worm' Murphy (Edward Norton) pay off loan sharks. This was the first film that truly depicted the mind of the professional poker player and accurately portrayed the compulsion to play. It was also my introduction to the WSOP.

I was getting sick of playing Manila, and one day while in Crown Casino I saw another game being played and didn't immediately pick up on it. I asked the floorman what it was, and he said Texas Hold 'em and Matt Damon and the movie immediately came back to me.

'Refresh me on how to play,' I said.

'It's like blackjack. You get two picture cards and play them.'

I thought, *Beautiful. This is the game for me.*

I remember my first game of Hold 'em as if it were yesterday. I'm sitting at a table where the blinds are $8/$16 and I'm playing very poorly, but because of my lack of experience, I don't know it. I have the whole table on tilt because I'm calling to the river with any two picture cards, pair or ace, but remarkably I end up winning all the money. I think I'm a genius, but I don't take long to realize that I've just been lucky and that I need to learn more about this game. I'm totally hooked and really like the fact that Hold 'em is played with a full deck, as opposed to the short deck used in Manila. This reduces the odds of your opponents getting lucky and drawing on you, and therefore the skilled player has a distinct edge. The opportunity to bluff increases significantly as it's much harder to make a hand with a full deck (52 cards) than it is with a stripped deck (32 cards).

One of the turning points in most pursuits in life is when you come to the realization that you actually know very little about what you're pursuing. From the minute I played my first hand of No-Limit Texas Hold 'em I loved the game, but in those early days the more I played, the more I realized how little I knew. I did some research and headed to Borders to buy my first book on poker, T.J. Cloutier's *No-Limit and Pot-Limit Hold 'em (Championship Series)*. It sets out the basic rules, the fundamentals and the strategies used in Hold 'em, and the format is non-technical and easily understood by the layman. I refer to this text constantly in years to come and have read it more than a dozen times. My next acquisition is Doyle Brunson's *Super/System: A Course in Power Poker*, the 'bible of poker', and I use it to further refine my game. These two books are exceptional: amateurs will find everything they need to know to progress, and intermediate players will find what they need to help them jump to the next level.

However, I also realize that reading a book or two won't make me a better player overnight; if it did, we'd all buy books on golf and be playing like Tiger within weeks. Reading provides me with the knowledge, the tools to develop my skills, but to test this newly acquired information I need to play in games. How else will I know if it is valid? Applying this knowledge in games greatly hones my level of concentration. I find myself recalling strategies that I've read in the books and checking them out after I've finished playing, in effect compounding my learning. Some of the information I discard, because it's not relevant to my style of play. The last thing a poker player needs is a cluttered mind.

It's early days and I experiment with different tactics and strategies, looking to find a style that suits me that I can consistently apply. I also closely observe others, which in some instances I find to be a better learning tool than actually playing in games. Sometimes I watch games from the outside, observing the complete table, while in others I hone in on certain players, learning from how they deal with specific situations.

My style of play in the beginning is fast, aggressive and loose — very loose in fact. As I start to learn more about the game I play much tighter but I'm still aggressive. I learn to switch gears, adapt my style — be it tight or loose — to the demands of the table. The constant theme underlying my play is aggression, which I'm very comfortable applying. I have a natural inclination to take charge of the pot and leave my opponents having to make the hard decisions. I find myself continually leading the betting and pouring on the pressure, forcing others to make the tough decisions. I learn very early that if you're the one who's always left to make the choices, you'll soon become a calling station. Next stop: Losers' Central!

I'm strictly a cash game player for the first few years and know very little about tournament poker. I play my first tournament, a $20 Sit 'n' go, at a mate's place in 2000 and manage to win it. I'm now bitten by the competition bug and start playing in the regular Sunday tournaments at Crown Casino. I'm winning just enough to cover my seats and entry into other tournaments on the Australian championship circuit. The first serious tournament I play in is Pot-Limit Omaha, and I make the final table as chip leader and end up coming fourth, mainly due to my inexperience. I'm not worried because I know I'm on a rapid learning curve, and from this point on there's no looking back, not ever.

Meanwhile, my daily life doesn't change; I'm a regular guy with a wife, family, and a career as a chiropractor. No matter how much I want to play poker, I can't abandon my career, forget my mortgage payments, steal time from the family I love, or cut back on my other social commitments. I continue playing poker at the tournaments in Melbourne and occasionally travel to other states for the action on their circuits. Poker for me is still just a hobby, but one that I have a deep passion for, and an obsession to learn more about.

I have a happy, fulfilling life, and have no inclination that I'm about to draw a blank on the river that will put my health, well-being, and career on tilt.

15

The Main Event — Day Six
A Part of History

For the first time, I'm not catching a cab to the tournament by myself; Ian is with me. I'm not superstitious about breaking winning routines — well, not this one, anyhow. We're running late. Binion's is situated in downtown Vegas, which takes a little longer to get to from the Mandalay Bay than the Rio. I ask the cabby to put his foot down and he asks me what my hurry is. I tell him I'm playing in a poker tournament and he says, 'Jeez, you're not one of the final 27 in the Main Event?' I tell him I am and he says that he wants to shake my hand before I get out the cab because he might just be shaking the hand of the next World Champ.

This is the 36th and last time that the tournament will be held at its traditional home. I've never set foot in Binion's before, not even for an exploratory visit, but my first impression is that it lacks a lot when compared with the casinos on the strip and is obviously long past its best days. As I enter the downstairs poker room I glance to my left, and there on the wall of the adjoining room are the famous photos of the past 35 years' winners — the Gallery of Champions. I stand below them looking up at Doyle Brunson, Johnny Chan, Stuey Ungar, Chris Moneymaker, Chris 'Jesus' Ferguson and last year's winner, Greg Raymer. The photos are arranged with three down and 12 across, and there's one empty space on the far right of the bottom row waiting for this year's winner to complete the set of 36. Strangely, it's at my perfect head height when standing, which I think is a good omen and one of my mates snaps a photo of me. Who said I wasn't superstitious?

While this is the first time I've been in Binion's Horseshoe Casino, I know something of its history and the world famous tournament it spawned. Benny Binion created the WSOP in 1970 by inviting six of his mates to play and then vote on who was the best player. Every year since then it has grown bigger and bigger, until, thanks to Chris Moneymaker's 2003 WSOP win coupled with his unique name, it became known around the world — even by non-poker players.

After Chris's win, Harrah's Entertainment purchased the Horseshoe together with the WSOP for $40 million. Shortly afterwards, it sold the property to another company to manage, while retaining the real prize, ownership of the WSOP. Greg Raymer would go on to defeat a record-sized field later in 2004, becoming the first winner under Harrah's ownership.

I take the escalator up to Benny's Bullpen, sucking in the atmosphere, and my mind turns to the history of this iconic room. If only its walls could talk. It's so small when compared with the Amazon Room and there's room for only about three hundred spectators and media, but it's packed and there's barely room to breathe, let alone move. I can feel the pent-up tension, the anticipation, and tell myself not to get carried away by the hype.

My goal for the day is to make the final table, but first I have to get through the initial session and down to the final 18. As with every other day, I have stepping stones, with the final goal of having the bracelet around my wrist.

Three of the five chip leaders are media favorites: Mike Matusow leads the field with $5,140,000 in chips, Phil Ivey is second with $4,635,000 and Greg Raymer fifth with $3,840,000. There's an expectation that the winner will come from those three — not an expectation that I share.

I'm on the feature table with Phil and Greg, while Mike is on one of the two outer tables. The instruction to 'shuffle up and deal' comes at 3.40pm.

The first big and crazy hand comes when Phil Ivey raises to $120,000 with Kh-5h, Andy Black raises another $300,000 and the rest of the table folds. Phil then tries to bully Andy and steal the pot by re-raising $500,000 more, but he couldn't have picked a worse opponent to try this tactic on. After thinking about it for 30 seconds or so the mad Irishman says, 'All-in.' Phil is a winner of five bracelets and one of the qualities that makes him so good is that he's almost impossible to read. However, when Andy moves all-in, not even Phil can hide his shock. When he folds, Andy shows him Ad-2d.

On a nearby table Mike Matusow and Shawn Sheikhan are at each other's throats. Shawn takes a long time to fold pre-flop and leaves Mike and Michael Kessler to fight out the hand, but when the flop comes, Shawn pounds the table in disgust. Mike looks up and says, 'You know we're in a hand. You should shut the f*** up.'

'What'd you say, Mike? What'd you say?' Shawn retorts.

This time Mike wises up, keeps his head down and doesn't say a word, but the skirmish has attracted the attention of the Assistant Tournament Director, Jack Effel, and Shawn lets him know what Mike said. Jack says he'll sort it out after the hand is over, which Mike wins, and then proceeds to call Shawn an idiot. Jack Effel exerts a firm hand, suspending Shawn for ten minutes for thumping the table and Mike for ten minutes for dropping the f-bomb. Mike must be near a tournament record for f-bomb suspensions.

Phil Ivey is sitting to the right of me and he raises to $130,000; I call with K-J and the rest of the table folds. The flop comes J-J-6, and unless Phil has A-J or pocket sixes, which is highly unlikely, he's in a world of trouble. He checks, and I quickly fire $150,000, representing weakness in the hope that he'll raise me. This is exactly what he does, raising another $500,000, and without hesitation I go all-in. He has made another misread, which is rare for him. His head jerks around toward me and there's no concealing the look of shock on his face. He asks me how much I've got and I let him know I'm sitting on about $3 million, but there's absolutely no way he can call. He folds, having lost more than a third of his chips in the two bluffs that he's tried to pull off against Andy Black and me. (I find out later that he had A-8) My team breaks out into, 'Aussie, Aussie, Aussie, oi, oi, oi!' Even after 35 tournaments, this must be a first for the Bullpen.

Meanwhile, the poker gods are about to unleash their wrath on Greg Raymer, who's going up against Aaron Kanter. Greg plays the hand astutely, has nearly all his chips in the pot and is a massive favorite with only the river to come. Aaron has played the hand very recklessly and now only a heart on the river can save him. When the dealer turns over the two of hearts, Greg is mortally short-stacked, and a gasp echoes around the room. He's the crowd favorite, and his hurt is felt by his many supporters.

Shortly afterwards, Greg goes all-in after the flop with a couple of overcards against my old foe, Ayhan Alsancak who has a small pair, which isn't a great hand, but he wastes little time in calling. The turn card and the river are no help to Greg and he is knocked out in 25th place — but it's the shocking beat against Aaron Kanter that's been so cruel to him. The room stands as one and gives him an ovation as he departs; he's been a great World Champion, beating 5595 in this year's tournament to add to the 2479 he defeated in winning last year — an incredible back-to-back performance. There is a sense of shock among the spectators and a respectful hush descends over the room. I can't say I'm unhappy to see Greg go. I'm not about to shed crocodile tears over the demise of a major obstacle standing between me and this year's championship. Phil Ivey is now the media favorite to win the tournament, and an amateur player, accountant and mortgage broker, Steve Dannemann, replaces Greg on the feature table.

A few minutes later, Tim Phan goes all-in against Andy Black. After the turn Tim is a 90 percent favorite, but as so often happens in this game he gets a bad beat on the river. Tim is very unlucky to be eliminated in 24th place.

I haven't had a hand for a while and when I get Ad-Kd I raise under the gun to $160,000 and the table folds around to Steve Dannemann, who calls. The flop is 9h-10d-5d and I think, *Wow, what a flop for me* — two overcards and a nut flush draw. I check so that I can re-raise by representing a big hand like A-A. I'm not worried about being called on my planned re-raise because I've got outs. All is going to plan when Steve bets $150,000, and I put a million back to him; he pauses for barely a split second before going all-in. *Shit! I hadn't expected this! What do I do now? Does he have a set, two pair or an overpair?* I have him covered but the pot is $3.5 million, and if I lose I'll be severely short-stacked and have to claw my way back from the dead. Should I wait until a better time to risk my chips? I don't know Steve so I decide to do a bit of talking to see what I can find out.

'You're staring me down like you've got nothing,' I say.

'Excuse me?' he responds.

'You're staring me down as if you've got nothing.'

'Everything else is extra credit for me from here, buddy,' he replies.

'Sorry?'

'Everything else is extra credit for me; I got past the first day.'

'All in, huh?'

'I'm just having fun.'

'So am I.'

I stand up and take a swig from my bottle of water; he's looking at me smiling. 'Did you flop a set on me?' I ask.

'Excuse me?'

'Did you flop a set there?'

'Phew.'

'Not sure? Check your cards again.'

'I'm checking them again.' Steve checks his cards again, let's out another phew, wipes his brow in mock concern and then starts laughing. 'Take your time, think about it,' he says, as I take another swig of water.

'Thank you.'

'Do you want me to put my glasses on? Will that help?' he asks.

'Put them on,' I jibe.

He puts his sunglasses on and then says, 'I'll take them off. You'll get a better read that way,' and then starts small-talking to Phil Ivey.

Next moment, he asks me, 'What's your name?'

'Joseph, Joe.'

He's taking it too easy, and he's relaxed and very confident. I think I've learned enough and my gut feeling tells me he has a set of nines or tens. A set is the only hand I'd crumble against, as even if I hit my flush I can still end up being crippled. 'I'll leave it to another time,' I say, and throw my cards in. I've taken nearly eight minutes to fold, my temples are throbbing, and Phil Ivey has called time on me.

'I have not been behind on a hand. I have not given a bad beat to anyone,' Steve says. 'What do you think I had, Joe?'

'Nice hand, whatever you had, nice hand,' I respond.

'Would you like to see it?'

'That'd be nice.'

'Okay,' he says, turning over a pair of nines.

'Nice hand.'

'We're still friends, right?'

'Always friends, mate,' I say.

I've made a great lay-down and when Steve shows me his nines I get a fresh surge of confidence, which helps me play even better. I didn't pay to see Steve's cards and he shouldn't have shown them to me; I bet in hindsight he regrets doing it.

We're down to 20 and when two more are eliminated we'll get a break and be down to two tables. The table folds around to me in mid-position and with Ac-6c I bet $120,000. Andy Black, who is on my immediate left, raises to $400,000 and I call. The flop could hardly be better for me — Qc-7c-9c — and I check with the intent of check-raising when Andy, who has me covered says, 'All in.'

Before he has turned his cards over I jump up and call, and for the first time in the tournament shout, 'Pass the sugar!' simultaneously slamming my cards down on the table. Then I see he's turned over queens and has a set, and if he pairs the board on the turn or the river it'll be the end of my tournament. I ease myself back into my seat knowing my call of 'Pass the sugar' could well be premature and I feel the blood draining from my face. I've barely sat down before I'm back on my feet again and this time I walk over to a group of strangers who've been supporting me, cross my hands in front of me and say, 'No pair, no pair.' *I can't believe I've shouted 'Pass the Sugar' when he's drawing live-so live.* I'm numb, almost senseless, and can't bring myself to face the boys. I return to the table to shake Andy's hand, holding my breath for dear life, and watch the dealer flick over the turn card which is a ten. I can't stay at the table and I can barely breathe as I stand facing the crowd, saying, 'I can't look. I can't look. I can't look.' The river is a king and the boys burst out into their now-famous catch-cry. I can finally show my face to them and Billy gives me a huge hug. I've been lucky.

This was the first time I'd shouted *Pass the Sugar* at the WSOP, it came out totally spontaneously and was an outpouring of relief. Of course after seeing Andy's hole cards I wanted to cut my tongue out.

I actually picked the saying up about 10 years ago when I used to play poker with an older Greek guy, Michael Marcos, and every time he won a pot he'd shout out *Pass d Shuga* in this thick guttural accent. We used to think it was hilarious and it just caught on but I had no idea I'd eventually be yelling it out on the world stage.

Soon afterwards, Aaron Kanter goes heads-up with Phil Ivey who goes all-in pre-flop with a pair of jacks. You can tell Phil is not happy when he sees Aaron's kings, and when the flop is K-4-8 Phil is in a world of trouble, his only hope being running diamonds on the turn and river. When the river is the three of hearts, Phil is eliminated in 20th place. Aaron has eliminated both the favorites, something I'm not in the least displeased about, and earns him the name 'Giant Killer'.

Minh Ly is knocked out in 19th place, and we're down to the final two tables. It's 7.12pm when we take a dinner break. At the completion of the session, I have $6.5 million in chips and am in equal second place with Daniel Bergsdorf just behind the leader, Aaron Kanter, who has $6,725,000.

16

The Ultimate Good Beat

In early 2001 my practice is booming and I even have a nice balance in my bank account when my hands begin to hurt. I dismiss the pain as a passing ailment and continue treating my patients, but my hands are getting very hot, almost to the point that I can't use them. This affliction then spreads to my feet, and they too become painful and burning. I've been working long hours and I put the pain in my hands and feet down to being over-worked and over-tired, so I ease off a little, but still there's no improvement. Three months go by and the pain becomes more acute. I'm now very worried — a chiropractor who can't use his hands has a very limited future.

I visit my local GP and he sends me off to have a variety of blood tests, covering everything that he thinks might be causing the pain, but the results are negative. I'm no wiser; the pain is increasing by the day and my hands feel like they're on fire. I'm then referred to a neurologist who puts me through a series of tests, but again the results are all-clear. My GP organizes for me to have MRI scans of my hands and feet but they reveal nothing. By this stage, my hands are so hot and sore I can no longer work. My GP refers me to a well-known orthopedic surgeon, but like all those before him he is unable to locate the cause of my pain. Ten months have elapsed and I am in excruciating agony, but worse, I have no idea what I am suffering from, let alone whether it's curable. Almost as a last hope my GP refers me to a vascular surgeon who diagnoses me with erythromalgia, an extremely rare condition affecting the blood vessels of the hands and feet. This is the first time in 30 years of practicing that the surgeon has seen or diagnosed it. It's a condition that causes the capillaries in my hands and feet to constantly dilate, forcing blood into them while I'm working, which stretches them and causes the extreme heat and pain. The only positive is that it's not degenerative, but I'm shattered. As a chiropractor, my hands are my tools of trade, and I've just been told that under no circumstances am I to try to use them.

I can no longer practice the profession that I first became enamored with 18 years earlier, and so I have no choice but to sell my practice and look for another line of work. I have no idea what I'll do or how I'll provide for my family. I'm devastated, depressed and need counseling. I think about studying law but I'm 35 years old, have four kids and two mortgages, and I know that my pay as a law clerk, pending getting my degree, will be a mere pittance and I won't be able to meet my bills. I discount the law option and start playing countless hours of poker at Crown Casino and online at PokerStars.com and other sites, and do quite well, but Jeanie doesn't like me trying to earn a living from my hobby and tells me I have to get a real job. Her concern is about the social stigma that surrounds poker, the long-held community prejudice that poker players are 'low-lifes.' Fortunately, thanks to television and the internet, poker has become more socially acceptable, and is now watched and played by tens of millions around the world. I do, however, respect Jeanie's opinion and can understand her concern, so I knuckle down and set myself to find a regular job.

Nearly a year has elapsed since I was diagnosed with erythromalgia and I've made a large dent in my savings. I check out the options and determine that I can make a good living as a mortgage broker, and while I work hard and am reasonably successful, I don't have the same love for selling mortgage finance as I did for healing people. I set up an office in Bell Street, Pascoe Vale, with two friends Michael Barkho and Sam Georges and when the phone is not ringing or I'm not chasing up a client, I take the opportunity to play a little internet poker. Now *this* is something I love, but for me it's only a recreational pursuit. I'm like a member of a local golf club practicing to win my club championship. I am resolved to play only local tournaments as playing the international circuits would mean leaving my family, and in my book my family will always come first. Maybe one day, when I can afford to take everyone, I'll play in the WSOP.

I'm consistently winning; I've outgrown the games at Crown Casino and am playing in bigger tournaments on the net. I feel my game is getting better but I need to do something to take it to an even higher level. I know that if you play golf against players with a 27 handicap you'll play to their standard. I don't see myself as a scratch poker player yet, but that's what I'm aiming to be, so I need to be consistently playing against the best, not the 27 handicappers. I don't realize it but I'm about to sow the seeds that will see me in Vegas in 2005.

The garage at my house is a strange size in that it's been designed for one and a half cars; I know that's weird, but the builder must have had his reasons. On the plus side it's the perfect size to accommodate three poker tables; a three-poker-table garage is something I like the sound of. I install an open fire place, which makes it a very cozy place to be on Melbourne's cold winter nights. I put a fridge in, organize a monthly tournament, and invite the city's best players to join me. It takes no time at all before the tables are filled with 30 eager poker players. We put in $330 each, of which $30 is deducted for food and drink, and ten percent is put toward a jackpot prize for the year's top point-scorer. The remaining sum is distributed on the night to those who make the final table. As expected, the standard of play is very high and I not only notice an improvement in my play, but in those who I'm playing against.

17

The Main Event — Day Six
The Last Eighteen

I 've achieved my first session's goal of making it to the final two tables, and when nine more are eliminated I'll be within spitting distance of my ultimate dream.

Even before a card is dealt on the feature table, Mike Matusow and Shawn Sheikhan are at it again with Mike calling Shawn a 'bad poker playing idiot', only to be told by Andy Black, 'There's no need for that, Mike.' This side show's been going all day and the crowd is pressing around the table.

Meanwhile, I'm on the other table with A-10 when John McGrane goes all-in with A-9. I have him totally dominated and the flop of K-J-5 provides him with no respite. Nevertheless, when the turn card is a five there is a distinct possibility of a split pot if he pairs the board on the river. Fortunately he doesn't, and when the dealer turns over a queen, I have the nut straight and John is eliminated, earning $350,000 for his 18th place finish. My supporters celebrate my win with their Aussie chant.

Just before 10pm Tiffany Williamson goes all-in with pocket fives against Tex Barch who has Jc-7c and comes up short when Tex draws a jack on the turn for a pair. Tiffany departs the table in 15th place to a standing ovation from the room, and takes home $400,000.

Bernard Lee kisses the photo of his two children, as he's done all through the tournament, before going all-in after the flop with a pair of kings. He's a red-hot favorite against Aaron Kanter. When the turn is no help to Aaron, Bernie's an 89 percent favorite and is out of his chair looking very confident, but I'm not so sure. I was on Aaron's table when the poker gods smiled down upon him to knock out Greg Raymer, and since then they've been literally laughing with him as he's been pulling cards from nowhere to knock out opponent after opponent. He's had one of the most remarkable runs of lucky cards I've ever seen. The run continues unabated when he draws a six on the river for trips and it's goodbye Bernie, who finishes in 13th place and collects $400,000. I'm to the left of Aaron and I'm laughing as I put my arm around his neck to congratulate him. Bernie kisses a photo of his wife, who, despite being very sick before he left home, said that he should still go ahead and fulfill his dream of playing in the Main Event.

On the feature table it becomes apparent just after midnight that the duel between Mike Matusow and Shawn Sheikhan is finally over when Mike shouts out, 'Nuts!' holding up a club flush, and then bounces around the table with both hands raised above his head. Shawn, despite earning $600,000 for finishing 11th, looks angry as he leaves the Bullpen. Obviously it's not just the disappointment of being eliminated but the ignominy of having Mike Matusow deliver the knockout blow. We're now down to one table of ten and I'm only one small step away from attaining today's goal; after the next elimination we'll have a final table. I'm in third place with $7,150,000 in chips behind the leaders, Andy Black and Aaron Kanter. The only bracelet winner left in the field, Mike Matusow, is in fourth place, but with just a little luck I sense this tournament is mine for the taking.

Steve Dannemann has been laughing and joking his way through the tournament but he's not without a serious side, and is extremely superstitious. He's worn the same lucky khaki open-necked shirt every day of the tournament, but unlike Mr Stinky, he either washes it or has minimal body odor, because he's certainly not on the nose. His wife walks him to his cab each day where he gives the cabby exact directions, and before getting out of the cab he forces the cabby to wish him good luck. After every level that he survives he phones his Mum and his wife, and he never plays the first hand of a new level. His wife didn't attend the first day at the Rio and because of this she's banned from all other days that Steve plays there, just in case she brings him bad luck. She's actually in the crowd supporting him today only because of the change in venues from the Rio to Binion's, with Steve reasoning that he has no personal history at the new location. For one so supposedly light-hearted and carefree, this is one very superstitious dude.

It's 2.30am when Andy Black, who's semi-bluffing with K-J, goes all-in in an attempt to knock out Tex Barch, who calls with a pair of jacks. It's the biggest pot of the tournament, a monstrous $9.5 million, and when Andy doesn't improve with the community cards, Tex is the new chip leader.

Twenty minutes later, Ayhan Alsancak has pocket queens and goes all-in with his final $840,000 against Scott Lazar. After the flop and the turn, Ayhan needs a queen on the river or he's going home; the odds are stacked against him, and he looks resigned to being eliminated when the dealer flips over a queen. The crowd erupts and we line up to congratulate Ayhan on his survival. We've been playing the table of ten for hours but seem no closer to a final elimination. The cards have gone cold on me again and my chip stack is down to less than $4 million.

At 3.10am Ayhan Alsancak is again dealt pocket queens but this time he's up against the almost unbeatable Aaron Kanter, who is a two-to-one underdog after the flop, but he's sizzling hot. Aaron's odds have stretched even further before the river and he needs a heart or we're going to be playing on. Yeah, you've guessed it — the dealer flips over a heart and Aaron adds yet another notch to his overcrowded belt, while Ayhan is heading home to Sweden $600,000 richer in tenth place. We commiserate with him and congratulate each other on making the final table. The last elimination has taken almost three hours. Jack Effel announces, 'Everyone at the final table is a millionaire. Let's hear it for them.'

I've been playing for 12 hours against some of the best and toughest players in the world, and I'm stoked to have made the final table. My brain is in overdrive and I can't imagine how I'm going to get to sleep, no matter how many sleeping tablets I take. My support crew has doubled and they've all stayed to the very last hand, cheering and in some instances praying for me. They're as happy as I am, but for the first time a little quiet and subdued, as if they're trying to give me a break and take my mind off what's going to occur on the final day. As if that's possible! We find a 24-hour McDonald's which, unlike in Australia, is actually licensed to sell beer, so I order a Big Mac and a Corona and most of the boys do likewise. I smile and find myself thinking about Jack Effel's words and I wonder how many other millionaires have celebrated their elevation to this lofty club by dining at Maccas.

18

The Final Day
The Storm Before the Storm

I've never liked doing deals or entering into contracts based around the possibility that you may be successful in some event or contest in the future. I've always thought that it's more advantageous to be successful or win in the first place, and then negotiate from a position of strength. I know there'll be plenty of deals on offer this late in the tournament but I'm not interested. I want to remain totally focused on winning. Besides, how could I check the credibility of those making the offers at this late stage? My word has always been my bond and I only want to deal with and mix with people of a similar ilk.

Unbeknown to me, my crew is working to ensure that I have a good sleep before I attempt to lift the holy grail of poker. I'll let Tony pick up the story: 'This is my first trip to Vegas and seven days ago I had no idea how big the WSOP was, or of the enormous prestige that went with winning the Main Event. I was just rapt to be on my first overseas holiday with Joe, but now he's made it to the final table, I find that it's bigger than Ben Hur. Everything is surreal and even though Vegas is a hyped-up city, I'm seeing everything clearly, almost in slow motion. I know Joe's going to need all the rest he can get on the final day, so I appoint myself as his unofficial manager and organize with hotel reception to have all his calls put through to my room. I want him to be relaxed and fully focused when he takes his seat at the final table.

'I field a stack of phone calls from online poker companies wanting to sponsor Joe, radio and television stations wanting interviews, and a few guys who want to talk about buying a stake in him at the final table. These are not people who are used to being told "No thanks" over the phone and some insist on meeting with me.

'I meet with the guys from some of the internet companies and tell them that we're not doing anything with anyone until the final table is over, that Joe's whole focus is on winning and that he doesn't want to be distracted looking at deals. One of them suggests that he'd better do a deal now, because he mightn't have anything to sell tomorrow. But Billy, who's with me, tells him, "Joe's gonna win this f***ing thing, and after he does you're gonna be paying a helluva lot more than what you've just offered."

'The television and radio stations are equally persistent and some of the amounts they offer me for a pre-final table interview with Joe are truly staggering, but I knock them all back.

'Finally there are the guys with the bags full of cash who want to buy a percentage of Joe at the final table. I've never seen so much cash in all my life, but my answer to these guys is, "Thanks, but no thanks."

'When we arrive at the Horseshoe that afternoon, it's packed; you can't move and there must be thousands of people trying to get in the Bullpen. There are lots of Aussies there and we even hear some Americans doing our chant. As I'm going up the escalator with Billy, this guy opens up a bag which he claims has $250,000 in it, but it looks like more to me, and he says it's all Joe's if he'll wear his company's gear at the final table. As if this isn't enough we've got nutters telling us that they want to manage him, and they're talking phone numbers. To this day I'm not sure if Joe knows how many offers we knocked back on his behalf.'

While all this is going on I'm sleeping soundly in my room. On reflection, I realize how lucky I am to have such terrific mates who formed themselves into a great support team. The public only see and hear the yahooing, screaming and of course the now famous (or perhaps that should be infamous) chant, but these guys are far more important to me than that. Each one of them has played an important part in getting me to the final table and I'll never forget what they've done. When I wake up, Ian says something to me like, 'This is the day you do it, Joe.' I don't think I made any dickhead plays when we were down to 27, but if I did Ian's far too sensible and supportive to tell me about them. I wonder how my opponents with lesser teams are handling the numerous distractions they are no doubt facing.

I have no commitments to anyone other than my family and friends, and my sole focus is to win the gold-and-diamond-encrusted bracelet that goes with being World Champion.

I phone Jeanie at around 3pm and let her know that we've won at least a million dollars, and to go out and buy gifts for all the kids.

Jeanie recollects going to the mall, buying watches and a stack of Play Station games, and then going up to the register to pay for them only to be told by the shop assistant, 'Anyone would think you've just won a million dollars,' which was really bizarre. 'I smiled to myself,' says Jeanie, 'but I didn't say anything and continued on with my shopping for a few more hours before heading back to my brother Freddy's house in West Preston for lunch. By the time

I get there the final table has commenced, and I'm finding it hard to focus on what's going on around me. My thoughts, heart and prayers are with Joe on the other side of the world.'

19

The Main Event
The Final Table

The targets I've set myself every day of the tournament have been achieved — I'm one of nine at the final table — and now I have to time my run to the finish line. The winner won't be a sprinter and I've steeled myself for a marathon that will test every ounce of concentration and stamina I possess. My nerves are already jangling and I know before the final day is over that they will be pushed to the limit. I've assessed the field and think there are probably only three others who can win, with home town boy, Mike Matusow, being the media favorite.

The Horseshoe is packed to the rafters as punters beg, bribe and probably even try to steal a ticket to the hottest event in town — a seat in the Bullpen to watch the finale of the most lucrative event in sporting history. And then there are those with a sense of tradition and sentimentality who want to be able to say they were there when Binions hosted its last final table.

The crowd is asked to stand and pay a moment's respect to those in the poker community who have passed away in the last year. We remain standing as a solemn rendition of 'The Star Spangled Banner' is sung, then Greg Raymer makes a short speech congratulating us on making the final table, and kindly calls us all champions before saying the words we're dying to hear: 'Shuffle up and deal.'

The blinds are $50,000/$100,000 and the antes $10,000, and play kicks off at 4.50pm. The final table's contenders, their chip counts and seat numbers are as follows:

Aaron Kanter: $10.580 million (Seat 6)
Tex Barch: $9.31 million (Seat 3)
Andy Black: $8.12 million (Seat 2)
Mike Matusow: $7.34 million (Seat 5)
Steve Dannemann: $5.44 million (Seat 8)
Me: $5.4 million (Seat 1)
Daniel Bergsdorf: $5.25 million (Seat 4)
Scott Lazar: $3.35 million (Seat 9)
Brad Kondracki: $1.4 million (Seat 7)

The former magician, Scott Lazar, is the only finalist over 40, by a mere two years, and student lawyer Brad Kondracki is the youngest at just 24.

In only the second hand of the day, Mike Matusow, who's on the button, goes all-in with pocket kings against Steve Dannemann, who folds, and Scott Lazar, who calls, turning over pocket aces. Mike looks sick around the gills when he sees those pocket rockets. When he hits a king on the flop he runs around the table jumping up and down and in the blink of an eye Scott's staring at the end of his tournament unless he gets an ace or running hearts. The poker gods are smiling on him and he hits the nut flush. Mike comes back to the table saying how unlucky he is, and his mother, Gloria, looks on in dismayed disbelief. Scott walks over to Mike and makes the obvious comment, 'The best hand won, right?'

Not long after, Brad Kondracki gets lucky on the river after going all-in against Steve Dannemann, and Steve wryly looks over at him and says, 'At least the best hand won again.' Steve's still wearing the same khaki shirt and I just hope he's getting it washed each night, and not sweating too much because he's about to be in the biggest hand of the day so far. He goes all-in on a semi-bluff after the flop with a possible inside straight draw against Mike Matusow, who, after a lot of thought, calls with pocket tens and says 'Was I right? I was right!' as he stands up and punches his fist into his palm. Steve looks like the little boy who's just been caught with his hands in the jam jar, but he still has outs with two overcards and a straight draw. Even as Mike's telling us how good his read is, the dealer flicks over a four and completes Steve's inside straight. Mike is totally shattered. 'There ain't no justice when I play great,' he moans. He's eliminated in ninth position and wins $1 million. It's 6.30pm and the first elimination has taken nearly two hours. Steve half-apologetically says to him, 'That's the first bad beat I've given anyone,' but it doesn't help. Despite his shocking beat, Mike maintains his composure as he departs the table.

Another hour elapses before Brad Kondracki, who has the short stack, goes all-in with A-Q and is called by Andy Black, who has him covered by about ten to one, with 8-8. The community cards are no help to Brad and he's knocked out in eighth place, taking home $1.15 million. He doesn't appear too disappointed, and his supporters are elated as they improvise on the Aussie chant with, 'Bradley, Bradley, Bradley, Kondracki!'

So far the cards haven't been kind to me and I'm only keeping my head above water by stealing a few pots from late position. Right now Daniel Bergsdorf and I are the short stacks. I decide it's time to add to my chips and when Steve Dannemann, who's on the button, raises to $400,000, and Scott Lazar in the small blind calls, I raise to $2 million in the big blind with trash, trying to steal the pot. Without even taking a moment to think, Steve, who's easily got me covered, goes all-in. Scott gets out of the way and now it's up to me. Its an easy fold as I am not going all-in in that spot without a hand, however I give a little Hollywood before folding whilst silently cursing my bad timing. I live to fight another day, but I've been seriously wounded and am now the short stack.

I revert back to playing cautiously, managing to steal a few more pots, but my chip stack is less than 20 percent of the size of the leaders' stacks. Soon, I sense an opportunity to claim a big pot when Aaron Kanter raises to $400,000, and I waste no time calling with 10-9 from the big blind. The flop is 10-4-5, which gives me a pair, and I'm sure I'm in the lead so I bet $500,000 and Aaron calls. The turn card is a jack so I bet $1 million, and then, just like Steve Dannemann earlier, Aaron goes all-in, not wasting a second. The crowd starts cheering in anticipation of me going all-in, and while I'm totally pissed off, I'm not about to do anything rash. I push my chair back from the table, not trying to hide my disgust. I say, 'Is it time for me to go, or time for me to double up?' as I riffle chips in my hand. I eventually fold, saying 'It's not time for me to go.' Much later I find out I've made a lucky lay-down because Aaron had Q-9, and had I called, the river would have been an eight, giving him the nut straight, which would've busted me. I'm still alive, but only just.

I'm short-stacked, not getting any decent hole cards and, because of my lack of chips, when I try to play a pot I'm easily bullied. The chip stacks are now:

Andy Black: $18.23 million
Aaron Kanter: $10.68 million

Tex Barch: $10.48 million
Steve Dannemann: $7.13 million
Scott Lazar: $5.37 million
Daniel Bergsdorf: $2.94 million
Me: $2.45 million

I'm on life support, frustrated and low on chips. I haven't been able to pick up any hands, or make any plays because I'm so short-stacked. I really need something to go my way, and to double up.

We adjourn for a dinner break at 8.15pm and I'm angry. I say to Dusan, 'Come on, let's get out of here. I need some peace and quiet.' We're going down the escalator when this guy shoves a camera in my face, and says, 'Hey, you look so relaxed. You sure don't look you're playing for $7.5m. You look so chilled.'

'I'm not, I'm playing for the bracelet,' I respond. As we walk out onto the footpath, the Fremont Street Experience, which is a huge light and sound show that runs every hour, erupts into life. So much for peace and quiet, and I kick a rubbish bin and let forth with a stream of expletives. All the time Duzh is saying, 'It's not your time yet. It doesn't feel right to me; you're not getting knocked out. You're gonna be fine, just keep doing what you're doing.' We grab some fast food and Duzh keeps at me, and when it's time to go back inside I've regained my composure and know I can still win. The dinner break coming at the time it did is the first good beat I've had.

I get back and for the first time during the tournament I order a Corona; drinking at the tables is normally a no-no for me, but in the circumstances a beer can't hurt. I've barely sat down before Daniel Bergsdorf goes all-in with pocket jacks and is called by Tex Barch with pocket tens. Tex gets lucky when the flop is Q-10-4 and his relatives and supporters holler out, accompanied by lots of fist pumping. Daniel gets no respite from fourth or fifth streets and is eliminated in seventh place, earning $1.3 million.

The blinds are $80,000/$160,000 and the antes $20,000, and I'm hanging on by the skin of my teeth, but despite the huge discrepancy in chips between Andy Black and me, I'm convinced I can still win. I just need a small break and I'll be on my way.

With pocket eights, Andy goes up against Tex Barch, who has pocket fives, but this is not the story of the hand. Scott Lazar in the big blind mucks A-5 only to see two aces on the flop and another on the turn; if he hadn't folded he would've had quads. He's played tight, controlled poker all week, but in the next ten minutes he'll tilt off all his chips.

The very next hand Scott, who's in the small blind, raises to $500,000 and I go all-in from the big blind. Without so much as a breath, Scott calls, showing Ks-9s, while I turn over As-Qs. Once more my tournament life is on the line, and when I see Scott's cards I breathe a sigh of relief and get out of my seat to face my supporters saying, 'Flop three spades, and don't worry about it.' The tightness I'm feeling in my chest eases when the flop is Ah-10s-4s, giving me the top pair, and when the turn card is a five of clubs, I've doubled up. My supporters haven't had much to cheer about for a while but they let everyone know they are still there with an almighty roar.

They've barely finished shouting when Scott, on the button, raises to $350,000 with Q-10 and Andy Black with pocket jacks goes all-in. Just as quickly as he had with me, Scott growls, 'Call! I'll give you a gamble,' and now his tournament life hangs by a thread. The community cards are no help to him and he's knocked out in sixth place with winnings of $1.5 million. He's played so well all week and now, in the space of three hands, has gone into a massive meltdown; maybe it's the ace he didn't play that would've given him quads or perhaps it's a build-up of tiredness. It really doesn't matter now. I shake his hand and tell him what a pleasure it's been to play with him. Andy gives him a hug and the others shake hands and commiserate with him. Scott's a real gentleman and a role model for all at the poker table. Later, when we become close friends, I find he's battled and won a huge personal fight with the drink demons, all for the love he has for his two young sons, Nick and Jake.

I'm still struggling with the short stack when Aaron Kanter limps in. I follow him in on the button, Andy Black limps in from the small blind and Tex Barch checks. The four of us see the flop Ac-Jd-4h; everyone checks to me, and I bet $500,000. Andy, who wears his sunglasses upside down, takes them off and spends a long time studying me while he considers his options. He wrestles with himself before finally mucking his hand, and the others quickly follow his lead. In total frustration I show them my queen high bluff. I'm still managing to survive without any cards, but right now I'd kill to be dealt pocket aces. My supporters break out into a deafening rendition of the Aussie chant. I've not only got the most loyal team but also the noisiest, and the ESPN guys are still making cracks along the lines of 'How did these guys ever clear US customs?'

Shortly after, Aaron Kanter on the button raises to $400,000, Steve Dannemann calls from the small blind, and I go all-in with Ad-Js from the big blind. Aaron gets out of the way quickly but Steve spends some time thinking before asking for a count of my chips. Johnny Grooms puts his microphone down next to the dealer who announces it's $3.5 million. Once more my tournament life's hanging by a thread and Steve's grinning like a

Cheshire cat while trying to get a read on me. He's really taking his time and says, 'I gotta check something. My notes.' He pulls a piece of paper out of his pocket. I laugh and say, 'Have you got notes on me, Steve?'

'I've got notes for the tournament.'

'Oh, for the tournament,' I say, grinning, as he starts to read them.

'Number one, have fun.' I'm finding it hard not to break up laughing. 'Number two, you have nothing to lose.' Steve's supporters and one in particular, Jerry Ditzel, who's on half of what Steve wins, starts laughing and cheering. 'Number three, play tight.'

I'm still chuckling when he says, 'But we'll flip it over to the bottom, and the last one says, not calling a raise is only a small mistake. It's only a small mistake,' he repeats, holding his thumb and forefinger close together.

'Compared to what?' I ask.

'So,' he says, showing me A-10 as he mucks his hand. I stand up and groan. I knew I had Steve dominated and I really wanted him to play that hand.

For a guy who's only here to have fun, Steve's not only superstitious but also very well prepared. Despite this, what you see is what you get with him, he's a really fun guy, but he's definitely not to be taken lightly.

A few hands later, I decide to call in late position with J-9 off-suit. Tex Barch limps in and Aaron Kanter checks from the big blind. The flop is 7-K-10 giving me a double belly buster straight draw, and when it's checked to me I raise to $450,000 only to watch Tex make it $1 million and Aaron re-raise to $2 million. I say, 'What have I walked into here, boys? I guess I've got to be behind. Let me check,' and I look at my hole cards again and fold. Tex takes a bit of thinking time before re-raising to $4.5 million; Aaron takes even more time to respond and I can see him replaying the hand in his mind. The crowd becomes restless while Aaron ponders his decision; it's easy for them because they're not playing for a pot that could either cripple or make them the clear favorite for the title. Finally, Aaron quietly says, 'All-in,' and the action's back on Tex, who now takes plenty of time himself before saying, 'I don't see how I get away from the hand. I call.' He pushes all of his chips into the pot turning over Kd-7d and Aaron shows K-5 off-suit. Tex is a huge favorite and Aaron will need a miracle to get out of this one. The pot is over $21 million, the biggest in WSOP history, and I grimace when the turn card is a queen because if I hadn't folded I would've had a king high straight. The river's no help to Aaron and Tex is now the chip leader. Tex has been playing really tight, only risking his chips when he has the goods, and I can't understand why Aaron didn't fold after the flop when Tex re-raised it to $4.5 million. Maybe he thought he was going to get lucky again, but this rush of blood has badly wounded him. Maybe he was tired or impatient but what I've just seen is an amazing meltdown. I briefly think back to what happened to Scott Lazar when he went on tilt after not playing his ace. I've no intention of going down that road.

It's nearly 2am when Steve Dannemann calls, and I take a little time before saying 'All-in' with a pair of sevens, the first pair I've seen for ages. Steve doesn't take long to call and shows me A-J off-suit. He's got me covered about seven to one; I'm only a marginal favorite so this hand could definitely be the end for me. 'Let me win a race, let me win a race,' I say, before shaking Steve's hand and wishing him good luck. My supporters, who've been on a white knuckle ride, are on their feet. I stand up, flicking a chip into the air, and when the flop of 9-10-6 is no help to Steve, I'm the clear favorite, but he still only needs an ace or a jack and I'm out of here. The turn is a nine, which gives him a ten as another out, but when the dealer turns over a three, I've won the race and doubled up. I hold my hands in prayer and look to the ceiling as the boys burst into a thunderous delivery of their chant. I sit down and breathe a massive sigh of relief, saying, 'Man, winning a race in this game is like a miracle.'

Soon after, Andy Black goes all-in pre-flop with 10-10 and when Steve calls with A-K he's in another race. Andy really shows his emotions and you can see the pain in his face before the flop comes 2-3-8, but he still looks strained and tense. Steve hits a king on the turn and Andy starts to put his jacket on knowing he has only two outs with one card to come. The river is a nine and Andy's knocked out in 5th place, taking home $1.75m. Not long ago he was playing the best of all of us, had the biggest stack and was bullying us around, but he made the mistake of getting himself into positions he didn't need to be in. Like Scott and Aaron, he's gone into meltdown and self-destructed. His large contingent of Irish supporters burst out into 'Hip, hip, hurray! Hip, hip, hurray!' but it's too early to ease his pain. It's 2.15am and Johnny Grooms announces the following chip counts:

Steve Dannemann: $26.25 million
Tex Barch: $20.15 million
Me: $5.05 million
Aaron Kanter: $4.83 million

I'm finally out of the short-stack position when this feeling of calmness comes over me. I think to myself, *You know what,*

Joe? If you bust out next, man, you've gotta be proud of yourself. It's your first World Series and you've done better than any other Australian player ever. Fourth place and a couple of million dollars is great. Just as I'm getting comfortable with this notion I clearly hear the words, *Listen here, dickhead, no one remembers who comes second, so hurry up and win.* It's not about the money; it's about the recognition, the immortality, the bracelet, having your photo in the Gallery of Champions and being one of only a very select group to ever win the Main Event. It's time to once again put my head down and my ass up. (I later realize that another Aussie, 'The Silver Fox', Mel Judah, a dual bracelet-winner, came third in 1997, so I'm happy that I didn't capitulate at that point.)

Aaron Kanter almost immediately wins a big hand; I'm short-stacked again and have nothing left to lose. I decide to take a stand against Aaron, who's been re-raising me non-stop, whether it's because he has had big hands or whether he has just decided he can push me around because I was short stacked. All day I've never limped on the button; I've always either raised or folded. So I decide, even before my cards are dealt, that I'm going to limp in, and if the pot's raised I'm going to re-raise all-in, representing a monster hand.

Surprise, surprise — this is exactly what happens. I limp in with Qd-7d, Tex Barch makes up the small blind, and then Aaron raises as I half-suspected he would. When it gets backs to me I move all-in, Tex gets out of the way, and Aaron, after a little consideration, calls 75 percent of his stack with only a pair of nines! I'm shocked that he's made such a call holding only a medium-range hand, especially after I'd limped in and re-raised from the button. Taking a big gulp of my coffee, I stand up to see the flop of Qh-2h-8s and I take the lead. I upper-cut the air and my supporters are cheering, but Aaron has been drawing some miraculous cards on the turn and the river and I know a nine or a runner-runner straight will see me out of the tournament. 'It doesn't mean anything, Lon,' Norman Chad, the ESPN commentator, says to his co-commentator. 'Didn't you rename the river the Kanter?' The turn is an Ah and now Aaron has only two outs to win the hand, but Norman emphatically says, 'When Kanter hits the nine on the river, "Aussie, Aussie, Aussie, oi, oi, oi" will be over and done with and Hachem will be headed home.' But this time Aaron's all out of luck, and when the river's the two of clubs I survive and double up. Ironically, Aaron's been knocking out everyone when he's had second-best hands, but against me pre-flop he had the best hand and it hasn't saved him — maybe it's the poker equivalent of poetic justice. Sure, my decision to go all-in was part defiance and part desperation, and if I hadn't done it I would have been pushed right out of the tournament. But it was also based on several key factors. First, I hadn't limped on the button all day; second, I hadn't limped re-raised all day; third, Aaron was a raising machine so I couldn't give his raises too much credit; and fourth, my all-in was seriously going to damage his stack if he got it wrong and was caught.

Norman's wrong about the chant being over and done with, and it resounds around the Bullpen as my crew goes crazy. I'm still churning inside; if I hadn't hit the queen on the flop I would've been out of here. It's just gone 4am. It's taken me nearly 12 hours of grinding, folding, scrounging and bluffing to get myself a respectable stack of slightly in excess of $13 million in chips, but then again I always knew I'd need the endurance of a marathon runner to win this tournament. For the first time, I have chips in front of me, and now no one can bully or bluff me. The winning post is in sight, and I'm calling down with ace high and re-raising with garbage because I now have chips to use. Forty minutes later, for the first time since play commenced, I hit the lead without having been in one confrontation during that time. The earlier chip leaders have made the mistake of battling each other, letting me steal smaller pots to stay alive.

I later find that Duzh, Emad and Arul didn't like the way I played the hand with Aaron, and were tightly holding hands, collectively willing me on to win. These guys are very macho, but it's amazing what the emotion of supporting a mate in a tough spot can make you do. Maybe it was their united wills that got me over the line or maybe it was my brother, Tony, standing behind them praying for me. He later tells me that when he was praying he was thinking of our deceased brother, Elei. It just shows that the pressures of this tournament extract the rawest of emotions from players and supporters alike.

Aaron Kanter is now the short stack and he goes all-in only to be called by his nemesis, Tex Barch. Aaron shows Ad-9s and Tex is a three-to-one favorite to win with pocket jacks. This time the community cards don't help, and Aaron is eliminated in fourth place, earning $2 million. We give him a standing ovation and his supporters chant, 'Aaron! Aaron! Aaron!' He's had a great tournament.

❧

When the shotgun-wielding guards escort the $7.5 million into the Bullpen just after 5am and tip it on a nearby table, the reality that I am about to play off for the World Championship hits home with a wallop. I can just about reach out and touch the money; I can smell it, just like I can sense victory. But it's not the cash I'm worried about. All my focus is on sticking to my game plan and taking down Tex and Steve.

We have a short break, just long enough for me to take a few deep breaths, take in the encouraging words of my crew, and then it's back to business. I look down at two jacks in the small blind as Steve raises from the button, so I call with the intent of trapping him on the flop when, much to my surprise, Tex Barch moves all-in for $6 million. I've got $26 million in chips, and Steve has $23 million when he calls the all-in. I now have a tough decision. Should I move all-in and face Tex heads-up, or should I call, check it down with Steve in the hope that one of us will eliminate him? Either play is acceptable, but I have two things going through my mind. Firstly, I want to face Steve heads-up and secondly, I don't want to risk playing a massive pot if I can't get him to lay his hand down, just in case he gets lucky.

I look over at Steve and hope he's experienced enough to check down unless he hits a monster. The flop is 10-3-8 and we both check, but even as we're playing I'm thinking that I've made a big mistake and that I should have pushed Steve out of the pot right then with a bet. Fourth street brings a queen and we both check; the river is a blank and we check again. Tex shows A-6 and Steve reveals pocket sevens. I win the hand and Tex is eliminated, winning $2.5 million. We both shake Tex's hand and he leaves to warm but subdued applause; I guess some of his supporters haven't lasted the distance. Steve says, 'It's a coin toss now,' but I think my odds are far better than that. Jeanie's original prediction that she's reinforced so many times since — that I would either finish first or third — flits through my mind, and I now know the latter is no longer possible.

It's 6am and the marathon is nearly over. I'm well in front as we enter the stadium with $40 million in chips against Steve's

$16 million. I also know I'm a far more experienced player and that Steve has only been playing for 18 months; in fact, he ranks himself only fourth or fifth in his home game. Despite this, one thing's for sure; I'm not going to take him lightly. After all, he's defeated 5617 others to get where he is now, including some of the best players in the world.

I take a deep breath. This is it. I'm about to go heads-up for the prized bracelet.

20

The Main Event
Are You Having Fun?

The long hours have taken their toll, and while the Bullpen is still packed, the crowd has thinned from the size it was 14 hours earlier. I later find that some of my buddies want to get closer to the action by moving down to the vacated seats near the table. Duzh is so bloody superstitious, though, that nothing can move him from his seat because he believes in his heart of hearts that moving might change the order of the universe and work against me.

Bruce Buffer, avid poker player and the main ring announcer for the Ultimate Fighting Championship Main Events, makes the final introductions at 6.30am, finishing with, 'Let's get ready to gamble!' Seven days of intense, grueling and combative poker is about to reach its zenith.

The blinds are $150,000/$300,000 with antes of $50,000. I've got Steve covered more than two to one in chips. I know with levels of this size the state of the game can turn on just a few hands, but I've worked too hard to get where I am now, and resolve not to do anything stupid that will allow him to get back into the game. I've had the same game plan all day, which is to avoid playing big pots with him unless I've made a hand, because he's been playing fearlessly and has nothing to lose. He hadn't expected to get this far, so everything after making the money was extra cream. That's how he's managed to be so successful at the final table; he puts everyone else under pressure. Every time he sensed weakness or uncertainty he pushed all his chips into the middle to force his opponents to make a decision for their tournament lives.

Before we start playing, Steve walks over to me and says, 'Joe, I just wanna let you know, I hope you win. You are the best player. I know it means more to you than me so we're going to get it over quickly, alright?'

'Okay, mate,' I grin. This gives me an extra confidence boost just as we're about to go into battle.

We play five hands, of which Steve wins three and I win two, but there's no significant change in chip stacks. In heads-up, the button has the small blind and is first to play pre-flop. It's 6.45am when Steve on the button raises to $700,000 compared to my $300,000 big blind and $50,000 antes; I've got $40 million so it's a relatively easy call for me, and when I look down at 7c-3s it's the type of hand where if I hit a nice flop I could end the tournament. I call and the flop comes 6h-5d-4d. I couldn't have wished for better, and now I think, *How can I get all of his chips and finish this thing right now*? I decide I'll check to him and, all going to plan, he'll bet and I'll check-raise. I know that all night whenever he's been raised he's moved all-in. I check and he bets $700,000 and I raise him to $1.7 million. He thinks about it and then just calls. *What's he doing? He's just called!* He's never called — ever. The whole day he's never made a call. He's always pushed. My only fear, remote as it is, is that he's holding 7-8, which would give him the nut straight and put me in a whole world of pain. As the ace of spades hits the felt on the turn, I sense from his body language that he's holding one. *Here's my opportunity. I've got to get him to commit all of his chips to the pot.* I lead out with \$2 million and he starts looking at me and acting all coy. He smiles and winks at me, and I say, 'Are you having fun?'

'My God, it's a ball. Two million dollars — that's a pretty large bet for a young man of your playing ability', he responds, taking his time before raising to \$5 million.

'I thought we were being friendly', I say. My whole strategy is based around the fact that he's here to have fun. He's been having fun, so I want him to get back to the mood of *This is fun; this is just a home game*, and to throw his chips in and hope for the best. I spend a few seconds looking at him before asking, 'How many chips have you got?' He starts counting, but before he can answer I say, 'Stop! I'm all-in.' I just wanted to snap him, and I can tell by the look on his face that I've taken him completely by surprise. Despite this, he takes no time to call; he's having fun and you can tell he's ready to go home one way or another. When he turns over Ad-3c I stand up and punch my fist into the air because I know I can't lose the hand. Now all I can think is, *There are three sevens left in the deck. Please don't turn one over on the river; please don't let him chop the pot.* 'I've got a chance', he says, remaining seated, while I walk around the table barely able to stand the suspense of waiting for the river card to be exposed. My mates are yelling and cheering. I look over at them and their faces are filled with exhilaration; as far as they're concerned it's all over, I've won. I hold my hands up so they'll be quiet, saying, 'Wait, wait, there's one more card.' Steve wishes me good luck, and I raise my hand to acknowledge him. My gut is knotted and I'm still praying, *Please don't let it be a seven.* The dealer turns over the river. It's the four of clubs. It's finally all over, and the room bursts into raucous applause.

Steve and I embrace; he's a great guy and he's played some fantastic poker over the past seven days. I turn and wave to the crowd and shout, 'Thank you everybody! Thank you everybody! Thank you so much!' I'm jumped on by Tony and Billy, who hand me the Australian flag, and my supporters burst into a noisy but raspy Aussie chant. Seven days of pent-up tension starts to dissipate; I feel the weight of the world being lifted from my shoulders and want to shout, *Yes, yes, it's over!* For the first time I lead the chant, flapping the flag in front of me and then proudly wrap it around my shoulders. I know I'm the first Aussie to be the World Champion, and the pride I'm feeling is not just for me, but for all the wonderful people who live in my home country. You couldn't live in a better place, and I know every Aussie will be embracing my victory. A few minutes later the boys hoist me on their shoulders, their fists pumping as they hoarsely yell almost indiscernible words of victory.

Tony phones Jeanie on his cell and shouts, 'Jeanie! He won it! He won it!' and then tells the crowd, 'That's his wife,' before passing the phone to me. She already knows of my victory and I sense she's in shock when she says, 'I told you, didn't I? I told you you'd win it.'

'I love you, hon,' I say. 'Now pack your bags and get over here as fast as you can.'

I hear her say that the kids don't have passports when the connection drops out, and I'm laughing as I look out at the crowd and say, 'I think she fainted.' Next thing you know there're a million people around me all talking at once. Jeanie is a superb organizer, and I know she'll be in Vegas as soon as is humanly possible. What I don't know about are the hassles that she's about to go through back home.

Flash bulbs are popping off everywhere and media from all over the world are asking questions at the one time. Pop, pop, pop — it's like standing before one huge strobe light. I pose with a glass of champagne, with the money, with my arms around the money, and holding the seven of clubs and the three of spades. Then I attempt to throw some money into the crowd but the Tournament Director stops me. After about 20 minutes the photographers finally have enough shots and I start doing interviews.

Norman Chad sits me down at the money table, which is covered in stacks of $100 bills, and asks, 'What does $7.5 million do for you?'

'A million dollars changes my life, let alone $7.5 million. Everything's gonna change. Apparently Australia's gone mad, and you know we're all sports freaks already, right? So someone comes to America and wins the World Series of Poker, they're gonna go mental.'

After the interviews are over I start to think of the responsibilities that go with being World Champion. I know I'm going to have to talk to someone who's experienced what I'm about to go through, which leaves me with just two possibilities — Chris Moneymaker and Greg Raymer. I don't know Chris but have played at the same table as Greg; I feel comfortable contacting him because I know he's been a great ambassador for poker.

I'm meant to be checking out of the Mandalay Bay in a few hours, so I phone to see if I can extend my stay but there's no way they can help me, so I have to get back to pack. The floor of the Bullpen is covered with empties, litter, food scraps and even a few unconscious and semi conscious punters. As I'm leaving, this young guy grabs my hand and starts telling me how great it is that I've won. He's treating me like we're best mates but I don't know him, and it must show, because he says, 'I got the first autograph ever signed by the World Champ,' and when he says that, the penny drops — it's the young kid who insisted on getting my autograph in the Amazon Room when we were down to 27. I apologize for not recognizing him and thank him for his good wishes.

I'm exhausted and emotionally wrung out when I get back to my room, but there's no time for even a quick nap and I hurriedly throw my clothes into my suitcase and head down to reception. One of the concierges shouts out to me, 'Hey, you just won the World Championship, right?' and I say, 'Yeah, that's right.' He looks at me and my luggage and says, 'What are you checking out for?' and I tell him I phoned and there were no rooms available. 'Hell, man, that's not right. We can put you up in one of our suites.' I thank him, but it's too late because I've already booked ten rooms at the Wynn for my mates, my family and myself. Later, some of my new-found American friends tell me that when I phoned reception at the Mandalay Bay I should've told them I was the newly crowned World Champ, and they would've definitely found rooms. That's something Aussies just don't do, and the ones who do are brought back down to earth quick smart. If I were to return to Melbourne's Crown Casino and preen and parade myself, there'd be plenty there who'd pull me back into line — well, maybe not because Jeanie would never let it reach that stage. She'd carpet me long before then. Anyhow, I'd feel like a tool if I were to run around saying, 'I'm World Champion so you'd better find some rooms for me!'

Ian is booked on a flight back to Australia today, but I won't hear of it and convince him to come to the Wynn with me for at least the next week where we can celebrate with the boys in style. I get into my room, pop a couple of sleeping tablets, crash into bed elated but exhausted, and sleep like a baby for the next four hours. I awaken and go to the bathroom, and when I actually see my reflection in the mirror, I burst into uncontrollable tears. It suddenly hits me, *My God is this real, did it really happen, or is it all part of a mean dream?* After I regain my composure, I think about how my mates and I are going to paint the town red tonight, which brings a grin to my face, and my emotions are put to one side — for the time being that is. It's going to be a night to remember.

I've worked so hard, reading, learning, studying how others played and holding tournaments in my garage, and while I've been on many final tables in Australia, I've never quite managed to win. Now this! Think about it: how many people get to be World Champion in anything, let alone in the richest event in sports history, an event in which the winner is immortalized by having his photo hung in the WSOP Gallery of Champions? In years to come my children and, later, my grandchildren will visit Vegas, look up at those photos, and say 'There's Grandpa. You know, he was the 2005 World Champion.'

The late and great Kerry Packer, once Australia's wealthiest man, said that he'd do anything to be a national champion or in a national side. When pressed about what sport or pursuit he would choose, he responded, 'God, man, I would've settled for tiddlywinks if it'd made me a national champion.' Australians love their sports and their champions, and being a World Champion is the ultimate accolade, something that money could never buy.

21

A Tale of Two Beats

I have a very good friend in Melbourne, John Dalessandri, whose character and style of playing poker is strikingly similar to the character Joey Knish (played by John Turturro) from the movie *Rounders*. John is short, stocky, quiet and unassuming, but when it comes to cards and poker he's like a bull terrier. Like Joey Knish, he's a tight, very skilled player whose family is never going to go hungry.

Because of my table demeanor and the way I play, John is always saying, 'Joe, you should be in Hollywood.' I'm not really sure what he means but at this stage of my life I far prefer Vegas. John and I have vastly different playing styles but despite this we always swap ten percent when we play tournaments. Whether I pay him or whether he pays me is irrelevant, as our exchange is not about money but friendship. It's great to exchange with someone like John because I know that while he may not win, he won't be eliminated early in tournaments because he doesn't make careless mistakes. He's too controlled and measured for that, and he not only does well in tournaments but in cash games too. In fact, cash games are his bread and butter, and over the years he's ground out a very good living.

Before the 2005 WSOP I asked John whether he's coming along to join the rest of the group because he's a great mate and we have a lot of fun together, but unfortunately he couldn't get away. At the time we had no idea that his decision would prove so costly for him. What a bad beat!

In direct contrast to John, Steve Dannemann has a close friend, Jerry Ditzel, who plays home games with a group of 12 mates in Anne Arundel County, Maryland, on Tuesday nights. According to Jerry, Steve's a good player among many good players. Anyhow, a couple of weeks before the WSOP, Jerry and Steve had just finished a game of golf and were enjoying a few beers when Jerry agreed to put up $5,000 to stake Steve for 50 percent of his winnings. When Steve was runner-up to me at the final table he collected $4.25million, half of which went to Jerry. Now that is what I call an incredibly good beat.

Jerry later said, 'It was so intense and so nerve-racking that it made the Super Bowl look like child's play. Until you see it first hand, you don't know how intense it is.' I can definitely vouch for that. Every day you're on edge, knowing the very next hand might be your last but that's the beauty and appeal of No-Limit. Jerry watched the action from a chair about 15 feet from the final table at Binion's with Steve's wife, Anita, sitting next to him. 'She was breaking my arm — she was squeezing it so hard. She was very emotional,' he said.

When you play high stakes No-Limit Texas Hold 'em, it creates the same excitement and tension that you feel when you drive a fast car. You have to make decisions or force others to make decisions, and in either case if you get them wrong you end up in the gutter. In poker, those decisions and the anxiety and stress that go with them, flow through to your friends, family and those supporting you. But they're best expressed in the faces of your backers and those who you've shared the experiences with. Imagine the friend who wrestles with the idea of taking a share in his mate for a small sum, decides not to, and then watches his mate win millions. Now that's gotta hurt. Or imagine what Jerry Ditzel went through from the time Steve Dannemann made the money right up until he was going heads-up with me? The good and bad beats in this game are not just confined to the players.

Part Two

Seeking Validation

22

Lighting a Candle

On the other side of the world my family and friends have gathered at my brother-in-law Freddy's house in the Melbourne suburb of West Preston to track my progress at the final table. Unbeknown to me, Jeanie's cousin Collette, who's visiting from Lebanon, lit a candle for me a week ago and the flame has never died.

Freddy and Collette are following my progress online in one of the bedrooms when Jeanie arrives at 1pm after finishing her shopping spree. She recollects: 'I hadn't been watching from the beginning, and I wasn't just going to plonk my bottom on a chair and start now for fear that the change might adversely affect Joe's luck. Instead, I sit on the couch in the lounge room, a blanket wrapped around me, in semi-shock wondering why this is happening to us. An ever-changing mass of friends, family and well-wishers cram themselves into the lounge room and we get regular running reports on how Joe's doing and the state of the game from Freddy and Collette, who won't let anyone into the bedroom to watch it live online with them as they're concerned that it might be unlucky. Joe mightn't be superstitious, but I am, as are most of his friends, and we're not going to do anything that might jeopardize his chances. The house is filled with a mixture of anxiety and happiness, and my Uncle Gabriel ('Gabby') thinks it's fantastic that Joe's won a million dollars, and that even if he's knocked out it's a marvelous achievement. Around mid-afternoon, Freddy informs us that Andy Black is a huge chip leader and that Joe's still short-stacked. Little is registering with me now; I'm dazed, not talking, and I've retreated into my own little shell. Deep down I understand what's going on around me but it's like an out-of-body experience where I'm seeing everything from afar.

There's a collective gasp when we hear Andy Black is eliminated and the table is down to four. Gabby goes nuts and grabs my shoulders, shaking me to death, saying, "Wake up, what's wrong with you?" as he removes the cork from another bottle of champers. The lounge room is packed and the overflowing guests are in the kitchen. It's mayhem and there's a lot of talk about how much money Joe has won. My brain is totally numb when I say to the others, "Look, it's not about the money. Joe has a burning passion to win the World Championship. He wants that bracelet so badly." Deep down I'm almost certain he's going to get it.'

Later, when Jeanie tells me what went on in Freddy's house I can totally relate to it. My relations thought that I was a bit of a punter who enjoyed playing poker; they didn't really understand the game or what poker tournaments were all about. Jeanie, on the other hand, had seen and felt my disappointment after I'd made so many final tables in Australia and yet never tasted victory in a major tournament. She totally understood what it meant to me to have a chance of winning my first tournament, which just happened to be the biggest and most prestigious in the world, and she knew and could feel exactly what I was going through.

Jeanie remembers the excitement back in Preston when Freddy bounded out of the bedroom and shouted, 'Joe's just won a huge pot against Aaron Kanter and he's no longer the short stack! He's going to win, he's going to win!'

'The word must have been traveling rapidly around Melbourne,' says Jeanie, 'because by now there're over 50 of us in the house and everyone's pulling for Joe. If anything, I'm becoming more withdrawn and subdued and am almost oblivious to what's going on around me. Collette continues to deliver reports every ten minutes, but the next announcement that's greeted with unrestrained cheering comes just after 9pm when Joe takes the chip lead for the first time. The noise that accompanies this is nothing compared with the ruckus that takes place half an hour later when Aaron Kanter is knocked out and they're down to three at the Horseshoe. Everyone except me is in party mode, and the beer and spirits are flowing freely. Now that Joe is in the lead the running commentaries become more frequent. At 11.20pm Freddy races out of the bedroom and yells out that Joe's just won a massive pot, and that he's now a huge chip leader. Tex Barch has been eliminated, they're down to two, and all Joe has to do is beat Steve Dannemann and he'll be the winner. The house erupts with roars of approval, but there are still a lot of tense, nervous smiles. Freddy then says that there's going to be a 15-minute break before they start the final battle and this is met with a collective groan. Mercifully, it takes only another 15 minutes of play before Collette and Freddy make the announcement that everyone's been waiting to hear: "Joe has won! He's the World Champion!" Our friends and relatives are jumping up and down, and I finally get off the couch I've been sitting on for the past 12 hours and start kissing everyone. But the shock is just too much to cope with. I go into the bathroom and start sobbing as I think of all the near-misses that Joe's had in tournaments in Australia, the interstate trips, the hours he's put into the game he loves, and how he's now been rewarded for all his efforts with the highest prize. I can't fathom the ramifications of what's just happened; I know Joe's bringing home the bracelet, and that we're going to be debt-free, but I can't help thinking, *Why us? Why is God giving it to us? How are our lives going to change?* It's scary, and as I think about it the tears are rolling down my cheeks and I have to fight to compose myself. I can't talk about the feelings I'm experiencing with our extended family because they're not really aware of what the game means to Joe or his love for it.'

I'm a poker player but I don't regard myself as a gambler. This may sound a bit strange but there's a feeling in the community that anyone who plays poker is some type of river-boat gambler who has an aversion to working. Fortunately, thanks to the advent of poker tournaments being televised, this perception has lost a lot of traction over the past few years — businessmen, housewives, lawyers, doctors, film stars and sportsmen all around the world play poker. In one of the latest James Bond movies, *Casino Royale*, Daniel Craig plays in a high stakes poker tournament. This is the first time in 40 years that 007 has drifted away from playing baccarat, so presumably poker must be doing something right. I play No-Limit Hold 'em because I love the game, I have an edge, and when I sit down to play I'm definitely not gambling. I love my extended family and I know they were over the moon with joy for me that wonderful morning I won the WSOP, but I also know they didn't appreciate the blood, sweat and tears I'd put into my poker leading up to the Main Event. When I went to Vegas they didn't understand what winning the WSOP meant, and some still don't. Their excitement and happiness for me was all about the amount of money I'd won, and they didn't have a real appreciation of what it was to be World Champion.

❧

'My phone rings and I can just hear Tony's excited voice above the pandemonium. When he put Joe on we were both dreadfully emotional but are only able to speak for about a minute before the connection drops out.

'The party rolls on until 4am and I borrow a pair of Freddy's pajamas, as it's too late for the kids and me to go home. I have to be up early to take Anthony to football training. Gabby's driving us home, and we've had less than four hours sleep. I'm still wearing Freddy's pajamas, and I'm going to shower and change at home before driving Anthony to training. Gabby pulls up out the front of our house and we're surrounded by press, photographers and other media. This is the last thing I expected and I plead, almost beg them not to take my photo, and I'm so grateful when they go along with my pleas. However, they're insistent on doing an interview, and Gabby asks them to wait for half an hour while I get cleaned up and change. I invite them into the house and they ask me questions about what Joe's win means and I answer as best I can. I still don't really know myself. Then they ask Anthony and me if they can take photos of us out the front of the house. I readily agree, and while they've really been quite good, I won't be unhappy when they're gone.

'The following morning there's a barrage of media on the front door step. *Have I heard from Joe? What'd he say? When's he coming home? How do you feel? Will it change your life?* I tell them I have an urgent appointment to get to, and this time beg them not to hold me up. The kids don't have passports and mine has expired. The authorities bend over backwards and within 48 hours we all have passports. Needless to say I think the people who work for the Australian Passport Office are fantastic.

'I haven't been out of Australia since going to Lebanon with Anthony when he was only five months old, so really this will be the kids' first overseas trip. Freddy, Gabby and Denise decide we can't go by ourselves and join us.

'The next morning I look out the window and let out a loud groan when I see the media congregating again on the footpath, and wonder if they're ever going to disappear. I drive the kids to school and when I'm leaving I get asked the same questions as the prior day but this time one of the reporters from a television channel is adamant that he's going to interview me. I promise to do the interview when I return, which I do, but at the end I tell a little fib and say that we're taking a flight to Los Angeles the next day (Wednesday), when in fact we're not going until Friday. Hopefully this should ensure that I don't wake up to a media scrum in the morning.'

My second youngest child, Daniel, was only ten then, and now four years later he's grown to 6'2", and certainly doesn't get his height from me. He's a fine 200 and 400 meters runner, studies hard and is a real quiet achiever. I'll let him tell you a little of what happened in those mad days after my victory:

'We rushed around with Mum, organizing passports and our travel on the Monday, but on Tuesday morning I was back at school. As I walked into the classroom my school mates rose and started applauding. It was the last thing I expected but I was bursting with pride. Dad had been gone for two weeks, which was the longest I could remember him ever being away from home, and I was really missing him. This would be my first trip overseas and I was just dying to get to Las Vegas to see him.'

Jeanie remembers peeking out the window on Wednesday morning and breathing a big sigh of relief. 'My white lie had worked and the media had disappeared, and better still I knew that Joe would handle any questions we got asked in Vegas. He's confident and articulate and I knew the press would hold no fears for him.'

23

Crown Casino
'I've Got a Hachem'

Although I don't know it, my progress over the last three days is being closely tracked at my home casino, Crown.

Jonno Pittock, who runs the poker room at Crown, still remembers July 2005 and the Main Event as though it were yesterday: 'There were a number of Aussies competing, but live coverage online wasn't easy to pick up. Also, the Hold 'em craze, while evolving, hadn't taken complete hold, and our poker room was nothing like it is today. Less than half the area we currently use for poker was being used to house just 27 tables, and we had about the same number of blackjack tables and a live band. As the tournament progressed we tracked it on the net through Cardplayer.com and then we'd see if we could find any blogs containing more details about the action. As it got deeper into the tournament we started to read more and more about Joe, and with three days left to go, he was the last remaining Aussie. We then started making announcements every time he took down a big hand or someone got knocked out. My staff and I all love playing Hold 'em and there's a very close knit poker community in Melbourne made up of regular Crown players, so everyone was right with Joe, willing him on. A huge burst of applause reverberated around the room when I made the announcement that he'd made the final table and was now a millionaire.

'I started work at 10am on Saturday, play on the final table in Vegas had just commenced, and we were immediately online tracking every hand. Mike Matusow's early elimination on the last day was greeted with raucous cheers, and the talk coming from every table was all about how far Joe could go and whether he could win it. We all know he's short-stacked and up against the odds, but the punters are literally holding their breaths and praying for him. There was a buzz in the room and his name was on everyone's lips. I continued making announcements about the eliminations, and each time I did I let everyone know the minimum amount of cash that he'd now won. That night the 27 Hold 'em tables were full, there were another 100 players waiting to play, the blackjack tables were booming, and the band was belting out Elvis. From 10,000 miles away it seemed that Joe was gradually working his way through the field, and they were down to four when he took the chip lead for the first time at 9.40pm. There was a real belief that he was going win.

'And then, just before midnight, it happened! Thankfully the band was taking a break and I went out to the poker room to make the announcement. I managed to get out "Joe Hachem has just ..." and the room erupted into pandemonium — there was screaming, cheering and clapping, and it was like everyone in the room was in Vegas celebrating with him. Stony-faced tough guys were crying like babies. To fully understand the magnitude of what he'd achieved you have to be a poker player. Winning the Main Event at the World Series of Poker is Mecca, the Holy Grail, and the conquest of Everest all rolled into one. If Joe never wins another tournament he'll always be remembered for what he had just achieved — he was sitting on the pinnacle of world poker. Everyone in the room had a mobile phone to their ear and word of Joe's great victory spread like wildfire. Later, in the early hours of morning, when anyone got dealt 7-3 you'd hear them say, "Have a look at that. I've got a Hachem." It certainly didn't take long to catch on.

'I finally got to go home and catch up on a few hours sleep but I was back again in the poker room in the morning, only to be greeted by television crews. They wanted me to stand up and do the "Aussie, Aussie, Aussie!" chant, but I was reluctant and felt a bit of a goose, not knowing how the room would react. I needn't have worried as a noisy "oi, oi, oi!" echoed repeatedly around the room. I can't adequately describe the feelings — the euphoria and the excitement we had all experienced in the past 24 hours. I ran across Frank Bianco, one of the floormen, and he says to me, "I haven't slept a wink since Joe won. I just couldn't sleep!" I can't think of a finer or more deserving winner than Joe. He's charismatic and clever, and poker will be all the better for his victory. He's also a humble and generous guy, and I just know he's going to put a lot back into poker, promoting the game and uplifting its image.'

Thanks for the kind words, Jonno. They'll take a lot of living up to.

24

The Biggest Times

I find that in my rush to leave the Mandalay Bay I've left my white shirt and black belt behind. There's nothing to worry about, though, because Ian and I find an up-market fashion label at the Wynn called Brioni. We waltz in and I soon have three shop assistants looking after me, showing me a range of shirts and belts. Ian's sitting on a couch looking on as I choose a fitted white cotton shirt and black leather belt. The shop assistant recognizes me, congratulates me on my victory as she neatly wraps my purchases, and says, 'That will be $1,400 thanks, Mr Hachem. And how would you like to pay?' I look over at Ian, who's normally pale, but in that instant he goes three shades lighter and totters on the edge of the couch. I'm dumbstruck. Can she be serious? $1,400 for a belt and shirt! I want to tell her I'm not taking them, but embarrassment gets the better of me and I smile and say, 'Charge them to my room.' This is another lesson in the ways of Vegas, and I realize I've made a big mistake not asking the prices of the clothes before the shop assistant wrapped them — a mistake I haven't made since.

Tony gets Uncle Vince on his cell phone and he says to me, 'What have you done? Did you really do it? What have you done Joe?'

'See Uncle, I did it, I did it.'

'Are you the champion? Are you the new champion?'

'Yeah, Uncle, I did it. I'm the new champion.' Then I hear the crying and my eyes well up and I start to gag. He's so proud and I can almost picture him beating his chest.

That night the boys and I dine at the Tableau Restaurant at the Wynn where the cuisine is to do die for. I'm a steak-eater and little changes for me that night; I savor a perfectly cooked piece of beef, enjoy a beer and later share an exquisite bottle of wine with my mates — make that several bottles of wine. There are about eight of us and for obvious reasons I can't really recall every detail of the night, but Chris Newton writes in his poker blog the following day, 'Dinner — some of the finest and most subtle tastes I've ever had.'

We finish dinner and head to the Blush nightclub where we get our own private niche and table. The alcohol is flowing freely; we're noisy and boisterous and the boys relive some of the great hands that were played on that long final day. At home there is nothing I enjoy more than finishing off a great meal with a cigar, so I order a box of the finest and we sit back in our chairs blowing celebratory smoke rings into the air.

One of the security guys sees us enjoying ourselves and is obviously under the impression that our table is lacking some female company, so he introduces us to six stunning young ladies. The boys, who are all single, think it's great, and more rounds of drinks and cocktails are ordered. I'm guessing the security man has told the girls that I've just won the World Championship, and the blonde sitting opposite me seems to know the basics of Hold 'em. I say to her, 'What do you do?' which is some indication of how new I am to Vegas. 'I'm an entertainer,' she responds, and like a muppet I ask, 'What sort of entertainer?'

'It starts at $1,000 a night,' she says, smiling sweetly. I'm just being social and engaging in small talk and never anticipated that answer. I know that Barracuda will be the most embarrassed of our group, so in a flash I look over at him and say, 'The man you need to talk to is this guy.' It doesn't take long for the girls to realize there are no easy chips at our table, so they fold their hands, thank us for the drinks, and leave us to look for easier pickings.

We stay at the nightclub until the early hours of the morning but no one wants the night to finish. When someone suggests a game of Hold 'em we're off to the Wynn poker room.

We set up a small tournament where I put up $3,000 prize money, winner takes all. It's the first chance the boys have had to play with the new World Champion, and we're still playing at 7am. It's about 24 hours since I battled Steve Dannemann for the Championship, $7.5 million, and the precious bracelet. Now I'm playing with the guys who supported me through thick and thin, who gave me an important edge over my opponents. I couldn't wish for better company or be enjoying myself more, even though they've taken great delight in inflicting the World Champ's first defeat by busting me out of my own tournament.

Barracuda finishes his blog for the day: 'For me, home at 7.30am, a not-too-unpleasant hangover. Yesterday, the reality of it all somehow became believable and totally real. As I said yesterday, the past three days will be one of the biggest times of my life and I didn't even win a cent.' Thanks Barracuda.

25

Tony and the Pope

Let me tell you a story about my brother, Tony, to truly illustrate his character. He's five years younger than me and has always been my most passionate and outrageous supporter. He has also developed a love for poker and has made it deep into many events; it shouldn't be too long before he wins a major tournament.

Our personalities are nothing alike. I'm a very social guy, though I do like to keep to myself, and I have a tight network of close friends, whereas Tony makes a thousand friends wherever he goes. After I had been playing in the Crown poker room for years and years, I had accumulated my small group of friends. Tony first went to the poker room in 2003 and within a year knew everybody. To see Tony in the poker room at the start of a tournament is something else — he's usually walking around the room with his mobile phone glued to his ear while talking to players on other tables at the same time and giving the thumbs up to others. And no, it never worries him that he's losing his blinds while he's socializing. I'd probably describe him as gregarious but that would be a monumental understatement for someone as completely over-the-top as Tony.

I don't think there's been a black book produced that's large enough to hold the details of all Tony's contacts in Australia and around the world. He took a trip through Europe a few years back with his good mate Micky, and as they travelled from city to city across the continent, Tony would keep bragging about his connections, saying that he knew this person and that person, and Micky would scoff in disbelief, only to watch Tony come up with the goods. He would say, 'We're having drinks with Becks in London tonight,' or 'Rafa's invited us for dinner in Madrid tomorrow,' and, sure enough, Tony would never fail to deliver. As they continued their travels, Micky started believing Tony, but couldn't completely get rid of his nagging doubts. They finally reached Rome, near the end of their trip. Micky, who is half Italian, has some pride here, so when Tony says 'We'll go to the Vatican and see the Pope,' Micky's all for it.

Their timing is perfect and when they get there, a huge crowd is waiting for a rare appearance by the Pope. They're looking up at the balcony where he's going to appear when Tony says, 'Stay here Micky, I'm just going up to say hello to the Pope.'

'Don't give me that f***ing bullshit, Tony,' says Micky. 'You don't know the Pope.'

Tony looks a little miffed but takes it in his stride. 'I'll be back in about 15 minutes. Just wait for me.'

A few minutes later, applause breaks out around the square, and Micky looks up into the sunlight to see the Pope on the balcony, splendid in his white robes. And then he gasps in amazement when he sees someone standing to the right of the Pope. 'Oh my God,' he says to himself as he sees Tony waving down at him, and he tentatively waves back. Then, a beautiful young lady pulls on Micky's arm, whispers something to him and he faints, collapsing to the pavement. Tony sees what's happened and charges down from the balcony to the square, pushing the crowd aside. He reaches Micky just as he's coming around. 'What happened? What's wrong?' Tony asks, stress written all over his face.

'Throughout this trip you kept on bragging that you knew this person and you knew that person, and even though I was dumfounded how you could know all these people I eventually came to accept it. When I saw you waving down at me with the Pope I kind of accepted that you knew him, but when the lady standing next to me asked, "Who's that guy on the balcony standing next to Tony?" I just couldn't take it anymore and passed out.'

Bro, I really do love you.

26

Good advice

I first met Greg Raymer when he was shifted to my table with a huge stack of chips in the last half hour of the third day of the Main Event. But such was the brevity of time that we only exchanged a few words, and I didn't contest any hands against him — however, I did know he was the reigning World Champion. It was just after 7pm on the fifth day when I was moved to the feature table where Greg had been playing most of the day, and I got to go heads-up against him and to observe his play. I was really impressed with the way he represented himself and the way he carried himself as World Champion, and while I wasn't overawed I simply had to give the man the respect he'd earned. I thought, *This guy's a great ambassador for poker, and more particularly, the WSOP.*

After I won the Main Event, Mel Judah comes up to my room to congratulate me. I ask him if he's been talking to Greg and he responds by saying, 'I've got his phone number. Would you like it?' I take his number and phone him, asking if he'd be prepared to have lunch with Tony and me the following day in the Terrace Point Cafe at the Wynn, and he readily agrees. It's funny, but when I hang up I think *I've just been talking to the World Champ* — then quickly realize that I'm now the World Champ. This is going to take some getting used to.

As expected, Greg is as good as his word and the following day we sit down for lunch; I'm on one side of the table with him and Tony's on the other. For the past seven days Tony's lived every minute I've played, has partied relentlessly, and still been up early the following mornings. He's had even less sleep than me, and as he takes his seat his mouth opens in a huge yawn. I start asking Greg what to expect as World Champion, what's going to happen, how I can be the best possible ambassador for poker, how I should represent the game, and, most importantly, what I need to do to be the champion that he's been for the past 12 months. He's polite but a little standoffish, and he answers my questions in a serious, detailed and analytical manner, probably as a result of his background as a patent attorney. I guess he's still hurting about the cruel river card that Aaron Kanter drew to cripple him two days earlier but he's too stoic to mention it. I didn't win my seat online, but some of the online promoters have already contacted me wanting to do a deal. I ask Greg whether I'll need an agent or manager, and each answer he gives me results in a fresh barrage of questions. I really appreciate him giving up his time and I don't think I could buy the advice that he's so generously giving me. He's looking at me, articulating some detailed advice, when I glance over at Tony. *Oh shit, this is a sight to behold.* His head is lolled back, his mouth's wide open, and he's out like a light. I don't know whether Greg's noticed, but I guess even if he has he's too polite to say anything so I give Tony a tap with the toe of my shoe under the table. He wakes up, grins, and says, 'Sorry, sorry, sorry.' While this is going on, Greg doesn't miss a beat and continues with his advice as if nothing's occurred. His face doesn't reveal anything as to what he's thinking about Tony, but yet again you wouldn't expect it to, given his status in the world of poker. No more than 60 seconds has elapsed when I hear this distinct snore; Tony's asleep again, only this time with sound effects. I let fly with an almighty kick to his shins, and he jumps out of his seat and in the middle of the café shouts, 'I'm all-in! I'm all-in!' We finish the conversation and I thank Greg for his time and advice. One thing he stresses is that I should take my time in making decisions, and I take this on board, which later proves very beneficial.

We're walking out the café and I suspect that Greg hasn't found Tony's dozing off amusing because he hasn't cracked it for a smile. Then again, he's a little aloof by nature and you'd never really know what he's thinking. We reach the front of the café and I shake his hand, thanking him profusely. Tony, who's about half Greg's size, walks up to him, reaches up, puts one hand on his shoulder and with the other starts rubbing Greg's tummy like a Buddha, saying, 'Thanks Greg.' Greg looks down at him as if to say, '*What the f*** are you doing?*' and Tony looks over at me, winks and shrugs. I steal a quick glance at Greg and now even he can't keep from grinning, but God only knows what he's thinking.

Greg's now one of my closest friends but it took me a while to soften him up. Once out of his shell, he's one of the warmest people you could ever wish to meet. Our families have become friends as well and these days Greg greets all of us with a kiss and a hug.

❧

While we've been at the Wynn, this guy who looks like a Vegas degenerate gambler has been doing his utmost to befriend us. He's been hanging around us like a bad smell and trying to get in on the action. As I'm talking with Mike Sexton — man about town, bracelet winner and fine poker player in his own right — about a potential future sponsorship and what it involves, this guy grabs my arm and says, 'Hey Joe, hey brother, I'm so glad to see you.'

'Yeah, what's up?' I reply.

'I've been driving around all day trying to get you sponsorships and deals, and, by the way, my car broke down and you've gotta buy me a new one so I can keep working for you.'

'With due respect, why don't you let me get a manager who's going to be a professional, and you just do your business, and I'll do mine. Right?' *How do these guys find me?*

I look over at Mike, and he appears totally unfazed, so I guess this is an everyday Vegas scam that he's seen many times before. Con artists like this guy work on the basis that they've got nothing to lose by asking, and if they can find a mark and pick up a few hundred bucks here, or maybe a thousand there, it'll keep them going until they find their next sucker.

The morning of my victory, I'm in my room with Tony, Billy and Ian when I get a phone call from Australia. Tony picks up the phone and in his best protective voice says, 'No, you can't talk to him. He's busy. Who are you anyway?' I grab the phone and it's some guy called Andrew Neophitou, who I don't know and have never heard of. He seems quite polite; he congratulates me on my win and wants to know whether I'd be interested in receiving some information that could help me. I say, 'Sure,' and let him have my email address. In the next couple of days I receive bottles of champagne and baskets of fruit sent to my suite at the Wynn from professional managers in Vegas who wine and dine me. I think of Greg Raymer's words of advice and take my time in assessing the propositions that are being put to me. In the meantime I receive a couple of emails from Andrew, saying, 'Look, I've read you're thinking of doing this, but before you do maybe you should consider the following.' It's just helpful stuff, nothing pushy or in my face. I get back to Australia and receive a few more emails so I say to Tony, 'Maybe we should meet with this guy,' and he sets up a meeting in a café in Bourke Street, Melbourne. Andrew is about 6' 2" tall, well built, and is immaculately dressed in a suit and matching accessories. He's unassuming, softly spoken, but has done his homework, and I'm particularly impressed by the way he presents himself. As it turns out, he is Director of Licensing for one of the biggest management groups in Australia, Sports Entertainment Limited (SEL), and they fly me up to Sydney where I meet the Managing Director of SEL, James Erskine. They go over what they would like to do and let me know that if I go with them, Andrew will be my point of contact. At about this time I'd been introduced to an agent for William Morris in Australia called Rob Marcus, who I met while I was appearing on the popular TV show *Rove*. I liked Rob and, as William Morris is one of the biggest talent agencies in the US, I was faced with a difficult choice. The fastest way to get to a decision was to lay my cards on the table, so I ask James and Andrew, 'What can you guys do for me in the US? Can you represent me? Do you have offices there?'

'No,' they say, 'we can do anything you want in Australia or New Zealand, but we can't help you in the US.'

'Well, what if you represent me in Australia and William Morris represents me in the States?'

'Fine.'

We shook hands, there was no paper work or documentation and we've been together ever since. Four years on, our relationship has grown stronger and stronger and I know I can sleep peacefully at night while Andrew — or 'Neo', as I now know him — is looking after my affairs. I can trust him to do whatever needs to be done, and over and above being my manager he's become part of my family. He must have phoned every hotel in Vegas to find me that morning and I'm so glad he persisted. Neo is one of the best things to have come out of winning the World Series.

We have the same philosophy in that it's quality and not quantity that counts, and even though there have been many offers along the way we've only chosen three sponsorship partners — PokerStars.com, Crown Casino in Melbourne and Wild Turkey — and I'm extremely grateful for their support.

27

Las Vegas
An Emotional Reunion

I've had five whirlwind days since winning the title. On one hand the time has flown, but on the other I've been dying to see Jeanie and my kids — it seems like they're taking ages to get here. I finally get the phone call from Melbourne that their passports have been sorted out and they're on their way. Tony organizes a couple of white stretch limos for the following day, and we're at McCarran Airport more than half an hour before their flight is due to land. I'm chatting with Billy and Tony at the baggage carousel when suddenly they appear, and with that I flood the place with my tears and am totally inconsolable. I've missed Jeanie and my kids so much, and now they're here I can no longer contain my emotions. I'm cuddling Jeanie, the kids are around me and I'm hugging them, and we all have tears pouring down our cheeks. I've been dying to see them and to celebrate and share the joy of my victory with those I love so much. I'm also embraced by Denise, Freddy and Gabby, and we're all choked up, but between the tears everyone's talking at once. It's a moment I'll cherish forever, I guess something like climbing Everest and having those you love waiting for you when you complete your descent.

28

Knock Yourself Out

The Harrah's public relations people do all they can to promote the WSOP and its champions, so on the Monday following my win they let me know that they're contacting Jay Leno's and David Letterman's people to set up an interview. They tell me that protocol precludes me from being able to do both, so if both Leno and Letterman agree I'll have to make a choice. I smile when I think back to my dream about David Letterman when I was on the plane over the Pacific. As it turns out, I can be on the Jay Leno show next Monday, whereas with Letterman I have to wait until the following week. I'm anxious to get back home and the kids have to go to school so I opt for Jay.

Jay's production people contact me by phone and put me through a mini-interview, the obvious intent being to find out if I can put more than two words together. They mustn't think I'm a klutz or a bozo because next thing they're organizing air tickets and accommodation in Burbank for myself, my family and all of my support team. The Aussie chant has had a lot of coverage in the press, and I guess Jay's people think they may break out in the audience while I'm being interviewed. They are very professional and treat us like royalty. We arrive in Burbank where limousines are provided for everyone — yes, everyone — and they take us out for a very enjoyable dinner the night before the show. I'll never forget the looks of amazement on the faces of my kids that night. A week earlier they were kicking a football or playing basketball on the streets of middle-class Preston; now they're jetting around the US getting picked up in limos. I've had a week to adjust since winning the World Championship and I'm still floating, but my family has just been picked up and dropped into my new hectic world.

I've done poker-related interviews on ESPN before but this is my first live interview on mainstream television anywhere in the world. I know Jay Leno is NBC's huge late-night ratings star, and because I've watched him on cable at home I have some idea of what to expect. Before the show, he comes to say hello and exchange pleasantries, I guess as a courtesy and to put his guests at ease. He does the same during commercial breaks and I glean that he doesn't know a great deal about poker, but with the cross section of people he interviews, you couldn't possibly expect him to be expert in all of their specialties. I know that other Australians such as Nicole Kidman, Russell Crowe, Ian Thorpe and Steve Irwin have appeared on his show and he's pretty clued up on us Aussies. He really is a class act and I'm not nervous; however, I am keyed up and feel sharp and alert. I'm on second and I watch him interview the stunning Mariska Hargitay, the Emmy and Golden Globe-winning star of the smash-hit series *Law & Order SVU*, and daughter of Mickey Hartigay and former Hollywood blonde bombshell Jayne Mansfield.

I'm waiting for my entry cue when I hear Jay announce, 'Alright! My next guest recently won the largest and most lucrative poker event in history, taking home a very cool 7.5 million dollars, playing cards in the 36th Annual World Series of Poker in Las Vegas. He's from Melbourne, Australia. Please welcome Joseph Hachem.' The crowd applauds, the band strikes up the show's theme tune, and I come on stage and shake hands with Jay and Mariska before taking a seat to the right of his desk. I don't know it at the time but most interviewers have a prepared list of questions, don't listen or respond to answers, and are more interested in promoting themselves than in interviewing their guests. In contrast, Jay is well researched, feeds off answers with brilliant and very funny adlibbing, and obviously has no need to promote himself.

'Is it Joseph or Joe? What do you like?' Jay asks.

'All my mates call me Joe, Leno, so knock yourself out.' I respond, stuffing up by using his surname, but he lets me off the hook. I know that, had he wanted to, he could've taken the mickey out of me.

'All your mates call you Joe and knock yourself out. Alright, sounds good. Now, have you come down yet from this? Are you still pretty wired up?'

'How can you come down from this, man? Somebody will tell me when I've come down. I haven't come down yet.'

'Very cool. Now, this is also your first time in the United States, right?'

'Yeah, yeah, I've been trying to get out here for a long time, but I've got a young family and the responsibilities that go with that. My wife finally decided this year, "Joe, it's your time, go take a couple of weeks with your mates and see what you can do," and here I am so I owe it all to her.'

'Where do you get these wives? Go with your friends for a couple of weeks and go to Vegas. Vegas!' The audience starts to laugh and so do I. Jay is a very funny guy and the tone of his voice and facial expressions are enough to break you up.

'She didn't know what was in Vegas, though.'

'Really, and you come to the United States and land in Vegas. What kind of shell shock is that?'

'Man, everything was big, the cars were big, the people were big, the food was big, the buildings were big, and there's no such thing as a street in Vegas, they're all six lane highways. I come from Australia where everything is quite modest.'

'So when did you start playing poker?'

'You know, like most of us, home games with the boys on a Thursday night about ten years ago. Maybe a bit longer, and over the last few years I've taken it a lot more seriously. I call myself a professional player in the sense that I take the game seriously, but I still have a full-time job; it's not my main source of income.'

'What *is* your full-time job?'

'At the moment, as a mortgage broker.'

'What's scarier than knowing your mortgage broker is a big time gambler? What's more frightening? You know you see a mortgage broker in Vegas — yeah, come on!' This time the audience laughter is louder and I find myself joining them. 'Weren't you a chiropractor?' Jay continues.

'I was a chiropractor for 13 years.'

'Okay.'

'Unfortunately, about four years ago I had to give it up. I developed a condition in my hands and I couldn't continue working. I couldn't do the physical work. I had to keep working, obviously, so mortgage broking was a good alternative.'

'Now your family, when you tell this understanding wife, "Honey, I'm gonna become a professional gambler." Do they think, *okay it's a phase*?' Jay leans across the table toward me, grinning.

'No, look, she said, "You have to have a full-time job. You can play poker if you like, but you have to have a steady income for the family," and I respected that.'

'Women can be so unreasonable. Okay, so it's $10,000 to enter.'

'Yeah, it's $10,000.'

'So you take that out of your family's savings — this comes from the kids' college fund — does it come out of the college fund?' Again the audience and I simultaneously break up.

'No!' I say. 'I have to do this separately from everything else. This has to be money that I've put away.'

'Oh, this is separate money?'

'It's my own little kitty.'

'This is gambling money.'

'Yeah, this is gambling money. Everything is paid for, all the bills are paid, everything's fine. I can say, "Honey, this is my own little kitty," perfectly truthfully.'

'Now, anyone with $10,000 can enter this tournament, right?'

'That's what's great about it.'

'What do you play — Texas Hold 'em?'

'No-Limit Texas Hold 'em.'

'Now explain this, real quick, to people who don't know.'

'Okay, it's a form of poker, right. Texas Hold 'em is a game where you get given two cards. Five cards are produced in the middle of the table which are community cards, and you've gotta make the best five-card poker hand. The thing about No-Limit is that it's the Cadillac of poker, meaning that your chips, everything you have in front of you, is at risk at anytime. You can push the whole lot in and bet the whole lot at anytime. Other forms of poker are structured so that you can only bet certain amounts, and that's what makes No-Limit Hold 'em so exciting.'

'Okay, you start and you've got $10,000, and you get how many chips — 10,000?'

'Yeah, 10,000 chips.'

'Did you ever get down to a couple of hundred chips and work your way back up?'

'I was fortunate that I never really struggled in the early stages. On the final table on the last day, when everyone else had 10, 15 and 20 million, I had 2.5 million.'

'Wow!'

'I was the real underdog on the final table; for about 11 hours I was struggling.'

'For 11 hours you were struggling?' Jay asks incredulously with an 'are you for real' grin and breaks me up again.

'The final table went for like 13 hours and 56 minutes, so for most of the time I was sweating it, thinking that any hand I could be gone.'

'Now, they show this on ESPN; I'm thinking, is this really a sport? Is it like tennis and boxing?' He's getting funnier and the audience joins in the mirth.

'I'll give you my version, okay, and you can make your own decision, right. I think any self-respecting poker player wants to consider it a sport, right.'

'I mean do you train? How do you train? Do you smoke and eat potato chips? How do you train for this? How do you get in shape? Do you drink? Do you drink when they come around with drinks? Do you have any liquor?' I'm sitting in my chair applauding and laughing, and Mariska who's on the right of me is giggling as Jay milks the training angle.

'As a matter of fact, I had a Corona at the final table.'

'Really? What other sport can you do that in, in the middle of a game? Hold it, that's my kind of game.'

'And you're sitting still for most of the time — what other sport can let you do that?'

'That's true. Now let me ask you about strategy.'

'Yeah.'

'Are you a good bluffer? Are you good at faking people out? Can you read? See, I'm a little dyslexic so I sit down at card games like blackjack and, say I've got 48, I don't know what I'm doing. It's a mystery to me. So is it all mostly in the bluff? It's not all luck obviously.'

'No, no, it's not all luck, and it's not all in the bluff, but you have to mix it up. Sometimes you have a good hand and you don't want your opponents to know you have a good hand, and sometimes you have nothing. Most of the time I had nothing, right, and you don't want them to know you have nothing either. So you've gotta keep that poker face.'

'Do you wear sunglasses?'

'I wear sunglasses.'

'Do you wear sunglasses so they can't read your eyes?'

'Hopefully not.'

'And how many people competed? How many started?'

'There were 5619.'

'Wow!'

'It was the biggest poker tournament ever in the world.'

'At what point did you start getting excited, like "Oh my gosh, I could win this thing?" How many people were left when it got to that point?'

'I gave myself a chance when there were two hundred odd people left.'

'Two hundred odd people? Oh, so you're like the only normal guy. Well, you always have a better chance against odd people.' I burst out laughing again and so does the audience. If I'd been paid to be a straight guy for Jay I couldn't have come up with a better line for him to work with. 'Is there any trash talking? Do people throw digs at each other?'

'Yes, obviously some people do. Most of it is banter — like for example you start advertising to the table, "Look, I don't bluff guys, I've gotta pair of aces, I never bluff," so that when you do bluff, hopefully they remember the aces and you get away with it.'

'Now, was there a good crowd? Did people gather around? Did they cheer often?'

'I reckon it was the best crowd you could ever imagine. I had my own little support crew there, which you probably read about in the papers.'

'Those were your mates?'

'My mates, my mates. There's some of them here somewhere in the audience.' With that they start chanting, 'Aussie, Aussie, Aussie, oi, oi, oi!' and I say, 'here you go.'

Jay leans over the side of his desk toward me and says, 'Wait till they find out they're not getting any of that $7.5 million. Okay, you win the money. Did you blow any of this money gambling? Did you say to yourself, "I've got 7.5 mil, I can afford to blow $100,000 on playing the machines," or something?'

'This is something that is interesting. I don't really play table games.'

'You don't?'

'No, poker is probably my only vice. My wife blew a little bit for me though, and went shopping.'

'So the game will air on ESPN in October, right?'

'Yes.'

'So if you wait 'til October you can find out who won again. Well, congratulations, mate. Come back and see us again.'

After the show my family and I chat with Mariska and she's kind enough to take photos with us. She's one of those rare people who looks stunning on television, but is even more beautiful in person.

Before leaving Los Angeles we visit Universal Studios and because I've been on television and my photo's been in the newspapers, many people recognize me, ask for my autograph, or to have their photo taken with me. My kids are totally gob-smacked as they watch their dad sign autographs and have his photo taken with total strangers. But they're also very proud of me, and their awe-filled faces say, *That's my dad. He's the champ.*

29

Heading Home

Somehow the people at the Bicycle Casino in Los Angeles find out that I've played there on my way to Vegas and pay me the enormous compliment of throwing a party for me on the way home, which coincides with the opening of their new high-limit section. It's a red-carpet function with about 1500 punters in attendance, and before the party begins I do the honors and cut the grand-opening ribbon. We Aussies pride ourselves on our hospitality, but you'd be hard-pressed to outdo the treatment that's being meted out to my family, my friends and me in the US.

A private table is set aside just for my family. Gabby, Billy and Tony are so paranoid about protecting my kids that they're carrying on like they're the Secret Service. When this big guy wanders up to the table and says to Jeanie, 'Hi, are these Joe's kids?' they spring into action. Next thing you know, Gabby, who's 6'4" and strongly built, jumps out of his chair and is nose to nose with the big guy saying, 'Who wants to know?'

'Hi, I'm Scott Lazar. I was on the final table with Joe.'

'Oh, sure,' says Gabby, immediately changing his tone as he shakes Scott's hand. 'I remember you.' It's a 180-degree change by Gabby.

I don't see any of the guys we played with on the way to Vegas, but the waitress who served me that enormous breakfast comes up and offers me a drink. I don't recognize her but Tony jumps up and says, 'That's our waitress, Joe. Don't you remember her?' She's bubbling and so happy for me, wishes me well, and again thanks me for the tip I gave her on the way to Vegas. I'm flattered and taken aback that she's remembered me.

❧

I'm faced with a small dilemma on the trip from LA to Melbourne. I'm not looking forward to sitting in the back of the plane again, but at this stage I don't have the $7.5 million in the bank. I can afford to bump my family and myself up to business class with what I've got on my credit card, but I'd need another $150,000 to get my mates upgraded, and I simply don't have it. It's not much of a dilemma, though. How would it be if I sat up the front of the plane while my mates, who have provided me with such magnificent support, sat up the back? It's just not on, so it's back to economy and the overnight goody bags once again. Besides, on reflection, I'm still floating along in a euphoric daze, and I think I could fly back to Australia on a bed of nails and still be smiling

It's early morning when our plane lands at Tullamarine Airport, and I'm surprised when the flight attendants usher my family and me off the plane separately, warning me that the press are waiting for me. I anticipate that there'll be one or two newspapers and a local radio station wanting to interview me, but as we clear customs and walk through the large stainless steel exit doors, flash bulbs go off everywhere, temporarily blinding me, and I look up to see television cameras, a gaggle of photographers, reporters and radio station journalists all talking at once. There's about three or four hundred people, including many of my relatives waiting in the arrivals area, but the media want to hold a press conference and there's no way I'm getting out of the airport without answering their questions. So I stand outside the exit doors fielding questions for about 20 minutes while the crowd, out of curiosity, press closer and closer. I'm sure many of them are expecting to see some famous Hollywood movie star and are probably disappointed when they see that it's not Brad Pitt or Matt Damon. I never anticipated anything like this, but it's a fantastic moment. Ever since I won the championship I've just been going from one high to another, day after day.

We do a detour in the limousine on the way home from the airport so that I can see my Mum and let her know that I'm healthy and well, because even now she still worries about me.

The following Saturday we're back in the regular routine and having our traditional barbecue at Uncle Vince's. I've been dying to see him and Amne, and I say to her, 'Go and book tickets to Lebanon. You haven't seen your family for ages. I'm sending you, Uncle Vince and Dib back for a holiday.' Amne nearly faints on the spot. I take care of their spending money and give Vince some more money to give away to his cousins so he can be the big man. I'm sending him back to his village to be king, but much to my disappointment, all he does is talk about me. Worse still, when he gives the money to his cousins, he says, 'Here, this is from Joe. Joe wants you to have this.' I so wanted him to be the successful man in the eyes of his cousins, but all he did was talk me up.

In the weeks that follow I'm interviewed by numerous newspapers, do countless radio interviews and appear on some of Australia's most popular TV shows: *The Bert Newton Show, A*

Current Affair, *Rove*, the early morning breakfast shows, and *The Footy Show*.

It's about 10.30pm on a Thursday night when I finish my interview on *The Footy Show*, and Crown organizes for me to be picked up and taken to my home-town poker room for my first visit since arriving back in Melbourne. I'll let Jonno Pittock tell you what happened after that: 'When Joe arrived at Crown we had about 200 players in the poker room. We brought him in the back way and made no announcement acknowledging him, instead preferring to let him make his own way around the room. When the players at the tables saw him they were out of their seats shaking his hand, patting him on the back and hugging him. He's very aggressive at the table but he's also very humble, and that night he actually appeared to be overcome by the attention. The press and internet coverage of his victory had been off the planet, and it seemed to have totally captured the public's imagination. I was with Frank Bianco when I called Joe up to the podium, but he was still busy talking and being congratulated by all of his mates. Frank then asked Tony to come up and say a few words. For years, Tony, when talking about Joe, had always prefaced his comments with "my brother Joe" despite us telling him that we all know who Joe is. When Tony came up to the microphone Frank introduced him as 'JB', Joe's brother, and he's been JB ever since. When Joe finally joined us he spoke for only a few minutes, thanking everyone for their support and assistance. He's had bigger receptions than this, but I sensed he was a little overwhelmed as the people who congratulated him that night were the guys from the Melbourne poker community who he had been playing with and against for years.'

I remember entering the poker room that night and waiting up the back for a few minutes. This guy who's spilling his beer all over the place and looking the worse for wear comes up to me and says, 'Hey man, ya look a lot like Joe Hachem.'

'Oh yeah?' I say, and grin.

'You muss get that all the time.'

'Actually, I do a bit.'

He's not all that steady on his feet, but he's okay and not hurting anyone. One of my mates at the tables looks up and spots me, shouting, 'Hey, it's Joe! G'day Joe!' and next thing you know I'm surrounded by well-wishers. I glance over at my new-found friend; he's drained his beer and he's shouting, 'I knew it was you, man! I just knew it!'

❧

Hold 'em was becoming increasingly popular at home before my win, but after I won the Main Event it was like someone lit a fuse under the game and it took off like a rocket. When I left for Vegas there was only one poker room in Australia but now they're in every state. Since then, the game has just kept on exploding, not just in the casinos and hotels, but in home games played all over Australia. By the time the Aussie Millions was played at Crown in 2006, the number of tables had increased from 27 to 46; there are now 65 tables in what is one of the best poker rooms in the world.

One of the privileges you have in winning the World Championship is that all sorts of sponsorship offers come your way, and the most important ones by far are the online deals. After doing my research and speaking to the management of a few of the sites it was an easy decision for me to go with PokerStars. I liked their site, which I had been playing on since late 2001, and I liked the way they ran their tournaments. My decision was made easier because the two previous champions were with PokerStars already, which made me feel more comfortable

I knew on that early morning at Binion's Horseshoe that my life was about to change forever, but I never imagined the demands on my time would be so intense; in fact, I'm still trying to come to grips with them. Life is incredibly hectic, but I'm not complaining. I wouldn't have it any other way.

30

The Real Action

My next trip to the US is never far from my mind, and I have strong views about what the role of the World Champion should encompass. These were reinforced in my discussion with Greg Raymer, who is a great representative of the game. I see myself as being an ambassador for poker around the world, with a duty and responsibility to promote it to the best of my ability for at least the next year. While there's been a huge surge of interest in Australia, I well realize that my home is a long way from where the real action is taking place, and if I'm going to do my job properly, that's where I need to be.

With Tony in tow, I head for Atlantic City to play in a WPT event at the Borgata Hotel and Spa. When we finally arrive in New York we've been in the air for over 20 hours, but there's no rest for the wicked, and on landing we organize a car to take us to Atlantic City, which is about 120 miles away. By the time we check into the Borgata we need matchsticks to hold our eyes open. I pop a few sleeping pills just to make sure I stay asleep, and the following day I'm nearly back to normal. It's the only way I know to cope with the difference in time zones and the jet lag.

Before the tournament starts I meet professional players Phil 'The Unabomber' Laak and Antonio 'The Magician' Esfandiari, and a group of us head off to a bar. Phil is tall, has fair, sandy hair, and appears laid-back and confident, while Antonio is lean, dark-haired and sports a little goatee. Everyone's wearing jeans and casual shirts, so I'm totally over-dressed in a suit, but this is just me. A thickset American–Italian guy with a gridiron player's neck and muscles on his muscles introduces himself to me as 'Willy Will' but he's real name's Willy Failla. Every second word that comes out of his mouth is f*** in an intimidating heavy Bronx accent — an accent I hear everywhere I go in Atlantic City. I get talking to him, and while he never says it in so many words, he conveys the impression that he's a wise guy with connections. We play a bit of cards together and get on fairly well. He doesn't seem like a bad guy, but I'm still a little wary of him.

I don't do any good in the tournament and get busted out on the first day, which is not the first time it's ever happened, but it is the first time I've ever traveled 10,000 miles to suffer the indignity. The people from PokerStars take the opportunity to do a photo shoot for an upcoming event out the front of The Borgata, and as the photographer is clicking away, Willy comes out of the hotel, bag in hand, followed by a porter with the rest of his luggage. There's a black limousine parked in prime position waiting for him when he looks up and spots me. 'Hey, Joe, what the f*** ya doin'?' he barks in his thick Bronx accent, and I immediately think of *The Sopranos*.

'I'm just doing some photos for PokerStars,' I call back.

'Ya outta the tournament?'

'Yeah, I'm outta the tournament,' I respond in my best Aussie version of Bronx.

'Let's go to f***in' New York then. Come on, get in the f***in' car.'

'Aah,' I pause, trying to think of what I'm going to say to this guy who's not really asking me to go to New York, but telling me.

'What are ya f***in' thinkin' about? Just get in the car and come to f***in' New York with me.'

I look over at Tony with a 'How the hell can I say no to this guy?' expression, but he just shrugs his shoulders. I half stutter, 'Alright, let me pack my bags,' and we race up to our rooms like a pair of rabbits caught in the cross-hairs of a 303. We pack, check out, and we're in the back of the limo all within 15 minutes. I'm not totally comfortable but my read on Willy is that he's not really the wise guy he's making himself out to be, and if he is, I've called when I should have mucked my hand. On the way to New York, Tony and I are ready for anything; it's a real case of expecting the unexpected. As it turns out, Willy's just a big Jaffa — an iconic Australian candy, hard on the outside but soft and sweet on the inside.

There's an awful lot involved in becoming a good poker player: you've got to be able to assess the odds — getting good cards sure helps — and, as Kenny Rogers sings, knowing when to hold em' and knowing when to fold em' will also make things easier. But the talent with which God blessed me was an uncanny ability to read people. It's that ability that took me to the World Championship but it doesn't just stop at cards. Every time we meet someone new we make an assessment of them. I choose my business partners and friends using my reads, and no matter how good the deal, I won't go into business with someone I don't respect or who I have bad feelings about. Despite Willy's portrayal of himself as a wise guy, I sensed a lot of it was bluff and I turned out to be spot-on.

In New York, we stay at the W on Lexington Avenue for the next three days and get to see a lot of the sights. We visit Ground

Zero and walk around the fenced-off area, reading the placards. It was a harrowing experience and I was deeply moved.

It's hard to believe that a guy who looks so tough and whose voice and accent is downright intimidating can be such a sweet guy, and while we are now comfortable with Willy, we are also ready for any surprise he might spring on us. We don't have long to wait when he invites us to dinner at a restaurant in Brentwood, the Bronx.

We go down to the foyer and ask a huge African-American doorman to organize a cab for us. He looks at us as though we're a pair of muppets and beckons two other equally large doormen over, before saying to us, 'What the f*** do you want to go there for?' He rolls his eyes and says to the other doormen, 'Hey, these guys wanna go to Brentwood,' and they look down at us as if we're a pair of lunatics fresh out of the asylum, asking, 'Do you *know* we're you're going?'

'Yeah,' I reply, as though I've been traveling to New York for years.

'Man,' they say, 'that's the roughest part of New York. You sure you know what you're doing?'

'Are you serious?' I say, thinking, *Willy's a nice guy but it sure sounds like he grew up in a rough neighborhood.*

'There's no way I'd be going there,' the biggest of the three responds, and his two mates nod in agreement.

We're sitting in the back of the cab ready to go when my cell phone rings. It's Willy, telling me that he has to cancel dinner because his old lady's got problems and that he has to go home. We walk back into the foyer of the W and the doormen all have big toothy know-it-all-smiles. One of them says, 'So you listened to us, huh?'

'Sure did,' I grin. 'Thanks.'

My first trip to New York and Atlantic City hasn't been very successful poker-wise, but I'm on a rapid US learning curve and the people on the east coast seem far more intense and demanding than their cousins on the west coast. I don't know it at the time but Antonio Esfandiari and I will become very close friends in the future. That alone makes the trip more than worthwhile.

31

That's Poker

On the way back home from New York I ponder how I'm going to handle my poker-playing and family responsibilities over the next year, frustrated because I can't come up with a plan that satisfies both. If I'm to fulfill my role as an ambassador for poker I'll need to travel constantly, but I have a wife and four children at school, I love my family and being away from them is not something I want to do. It's a dilemma, and I just can't come up with a solution.

In the end, I don't need to worry because Jeanie's mind has been very active while I've been away and she reminds me of something I said before going to Las Vegas. It went along the following lines: 'Honey, if I win the World Series we'll travel around the world for the next year, and don't worry about the kids' education because I'll take a tutor with us.' In all the excitement this was something I forgot I said, but as soon as Jeanie reminds me I say, 'Okay, let's do it.' However, for the sake of the kids' schooling, we trim the year back to five months.

We lack for nothing in the way of luggage because for ten years Jeanie has been collecting suitcases, travel bags and back packs. Every time one of our major department stores has had a sale she's been there buying, and it's one of the very few things we argue about. I say, 'What are you doing? Where do you think you're going?'

'For when we go to Europe,' she'd reply, giving me a beautiful smile.

'I've got mortgages up to my ears and kids to educate. Don't you understand?' I'd ask in exasperation. 'What are you even thinking about travel for?'

Invariably she would just laugh at me, and now when her luggage collection is finally about to be fully utilized she gives me a *told you so smile* and says, 'I bet you're glad I went to all those sales now.'

We decide to start in the US and then head to Europe before finishing in Monte Carlo, and as I travel I'll play in a few tournaments and satisfy my commitments to promote poker. This is the perfect solution to my dilemma, and I'm relieved to have some structure in my frenetic new lifestyle.

In late October we depart and head to my all-time favorite US city — yeah, you guessed it: Vegas. It's funny — I've only ever been there once before, but it's a city I feel very comfortable in, my home away from home. I decide to play in one of the WSOP circuit events that are held regularly across the US, similar to the non-Grand Slam tennis tournaments played around the world. There's a lot of money on offer and the winner gets a ring, but they don't quite have the prestige of the bracelet events. I enter the $10,000 buy-in No-Limit Hold 'em event at Bally's, in a small but very high class field of 134, made up mainly of professionals. This will be just the third tournament I've played in Vegas but I'm eager to do well and prove that I wasn't just a flash in the pan when I won the World Championship.

The very first hand I play I have a pair of kings, the blinds are $25/$50, and I raise it to $150 from middle position. An older gentleman in the big blind raises to $600. He's out of position, and this, coupled with his age and demeanor, tell me that he's almost certainly not making a play and that he's got a big hand. The first thing I think is *Don't tell me I've run into aces here; I don't want to go broke on this hand,* so I call, opting to see the flop, which comes queen high. He bets $1,000, and when I smooth call I can tell by the look on his face he's petrified I might have queens. The turn card's a blank. He checks and I bet $2,000, and once he calls I know he has a monster hand, either the other two kings or aces. I resolve that unless the river's a king I'm checking; I think I've put enough fear in him to stop him betting as well. The river's a blank and, as expected, he checks and I check behind him. When he turns over aces, I show him my kings and I'm kind of relieved. I give myself a pat on the back because I could've easily gone broke on the very first hand of the tournament. I've minimized my losses, dropping only $3,600 when it could've been much worse.

For the next two and a half days I'm battling all the time, scrapping and scrounging just to make sure I stay in the event. Then, in the latter part of the third day I gain some momentum and surprisingly travel to the final table as chip leader. I can feel the buzz in the room and there's an expectation, or perhaps a hope, that the World Champ is about to go back to back.

I'm playing very solidly and am in a strong position when we get down to the last five. My remaining opponents are all top pros: J. C. Tran, Scotty Nguyen, Thang 'Kido' Pham and my old adversary who was so critical to me winning the World Championship, Lee Watkinson.

I get a pair of kings in late position, J. C. Tran raises to $18,000, Kido Pham re-raises another $50,000, and I ponder how I can milk as many chips as I can before re-raising to $150,000. I'm still the chip leader, have the table under control, and am thinking, *If I can win a big pot I'll be well on my way to winning another WSOP title only four months after that great morning at Binion's.* J.C. folds and Kido moves in over the top with an all-in re-raise of $160,000. This is a big move by Kido and I know there's a distinct possibility he has aces, so I ask for a chip count, but halfway through it I say, 'What am I wasting my time for? There's no way I'm folding. I'm calling,' and on hearing this, the color drains from Kido's face. He looks like he's just been caught with his hand in the cookie tin as he sheepishly turns over J-10, and knows he's in deep trouble. There's $650,000 in the pot, which I'm a red-hot favorite to win. Despite this, he gives me a weak grin and says, 'I'm feeling lucky.' I walk away from the table and I hear a loud collective gasp when the flop is J-J-2. The other players leave the table in shock, and when the dealer flicks over blanks on fourth and fifth streets I've suffered a shocking beat. My face is racked with pain and disbelief; I've put myself under so much pressure to follow up my win in the Main Event and now this one hand has all but crushed my chances. I'm sick with disappointment, Kido doubles up and I'm knocked down to $40,000. That's poker, and just goes to prove my point about having to avoid bad luck if you're going to win. A few hands later I'm knocked out in fifth place.

Kido goes on to win the ring and the first prize of $453,456, and while I have a good result, I'm sick with disappointment at having come oh-so close, but oh-so far, from winning back-to-back WSOP events. I'll never forget the Kido hand but I don't dwell on the negatives. Instead, I use it as a positive and become more determined than ever to attain the validation which will only come when I win another major tournament.

Antonio Esfandiari has very kindly let us stay in his Las Vegas house and use his car while he's away. He let me know that his Land Cruiser has satellite navigation and that I'll have no trouble getting around. I haven't driven on US roads or on the right-hand side of the road before, but with sat-nav how difficult can it be? I punch in 'Bellagio' and 15 minutes later I'm handing the keys of the Land Cruiser to the valet.

The only game they've got going is $10/$20 No-Limit Texas Hold 'em, so I cash in $10,000 and amble over to the table. As I'm about to take my seat, this guy who looks and sounds like he's had one or two beers too many pipes up with, 'Hey, that's Joe Hachem. He's just won the World Series. Let's take him down.' I think, *Oh great, my first trip back to Vegas and I'm already having to put up with this.* I grin, say hello to the other guys around the table, and settle in. On the very first hand I'm dealt a pair of red kings so I raise to $80, and — surprise, surprise — rowdy guy re-raises out of the big blind. I immediately check the size of his chip stack so that I can work out how I'm going to play the hand. He's got about $2,500 and I think about re-popping him right then and there, but instead I decide to smooth call, avoid an ace on the flop and then bust him. The flop comes J-3-7; he bets, I raise, and he goes all-in. I call, and when the turn card and the river are blanks, he turns over pocket aces, and as he drags in the pot his smirk seems to cover all of his face. That's poker. I played to bust him and not give my hand away, but at the end of the day he had the better hand — it happens all the time. This is not the end, though, as my noisy adversary wants proof. 'Excuse me, Mr Hachem,' he says, grinning, 'would you mind having your photo taken with me, you holding up your K-K and me with my A-A, so I can show my wife and family? I wanna show everyone how I knocked off the World Champ.' I can understand this, and if it had been anyone else at the table I would've been gracious and sporting, but with this guy I'm spitting chips and feel bloody sick. Still, what choice do I have? I do the honorable thing and hold my cards up like a muppet, forcing myself to smile as the flash bulb pops off.

Forty minutes later the same guy raises from early position and I decide to take the flop with 5-6 suited. We're three-way in the hand and as is usual in these situations the flop comes 5-5-6 (for those who don't know me, that's meant to be a joke, but for rowdy guy it's a disaster). I have him covered and all I'm thinking about is how I can take all of his chips. I know he's eager to play against me and that he's going to find it very hard to fold, particularly if he's heads-up with me. He bets, the other guy gets out of the way, and I take plenty of time before I call. The turn card is a blank and he bets, I raise, he calls quickly, and at this point I put him on an overpair. When the river is another blank, he checks and I move all-in. He takes an eternity thinking about whether he'll call or not but his desire to crush me is so great that he just can't concede in his own mind that I might have him beat. He's thinking, thinking, thinking, and I help him along the way by saying, 'Here's your chance, buddy, you know you want to. Here's your chance for another big payoff.'

'Alright, I call,' he says grinning nervously, and tentatively turns over a pair of queens. I haul in a huge pot of about $12,000, and he says, 'Nice hand.' As he gets up to leave, picking up his sunglasses, iPod and cigarettes, and downing his beer, I look up at him and ever so politely ask, 'Before you leave would you mind posing for a photo with me, you holding your Q-Q and me with my 5-6?' His grin is now a sickly smile but there's no way he can refuse me and the table bursts into laughter. I wouldn't normally do this and as the shot is being taken I'm thinking of the old saying, *What's good for the goose is good for the gander* and reminding myself to always be humble when I'm fortunate enough to enjoy a victory.

It's early morning when I get back in the Land Cruiser and hit home on the sat-nav. I'm thinking, *How good is technology these days? You can be on the other side of the world and find your way around as easily as if you were at home. Fantastic!* About 25 minutes later I'm traveling across the desert with hardly another car in sight when I get to thinking that this isn't the same route I traveled to get to the Bellagio, and maybe the technology's not all it's cracked up to be. I pull over and phone Antonio but wherever he is I can't raise him. Luckily, however, I have the number of one of his mates, who lets me know that Antonio also has a house in San Francisco and that's probably where home is set on the sat-nav. He tells me what to punch in and a few minutes later I'm on my way again, this time heading in the right direction. The road is desolate and, as I'm driving along, I notice the headlights of a vehicle in the distance giving the illusion that it's coming straight at me. In the space of less than a minute its bright lights seem to be boring down on me at a rapid rate and I think, *Oh shit, this is no illusion. What's going on?* And then the penny drops: I'm driving on the left hand side of the road, just like I would if I were back home. I veer rapidly over to the right and 15 seconds later this huge truck with the bright lights zooms past me. I love technology and how much easier it makes our lives but it really should be idiot-proofed; in my case, rather than providing directions, the first thing the sat-nav should've said was, *You're driving on the wrong side of the road.*

From California we head to the Bahamas and then on to Europe where Italy has a particular attraction for my 13year old daughter, Justine—'the cute looking young Italian boys,' as she describes them. Even at this tender age she's already been a young lady for four years, is very prissy and just loves the mirror. I'm not worried about the young Italian men though, because she's had to cope with three boys all her life and she can give as good as she gets. She's also smart and ambitious and has taken her text books with her, so in lieu of a tutor, I'm helping her.

Justine is now 17 and says that little has changed since her Dad's big win. 'Our parents had always taken us on great holidays around Australia and the only change is that we're now lucky enough to get to go overseas as well. Dad's always helped me with my studies and even though he's very busy, he still does. He's very open minded and when I don't do so well on an exam he's always encouraging and positive telling me that I'll do better next time. The other thing is that he's so cool, and having cool parents is really great.'

In March, 2006 we're preparing to head home but I still have the EPT Monte Carlo Grand Final to play. I don't get past the first day when I go all-in with pocket aces only to get knocked off by Q-10. I stay on for some sight seeing with my family and to fulfil my ambassadorial poker obligations. I'm honoured when the tournament organizers ask me, as reigning World Champion, to say a few words to the final table, and as I'm doing this they roll out a giant poker-chip birthday cake to celebrate my birthday. It's the biggest cake I've ever set eyes on, and for once I'm totally lost for words. My family are with me and we're absolutely thrilled and so grateful to the EPT for organizing this wonderful surprise. What a fantastic way to finish what has been the trip of our life time.

In front of Caesars in '06, back to defend my title.

In the heat of battle at the
Five Diamond.

Cursing the poker Gods for delivering an Ace on the turn.

'Yes, looks like I have.'

'Oh my God, I've nearly won this.'

'Can you believe it honey?'

Validation, finally!

Greg catching me bluffing in Monte Carlo.

The blow up: 'Are you talking to me?'

Me and Shane doing
a shoot to promote our
Charity Poker Tournament
for the Shane Warne
Foundation.

Playing poker with
Oceans 13, Cannes.
Someone please pinch me.

Me and the family at the
Voodoo lounge on top of
the Rio. What a view!

Matt with Jeanie and me after dinner.

My boys playing footy in LA (yes LA!)

Visiting Universal Studios.

Jeanie and I outside Hotel Du Cap in Cannes (Wow!)

My Hero, Uncle Vince.

32

Jason Alexander
That's What I'm Here For

One minute I'm a typical suburban guy, husband and father, and in what seems no more than a split second I'm plunged into a world that I didn't even know existed. If you can imagine going to bed as Joe Average one night and waking up the next morning as Joe Celebrity, you'll understand the change in my life. It's not just me either; it affects Jeanie and the kids as well. Don't get me wrong — I'm definitely not complaining, but this new life is like being hit by a tsunami. No matter how hard I try I just can't get my head around the monumental transformation, but I resolve very early that I'm not going to let it change me, and to this day I don't think it has. But I can't stop, nor do I want to stop the changes that are going on around me and in my life. Suddenly, movie stars, rock stars and athletes are following my progress in tournaments, either in person or watching me on television, and making contact by email.

Ian Schoots probably best sums up the changes when he says, 'I think I was probably the only supporter of Joe's in Las Vegas who felt a little flattened as he was winning that final hand. I knew that life as we knew it would never be the same again. The tournaments in his garage at Preston would be over, sitting cramped up with him in the back of a plane would never happen again, and playing small tournaments at Crown would be a thing of the past. I knew that his life was about to change, but no one at that time could have guessed the extent.'

Two traits I really admire are humility and an ability to be able to take the piss out of yourself, and I don't think I've lost either of these. I'll sign an autograph or have my photo taken with anyone; in fact, I derive a lot of pleasure from it. Think about it: for the sake of 20 or 30 seconds I can bring a bit of happiness into someone's life and perhaps even give them a leg up. I also think those of us who are lucky enough, privileged enough, and blessed to be able to earn our living from playing poker have a responsibility to put something back into it. It really irks me when I see some of the big names in our game selling their autographs, or insisting that fans buy a photo before they'll sign it, or point-blank refusing to sign autographs or have their photos taken. Sadly, those particular people have no appreciation of how lucky they really are.

This doesn't just apply to poker but to all of those who are fortunate enough to be in what I call the *lucky professions*. These are the pursuits that so many average people aspire to, be it footballer, actor, tennis player, singer, golfer, talk-show host or poker player. I remember the first time I met Jason Alexander, who's a great poker fan, at a tournament for a charity in Hollywood. I'm with Jeanie and Denise, who are both great fans of Jason's, when he enters the room sporting a most un-George Costanza beard. The girls immediately start cooing and Jeanie says to me, 'Wouldn't it be fantastic to get a photo with him?' Denise quickly agrees and I say, 'Well, why don't you ask him? The worst he can say is no.' They're embarrassed and a little nervous, so I say, 'Come on, I'll take your photo,' and drag them over to where he's standing. 'Hi

Jason,' I smile, 'we're from Australia. We're really big fans of yours and the girls would love to have their photo taken with you.'

'Sure, sure,' he responds, 'of course. That's what I'm here for.' He's very charming and nothing is too much trouble for him. In less than a minute he's made the girls' night. I shake his hand, thank him very much, and go back to my table.

About 20 minutes later the announcer asks everyone to take their seats and that the tournament is about to begin. Quite unexpectedly, he adds, 'We're really fortunate to have the reigning World Champion, Joe Hachem, with us. Stand up and take a bow, Joe.' Suddenly, Jason Alexander is bursting through the crowd, but now he's in George Costanza mode. 'Oh my God, Joe Hachem!' he says. 'I'm such a big fan. You're great! I love watching you play. I'm sorry, I just didn't recognize you. Jeez, I dunno how it happened.' I laugh and tell him not to worry about it, but all I can think is, *Oh my God!* Here's one of the stars of *Seinfeld*, probably the greatest sitcom ever made, apologizing to me. It's incredible: this great actor and comedian who I've been watching on television for years is going *ga ga* over me!

It's not really about me, though; it's about poker, and about the sustained wave of world-wide popularity that the game's enjoying. I just happen to be the guy who won the last Main Event.

Celebrities all around the world just love the game, and Jason, who I'm now lucky enough to count as a friend, is at the forefront of them.

33

Antonio Esfandiari
Value for $1,000

D uring the WSOP in 2006 Antonio and I participate in a number of large No-Limit cash games at the Rio, and on this particular day I go heads-up against him.

We have a single $50 blind with $25 antes and a twist. If anyone drags the pot and shows 7-2 we all have to pay $100 to that player. Of course it's just for fun, but the small twist introduces bluffing which at times is ridiculously improbable. After an hour or two, I have about $50,000 on the table, Antonio has roughly the same, and between us we have the table covered. The game is pretty pumped and there have been quite a few bluffs with 7-2, so those $100 chips are flying everywhere.

I'm in a hand where I limp in from middle position with 7c-8c and there are two other callers when it gets around to Antonio on the button and he too calls. He could have absolutely anything at this point, and when the blind calls we have some five-way action. The flop comes 7-2-2, the blind checks, I bet $100, there's one caller, and Antonio makes it $900 to go. The blind folds instantly and I pause to ponder what Antonio's up to. We've been playing this game for a fortnight with hardly a break, and we've been bluffing and robbing each other at every opportunity, so there's a lot of history between us. I decide to represent a deuce, re-raise to $2,500 and the limper gets out of the way. Antonio thinks long and hard before calling. With the benefit of hindsight and replaying the hand, my $100 bet was absolutely pathetic.

I'm already thinking, *What have I got myself into here?* The turn card is a jack, and I take my time before betting $5,000 but I'm feeling queasy. Antonio calls quickly, and I start convincing myself that all he's holding is a seven, perhaps a pair of eights or possibly nines. So when the river's an ace, I decide it's a great bluff card for me. I deliberate for a few minutes before firing $12,000 into the pot. Antonio thinks about it for all of ten minutes before making the call and takes the pot with a pair of eights. He high-fives everyone at the table, anyone else within reach and, for good measure, himself; he's really rubbing it in and letting me know about it big-time. He's made a great call as $12,000 is a lot of money to be calling when you only have a third pair.

Antonio has studied me well and knew that my pre-flop bet of $100 into a $700 pot was way too small. When I talked with him after the game I argued that I was representing A-2 but he said that was one of the first hands he ruled out because it just didn't make sense. He deduced that I either had 7-2 or nothing, stayed true to his read, and was richly rewarded for his deduction and conviction. In the end, Antonio benefited because of his careful consideration, and I was punished for my inconsistency. In retrospect I should have given up my hand on the turn — I think it's known as *20-20 hindsight*!

A week goes by and we're still playing a lot of poker but I can't get that particular hand out of my mind. It has nothing to do with getting a bad beat and everything to do with me playing like a rabbit. You can't do anything about bad beats but when I lose because I've played badly it really irks me. Of course Antonio isn't helping, and whenever he gets the opportunity he takes me back to that hand, exactly what you'd expect from a good mate. Surprisingly, we're playing very few big pots against each other, and it's the others sitting around the table who are getting caught in our cross-fire and losing all their money.

Antonio and I have a lot of fun when we play together and I really love him; however, there is nothing sweeter in the world than taking his entire stack, particularly when he's still rubbing my nose in that hand. We're still playing No-Limit Hold 'em with a single $50 blind and $25 antes all round on a full table where the average stack is about $50,000. We play a hand that folds around to me in the cutoff, and I make a pretty standard raise to $250, with 10-8 off-suit. It's not a great hand, but at this point in our month-long battle our starting hands have become irrelevant because we're playing the player and not the cards. Antonio re-raises me to $650; I'm getting sick of him re-raising me every time I raise so I decide to play back at him, making it $2,500 to go, which is a little more than the pot and represents a very big hand.

Antonio thinks about it for a few minutes before calling. The flop comes As-8h-4s, which is nothing for me to get excited about, but I still make a continuation bet of $5,000. Antonio quickly calls, and to my delight the turn card is the ten of diamonds. I've made two pair and I'm almost certain that I have the best hand. I'm not sure what Antonio has but he's likely to be calling me down on nearly anything based on the big hand he caught me bluffing with earlier in the month. In fact, what I lost on that failed bluff was really a small investment for the future, as it enabled me to set the trap I'm about to spring and hopefully get paid off in a big way.

I decide to bet $10,000 and draw him out a bit, even though it's a fairly risky play; if the wrong card comes on the river, I could well go broke. But he calls again, and now I'm hoping to fade one of many danger cards. Fifth street brings the sweetest card I've seen all day, the eight of hearts. *Bang!* I've just made a full house and without hesitation I move all-in for $31,000. Antonio looks more than a little frustrated, not really expecting that bet, and asks for a chip count while he counts his own stack. I can see that he's dying to call, especially because he knows there's a distinct possibility I'm holding fresh air. *Zilch, zippo, nothing!* Knowing that he still thinks I have nothing and that I'm trying to pull off a gigantic bluff I decide that I need to give him an incentive to call, so I say to him, 'Because we're good mates I'm going to let you call for $22,000 if you want.' He's still hesitant when I say, 'If you call right now, you can do it for $20,000 but this is my last offer.'

Antonio can't stand the thought that he might be being stung, so he takes me up on my offer and calls, and I flick my cards over and rake in the pot. To this day he hasn't told me what he was holding, but assures me that he didn't have an ace.

§

I don't want to play cards continually when I'm with my family so we leave Vegas and head for sunny California where we find a comfortable apartment opposite The Grove shopping village in beautiful Los Angeles. The Grove's most prominent aesthetic feature is its water fountain, not unlike a mini Bellagio without the music and lights. I invite Antonio and his gang to join us for lunch at Maggiano's, a small Italian restaurant in the shopping village.

On the way, my youngest son, James, is running around and being teased by Antonio. Even though he's only nine he has remarkable balance, is a good runner and footballer, and thanks to his Uncle Tony has been brain-washed into being a passionate supporter of Carlton footy club. Of my four kids James most resembles me in looks, mannerism and attitude and it doesn't take long for Antonio to pick up on this. He nicknames James, 'Mini', a name that's stuck to this day.

It's a stunning afternoon in LA, the weather is warm and balmy, and about 20 of us take over the mezzanine level of Maggiano's feasting, imbibing and telling each other outrageous stories until the sun starts to dip below the horizon. I've indulged myself to the max and am reluctant to end what has been a wonderful day with family and friends. I call for the check, but the waitress informs me there'll be no charge because the manager and owner is so thrilled that I've chosen to dine at his restaurant that he's personally taking care of the bill. 'I can't tell you what an honor it's been to look after you this afternoon, the waitress gushes, all smiles, and despite my repeated attempts to pay, she simply won't hear of it. 'The meal is on the house, and the pleasure has been all ours,' she says. I start to blush like a little girl who's been told how pretty she is and I look sheepishly over at Jeanie, with my palms face up as if to say, 'What can I do?'

I thank the waitress once more, take Jeanie's hand, and as we start to head for the stairs, we notice a cheeky smile on Antonio's face. Jeanie twigs immediately and nudges me, saying, 'Honey, it's a setup. I'll bet Antonio's paid the bill in advance and told that waitress exactly what to say.' Bugger! What can I say? I've been well and truly punked by Antonio. I follow the rest of the crew over to the fountain for some group photos, and I can't stop chuckling about Antonio's little stunt. All I can think about is how I'm going to pay him back. The opportunity presents itself far more quickly than I anticipated when Antonio idly threatens to throw his girlfriend, Vicki, under the fountain. I immediately offer him $500 if he's got the guts to follow up on his threat. 'No way,' Vicki screams. 'My hair, my makeup, my phone, my clothes....' Not wanting to surrender the moment, I re-raise to $1,000 if they'll both jump under the fountain, and simultaneously they whip their heads around and ask me to hold their phones. In the blink of an eye they're both saturated from head to foot, but the security personnel don't see any humor in their antics and we're asked to leave. As we are being unceremoniously escorted from the fountain, I relish the comedy of watching Antonio and Vicki stumble along the mall, chafing and dripping water everywhere, desperately searching for stores where they can buy new clothes. Now that's what I call getting great value for $1,000.

34

WSOP 2006
Seeking Validation

One of Greg Raymer's goals when playing in the 2005 Main Event was to attain recognition and respect. It may seem strange that a man who defeated a field of 2,479 to become World Champion in 2004 would still be seeking respect, but there are always those who'll say it was a fluke or that he just got lucky over a seven day period. Greg readily acknowledges that you have to be lucky to win the Main Event, and I don't think you can win it without avoiding bad luck. But No-Limit Texas Hold 'em is also a game of skill, and all the luck in the world won't help a novice or unskilled player become World Champion.

Because poker is a card game, the dangerous misconception has arisen that the game is so easy that anyone can walk in off the street and win the World Series. When I first went to Vegas I wasn't some rank amateur who'd been playing in pub events. I'd been playing in serious high stakes tournaments and cash games at home for years and made many final tables. It takes skill and dedication to win the World Series, combined with just the right amount of luck. Without the skill, though, it won't matter how much luck you have because luck alone will never win you this tournament.

I know that I, too, suffered the same knocks as Greg after I won the 2005 Main Event, and immediately set myself the task of winning another tournament in quick order. I was unlucky against Kido Pham in the Bally's event, but I resolved to win another major tournament in 2006.

Since my win I've noticed a big difference in the way others play against me. In cash games I'm constantly called on the basis that my opponents want to claim the scalp of the World Champ. This is fantastic, as most times I'm holding big hands and playing for bigger pots, so my win percentage goes up dramatically. In tournaments it's different — when I have a large stack my opponents steer well clear of me — but when I've got a small stack they're like sharks in a feeding frenzy and are dying to knock me out. In either form I can't get away with bluffing as much as I did when I was completely unknown, but this applies to any player with a reputation. I've always adapted my game to the table and the circumstances and it's no different now that I'm faced with a few more challenges. The real plus is the additional edge I have in cash games.

One of the great pleasures I derive from my new-found poker fame is playing at a table all day, only to have one of my opponents, who's hardly said a word to me, come up to me and say, 'Joe, I've always wanted to play against you. It's been a pleasure,' or 'Joe, would you mind having your photo taken with me?' These are truly humbling experiences and I can only think, *How lucky am I?*

♣

I finish third in the Melbourne Championships before heading back to Vegas in July 2006 to defend my title. I've been warned that

WSOP 2006 *Seeking Validation*

my photo is at McCarran Airport, but I'm totally unprepared for what I'm about to see. As I'm coming down the escalators to the baggage carousel, a picture starts to slowly emerge and then grows and grows until I'm looking at myself in landscape — about 20 feet long by about ten feet high. This is an unreal experience and I guess helps explain why my face is now so well known in Vegas.

The first big event in which I figure prominently is the $2,500 Short-Handed No-Limit Hold 'em at the Rio where 1066 entrants greet the starter. After three days and nights I'm going heads-up with Russ 'Dutch' Boyd who has a significant chip advantage over me. For nearly two hours I've been pouring on the pressure, but every time I think I'm about to pull his stack down, he rebounds stronger than ever. The vast Amazon Room is packed with spectators and I can't remember playing before a bigger or noisier crowd, even on my run to the world title the year earlier. It's just gone 7.30pm on Sunday night and although I've just doubled up, Dutch still has me covered more than two to one in chips. The very next hand he limps in, I raise to $60,000, and in a heartbeat he goes all-in. I take no time to call, and when I turn over A-Q he looks shaken as he realizes I have his A-5 totally dominated. I punch the air knowing I've finally snared him. All going to plan, I will have doubled up in a few minutes and taken the chip lead, severely wounding Dutch in the process. Hopefully, I'll now be on the way to my second bracelet. I walk over to where Jeanie and Greg Raymer are standing and say, 'One more time. Just one more time.' The flop is 9-A-K. We both have a pair of aces, the turn card is a jack, and I'm a 93 percent favorite to take the pot and the lead. If a jack or nine comes on the river we'll split the pot; the only card which can knock me out and give Dutch the win is a five. I'm still facing Jeanie and Greg when I hear an enormous cheer from

Dutch's supporters. I turn to see him being mobbed and know I've just been eliminated. I came so close; I was outplaying him and could almost taste victory and feel the coveted bracelet around my wrist when I was brought back to earth with a thud. Once again I've had what was to be a certain victory torn from my grasp.

Jeanie and Greg console me as I walk dejectedly from the room. We're about halfway to the door when, surprisingly, the players at an adjoining tournament in the next quadrant begin to rise and politely applaud, and then they're all on their feet bursting forth with spontaneous and unrestrained cheering. I haven't won, but this is an incredible gesture and it eases some of the pain. I feel I'm getting closer to validation.

Two weeks later I'm competing in the $2,500 Pot-Limit Hold 'em event in a field of 562. Once again, I've fought through the big field and find myself at the final table in real contention for another bracelet. Getting through fields of this size is no easy task and doesn't happen often, so it's crucial to make the most of every opportunity.

We're down to four when I raise to $38,000 from the small blind with K-9, and the chip leader, Englishman John Gale, makes the call from the big blind. The flop comes K-4-3, I bet the pot of $76,000, and he wastes no time making the call. The turn card is an eight, so I move all-in for $90,000. I look over at him and say, 'I've got you beat, John.'

'I know you have, Joe,' he replies. 'I may be forced to call because of the pot, mate.'

'You can let it go, I'll forgive you. Let it go. I don't want you to call. I don't want you to suck out on me.'

'The only way I can win it *is* to suck out on you, Joe. I just can't give this pot up for 90."

'Yes you can. It's easy.'

'If I had more I would.'

'It's easy to give up, it's easy. The best result is to let it go.'

'I call, I've gotta call,' he says, showing me A-3. *Jesus. How could he bloody well call with bottom pair?* Anyhow, I'm not worried as he's only got five outs and, unless he gets really lucky, I'm going to be the new chip leader and in a great position to win. I stand up, cross my fingers and say, 'King, king, king,' but it's in vain — the river's an ace, he spikes two pair and I'm eliminated. Norman Chad calls it a 'brutal beat', and John comes over and gives me a hug, saying, 'I'm so sorry, Joe.' I finish fourth and still seeking validation while John goes on to win the bracelet. I'm not winning, but I'm playing well and am becoming increasingly confident about my chances in the Main Event.

❧

The 2006 Main Event breaks all records, a staggering 8,773 players either forking out the $10,000 entry fee, winning their seats online, or by playing satellites. For the first time there are four first days, two second days and first prize is a mind-blowing $12 million.

I've been using my step–by-step strategy and am happy to be getting through each day still intact. I'm the last former champion left in the field, and my good form is holding up. On the third day I get to start the session with the immortal words, 'Shuffle up and deal.' Late on the fourth day I'm starting to think about the following day when I get into a hand against Andrew Schreibman. The player under the gun goes all-in and is called by Andrew. I come in over the top with A-A, raising another $30,000, and Andrew calls that as well, showing me J-J. The other player turns over A-Q and I'm a short priced favourite to triple up. The first card sighted on the flop is a jack and I curse my luck: it's the end of the 2006 Main Event for me. I earn $42,882 for finishing in 238th place, defeating 97.3 percent of the field. I'm humbled when living legend Doyle Brunson joins the rest of room in standing and applauding my exit.

It's tradition for the reigning-but-soon-to-be-former champion to make a short speech before play commences on the final table. I say that it has been an honor and a privilege to be the World Champion for the past year, and that I hope whoever wins this year appreciates and enjoys it as much as I have. I then wish them good luck before handing the microphone back to Jack Effel. I can still remember how anxious I was while waiting for play to get underway a year earlier, so I keep my words to a minimum. Jamie Gold is starting with one-third of the chips on the table and will be very difficult to beat.

I've won nearly $500,000 in the last month, which is not be sneezed at, but I still haven't added the title or bracelet I so desire.

Whilst the bracelet will have to wait, I did receive a very special gift from a new WSOP sponsor, a Swiss company, Corum, that crafts fine, high-quality watches. They had created a gold and diamond watch with a royal flush somehow encrusted into it, and asked me, as the reigning World Champion, to wear it during the tournament. In return they made beautiful watches for Jeanie and me, which was an incredibly generous gesture. They then said that they were going to craft a watch for me with my famous hand, the seven of clubs and three of spades, painted on its face to commemorate my victory. It is nearly two years before I receive this beautifully crafted white gold watch, which is testimony to the effort that they have taken in creating this stunning item.

35

Nice Hand

Icut my teeth on cash games and love playing them; tournaments and playing online only came later in my poker-playing career. They each require different sets of skills, and they're all challenging and enjoyable. Cash games engender patience and tight plays, and they also provide more time for players to develop the skills required to assess the best betting and bluffing strategies, to spot tells, and to read opponents. In my experience, a good cash player can make the transition to tournament play much easier than a tournament player making the transition to cash games.

One of the high stakes No-Limit cash games I play in during the 2006 WSOP is against some of the best and toughest players in the world. Little did I realize that one of my all time favorite hands would soon unfold.

The blinds are $50/$100, the antes $25, and Antonio Esfandiari, Kevin O'Donnell, Daniel Alaei and a few other tough Las Vegas players complete the table. The first and easiest assessment I make is that there are no rabbits at the table and, consequently, no easy money. We each have about $50,000 in front of us and play is fairly tight. On several occasions Daniel has raised the pot after there have been a few limpers and taken it uncontested. I knew what he was doing, as limping into the pot indicates weakness. I know Danny's thinking, *Well, if you guys are too weak to raise, then I'll just take the pot, thanks very much, and if you do call my raise I have position.*

I wasn't going to take this lying down, so after two players in early position limped in, I called $100 from middle position with Kh-Jc, and true to form Danny raised to $800. The other limpers folded and as I'm sitting there my Australian and Lebanese stubbornness tells me to re-raise him but my weak little heart decides to call instead.

The flop comes As-Js-3d, I check, and Daniel bets $1,850 into a pot of $2,750. I decide I have the best hand, and again, instead of raising, I call to see what he does on the turn. The turn brings the eight of spades, so now there's a flush possibility on the board. I cautiously check, and after a moment of thought so does he. The river brings the seven of spades. Wow! Any spade is a winner.

In the absence of him having a nasty little spade, I still think I've probably got the best hand. I check to him and he bets $4,000, which at first thought seems like a value bet screaming for a call. However, I know Danny well enough to know that's he's more likely to have over-bet rather than under-bet. I put him down as attempting a double reverse maneuver, where he's making it look like he's trying to steal the pot. I'm certain he doesn't have the king of spades, suspect he doesn't have a spade at all, and doubt he even has a pair, so I raise him to $10,000. What a bad play by me; I'm supposed to just call and take the pot. He thinks for a long, long time, which is a good sign, but then re-raises me another $6,000, which I just didn't see coming. Sugar! Don't tell me he has the nuts. He couldn't have the king of spades could he? It's the only card in the deck which could warrant that re-raise.

Now it's my turn to think for a long time, and I can actually feel the pain above my eyes as I rack my brain trying to work out what he's holding. In the end I decide that he must have me beat, and reluctantly fold my hand. In a heartbeat Danny flips over his cards to reveal 9h-2h … no flush, no pair, nothing. Yikes! I got what I deserved.

Nice hand, and what a great play. I can clearly see what happened now as you always can after a hand is over. Logic and gut instinct told me I was right, but nerves, with a little help from Danny, convinced me that I was wrong.

Okay, now for the best part of the story. Danny tells me later that while he was thinking and taking forever to determine his play, he worked out I knew he had nothing and that I was trying to take the pot away from him. He then deduced that the only way he could win the pot was to come back over the top of me with a re-raise. What a great play, and it worked a treat. It's great playing with guys of the caliber of Danny, Antonio and Kevin where guile and cunning is pitted against guile and cunning.

I said that there were no rabbits at the table, because most poker theorists subscribe to the view that so long as there are rabbits at the table then you shouldn't leave it. However, my cash game experience is that sometimes the rabbit has the gun, and, worse, that on a bad night it just might be a shotgun that takes the whole table out. If it seems not to be my night and I keep getting beaten by a rabbit, I prefer to leave the game and come back another time. My reasoning is that we're all prone to tilting and I know that I'm certainly more than capable of going off the rails. So rather than let my 'A' game drop out of frustration, I prefer to leave the table. I know there are plenty more rabbits out there without guns, and there'll always be a game of poker I can play in tomorrow.

36

December 2006
Validation

The first thing that hits you when you arrive at the magnificent Bellagio Hotel and Casino on the Vegas strip is the vast water expanse at the front of the hotel and the fountains that rise hundreds of feet into the air in perfect harmony with the accompanying music and light show. It's a breathtaking sight and the entrée to what is a superb hotel. However, I'm not here to sight-see but rather to attempt to win the prestigious Doyle Brunson Five Diamond World Poker Classic, a $15,000 buy-in tournament in which 583 entrants took their seats on 14 December 2006. They included Doyle Brunson, T. J. Cloutier, Dan Harrington, Daniel Negreanu, Freddie Deeb, Minh Ly, Mike Matusow and Chip Reese, to name just a few of the top professionals. This is a tournament in which there are more pros than amateurs, and day after day I've been made to earn every chip I have. At the end of Day Three I get desperately short stacked and I know that my family's arriving the next day from Melbourne. The one thing that keeps flickering through my mind is the look of disappointment on my sons', Daniel and James faces if I were to be at the airport to greet them. This would mean I was out of the tournament and they would be shattered. This single thought gives me strength to play my super best and I resolve not to get unlucky. Fortunately, I get through the night and the next day I have a nice rush, becoming chip leader for most of the day, before ending in third position. I go to the final table of six, along with Daniel Negreanu, and many think we'll end up going heads-up against each other — although I'm sure the other four: Ed Jordan, Mads Anderson, Jim Hanna and David Redlin, have other ideas.

Late on the previous day, when we were down to seven, I was involved in a much talked about hand. The blinds were $30,000/$60,000 with $10,000 antes. Dane, Mads Anderson, who'd just doubled up twice in a row, had about $1.5 million in front of him when he raised $175,000 from early position. I had $2.7 million and made it $475,000 from the button with a pair of queens. The blinds folded around to Mads, who peeked at his hole cards again, glanced over at me, and then crossed his arms defiantly in front of him before going all-in. I think he'd raised quickly because he wanted me to think he was weak, and then he was all-in sending a message that he was bluffing; it's a reverse tell designed to trap me. I went over and over the hand in my mind and came to the conclusion he was really strong and he mostly likely had ace/king, or kings or aces, probably the latter. If he had an ace/king it was an even money proposition but if he had kings or aces I was a four to one underdog. This is not some amateur but a seasoned veteran deserving of my respect. The more I pondered the more I was sure I was beaten; I just didn't need to risk my chips in this spot, so I folded my queens face up. Mads slid his cards into the muck face down, and I didn't ask him what he had.

That night the poker forums and chat rooms on the net go into meltdown with comments like, 'What a donkey that Hachem is, mucking queens,' and 'Give me two queens as hole cards anytime and I'm going to play 'em,' and 'How weak. How did this guy ever win the Main Event?' I think in the old days they called it being pilloried, and I cop a complete shellacking for the way I've played the hand against Mads, but I survive to fight another day. The burning question at the end of the day for poker aficionados is, *What did Mads have?* But he's not talking yet.

Play at the final table kicks off at 5pm. Daniel goes on an early rush and 45 minutes into play he eliminates Ed Jordan and wins himself a huge pot. He now has a $9 million stack and more than half the chips on the table; I'm a distant second with $3 million.

Soon after this, young David Redlin, who won his seat in a $70 satellite, raises from under the gun to $180,000, and the table folds around to me in the big blind. He's the tightest player at the table and I check his chip stack out to make sure I have him covered, and then after some consideration I raise to $500,000. He checks his cards again, shuffles his chips and then goes all-in. I call in an instant and he grimaces when he sees my Q-Q; he has A-Q and there's nearly $3 million in the pot. As we wait for the flop I say, 'I can't look,' and David responds with, 'Dammit, Joe, I was going to fold, man.' I put my hand over my eyes and as I look up I breathe a sigh of relief when I see 4-7-4. He's a four to one underdog but I'm still not confident and say, 'I can't look, I can't look, I can't look,' but the uproar from his supporters tells me he's spiked an ace on the turn. I stand up and walk around the table cursing, knowing that there's only one queen in the deck and the probability of hitting it is near zero — two percent to be exact. The odds are totally stacked against me and if ever I've needed a miracle I need one right now. The announcer comes over the PA and says, 'Joe Hachem needs any queen of diamonds to win,' which does nothing to help my mood. Then it happens — a miracle! The river is the queen of diamonds and the whole room erupts. I shake hands, embrace David and go over to Jeanie for my celebratory hug.

After 90 minutes of play the blinds are increased to $50,000/$100,000 with $10,000 antes. Daniel Negreanu knocks out Mads Anderson who, not surprisingly, has played extremely well. We're down to three but Daniel's position is not as dominant as it was earlier and the chip stacks are:

Daniel Negreanu: $8.1 million
Me: $6.5 million
Jim Hanna: $3.4 million

Daniel, who has Kd-9h, is soon in a big hand against Jim Hanna, and after the turn he goes all-in and is called by Jim who turns over Ks-Jh. Daniel needs a nine and only a nine on the river or he's going to lose a very big pot and, for the first time today, also lose the lead. The river is the six of diamonds and Jim doubles up.

The blinds are now $80,000/$160,000 and $15,000 antes when I raise to $450,000 from the button and Daniel moves all-in from the small blind for an additional $1.125 million. I call, showing 4-4, and Daniel turns over K-10. When the flop comes A-Q-2 he has plenty of outs including a gut-shot straight draw, but when the turn is a queen and the river a two he's knocked out in third position, winning $592,000.

I'd become very close friends with Kevin O'Donnell, who I met through Antonio, and had stayed with him at his home in Arizona a few times. He's an extremely aggressive player; in fact, the way he plays sends shivers up my spine and I tell him he shouldn't be playing that way. On the third day he has a huge stack of chips and is playing on the same table as Daniel and me when Daniel traps him with a pair of aces and busts him out. Kevin's not happy and as he's leaving he says to me, 'Brother, I'm going to fly back for the final table.' True to his word, he flies back with his daughter Jennifer and he's watching when I bust Daniel out. I point at Kevin, and say, 'This one is for my Irish friend.' It's a really cool moment and Kevin gets a big kick out of it.

I'm now about to go heads-up against Jim Hanna, the brother of professional poker player Mark Hanna. He's an ex-gridiron player who played defensive end for the New Orleans Saints in his younger days. He has a slight chip advantage with $9.52 million against my $7.985 million. He's fairly new to the tournament circuit, being mainly a cash game player, and I resolve to up the tempo and play very aggressively against him. I'm just lucky we're playing poker and not gridiron.

We're soon into a big hand. I know he's getting sick of me raising and is looking for an opportunity to re-pop me with any hand. I raise to $450,000 pre-flop, he raises an additional $900,000 and I call. The flop is 9-6-5 and he bets $3 million — a huge bet — and tells me he doesn't want to get called. This is exactly what I thought he'd do; after all, he's represented a big pair or perhaps A-K with his pre-flop raise, and now with a rubbish flop he bets $3 million. I move all-in and leave him with a very hard decision. He thinks for a few minutes before folding his hand and I rake in a huge pot and take a massive chip lead.

Three hands later Jim raises to $720,000, I go all-in and he makes the call showing Qc-Jc. I have him dominated with As-6c and maintain my lead when the flop comes Ac-Qd-3d. Jim needs a jack, queen or running clubs on the turn and river. The turn is the eight of clubs, so he still has lots of outs on the river, but when the dealer turns over the two of diamonds, Jim is eliminated in second position, taking home $1,099,430. I win the gold bracelet, a $25,000 entry into the WPT Championship in April, and $2,182,075, the second richest prize in world poker. But most importantly, I finally secure the validation I've been so desperate to attain.

I feel fantastic. My feet are hardly touching the ground and I'm more excited than I was when I won the World Championship. This was the toughest field of the whole tour, and to get there and take it down has put me on an incredible high. Amanda Leatherman from PokerWire interviews me soon after I've won and asks, 'How does it feel to join the ranks of Doyle Brunson, Carlos Mortensen and Scotty Nyugen, being the only three people to win a World Series of Poker Championship and WPT title? How do you feel?'

'How cool do you reckon it is to belong to a club that has only four members?' I respond. 'Pretty cool, yeah.'

By now Mads Anderson has been interviewed and the video is already on the net. The commentators, like everyone else, are just dying to know what he had in that hand we played late on the second last day. When he tells them that he had a pair of aces they go into raptures about how good my play was in laying down queens. That night the poker forums and chat rooms go ballistic again, this time with comments like, 'How good is that Hachem?' and 'He has to be the best player in the world,' and 'What a great lay-down that was.' In fewer than 24 hours I'd gone from being a donkey to being a champ. It's a fickle world but what's really important to me in winning the Five Diamond is that I've forever removed the self-imposed validation monkey that I strapped so tightly to my back after becoming World Champion.

Jeanie was in the audience during the final table and when we went back to the hotel to see the kids they were louder than fireworks on the fourth of July. This was a fantastic contrast to the vision I had of greeting them at the airport with the news that I'd been eliminated.

Part Three

Fame and Family

37

Cannes
Holy Shish Kebabs!

O ne Thursday night, late in May 2007, I get a phone call from one of the bosses of PokerStars inviting me to attend the premiere of *Ocean's Thirteen* at the Cannes Film Festival, do a photo shoot with the cast, and attend a charity ball on a private yacht. 'You'll only be there for two days,' she says.

'Look, I'm happy to come, but only if I can bring my wife,' I respond.

'Of course, of course,' she replies. We pack our bags that night and the following day we're on our way. The flight is booked for us, everything is taken care of, and all we have to do is turn up at the airport.

Cannes is beautiful at this time of the year, the weather is perfect and it's buzzing with excitement. We're picked up at Cannes Airport and driven to the Hotel du Cap, which is the finest of fine French hotels — the place in Cannes where Hollywood film stars like to stay. Situated on the southernmost tip of the Cape of Antibes, it sits on 22 acres overlooking the Mediterranean Sea and on the other three sides it's surrounded by a magnificent pine forest. As the hotel comes into sight it reminds me of a French provincial castle and I later find it's a Napoleon III structure. There are 53 guest rooms and private suites, all featuring Italian marble bathrooms, polished wood furnishings and views over the ocean or pinewood gardens. It's amazing and just the type of structure that Vegas architects are so expert at duplicating, at 20 times the actual size, of course.

A poker table is set up outside for the photo shoot and then, without any warning, the actors from *Ocean's Thirteen* turn up. Matt Damon, Don Cheadle, Brad Pitt and George Clooney amble out from the hotel and Jeanie's chin is on the ground. I have to say to her, 'Please, honey, close your mouth.' While we're waiting for the rest of the cast to turn up, Matt Damon comes over to say hello, and we hit it off immediately. I already know that he's into poker and he tells me he's a big fan. He followed my progress, he says, in winning the World Series and the Five Diamond late last year. I'm flattered and floored when he tells me that he admired the dignity and grace with which I carried myself after winning the World Championship. He's very easy to like, a what-you-see-is-what-you-get type of guy. I also get on really well with Don Cheadle, maybe because he's into poker, too, but he's a real natural, one of those guys who would be easy to get on with even in the absence of a shared interest. Brad Pitt and George Clooney are pleasant enough but a little aloof; I get the impression that, unlike Matt and Don, they're not into poker.

Before the photo shoot gets underway, an extremely well-groomed and well-attired young lady carrying a large leather pouch and accompanied by a huge security guard approaches the table. I think, *Who the hell is this?* as she pulls a bag out from the leather pouch and opens it on the table. This time it's my turn to gape. It contains an assortment of jewelry from the very exclusive European jeweler Chopard: watches, bracelets, pendants, cuff links, necklaces — virtually any piece of jewelry you can imagine. The producer of the show, Jerry Weintraub, who's a larger-than-life American guy, says, 'Come on guys, get over here and pick something to wear to your media interviews.' After everyone's made their selections the lady looks over at Jerry and says, 'I need you to sign for what's been taken.'

'Sure,' he responds, but as he starts to sign he looks up at her. 'You know you're not going to get them back, don't you?'

'Yes, of course,' she replies, and with that he signs away.

We do the photo shoot, and Matt and Don say that after the charity ball tonight they'd like to have a little 'sit-and-go' with me. After I resuscitate Jeanie we head back to our room to get changed for the ball, but on the way I organize with one of the guys from PokerStars to get cards, a chip set and a poker table setup at the hotel.

I'm wearing a tuxedo, Jeanie looks fantastic in her ball gown, and along with three PokerStars representatives we get picked up and driven to the pier, which we're amazed to see is covered in red carpet. At the end of the pier and just before we board the yacht there is a small marquee: 'Could you please sign in, could you please leave your cameras with us, and could you please take your shoes off?' Jeanie's in stilettos, so I say, 'What are you talking about?'

'The floors are teak and we don't want any marks or scratches. It's a 100-million euro yacht that we've hired out for the evening and we don't want to have to repair anything.' In lieu of shoes we're given floppy white slippers, which I don't have a problem with (although I have to say that a black tuxedo and white floppies is not a good look). I feel sorry for the ladies who've gone to so much trouble preparing themselves and who look great in their beautiful gowns — until your eyes reach their feet, that is. We board the yacht, which remains moored at the pier, and nearly everyone is wearing floppy white slippers — Matt Damon, Brad Pitt, George Clooney — with the only exceptions being those who've opted for bare feet. We have a drink and mingle for a few hours, and I notice one particular girl who, for the whole night, stands on her toes rather than put up with the flat look in the white floppies. Matt, Don and I agree that we'll meet back in the bar of the hotel and then get a little poker action on.

We walk through the hotel lobby and into the bar, and it's like we've entered another world. Angelina Jolie, Robert De Niro, Martin Scorcese — everywhere I look there are famous faces. I think, *Holy shish kebabs,* but it soon gets even worse — or perhaps that should be better. We are ushered from the bar to a room immediately behind where a poker table has been set up with Matt, Don and a number of others sitting around it. We have a few drinks and then they want to start playing, so I say, 'Look, let's just play for $100, that way my wife can play, your wives can play, and we can have some fun.' The only one who is carrying any money among them is Don, who pays for everyone, and the game is soon underway.

The room has its own balcony overlooking the water and we can see a large yacht about 400 meters offshore. It must be someone's birthday or a celebration of some type because the grand vessel is lit up with a magnificent fireworks display that lasts for all of five minutes. By now the balcony is filled with Hollywood stars and producers, and Andy Garcia, Brad Pitt and George Clooney are glancing over at us while we're playing poker. They are obviously interested so I ask Matt why they are not sitting down with us and playing. Before he can respond Daniel Craig, who's a very big, well-developed guy in real life, comes in from the balcony, and, knowing he's played a lot of poker in *Casino Royale*, I say, 'Hi Daniel, would you like to join us?'

'Hello, no thanks,' he responds pleasantly, but a touch timidly. I say to Matt, 'What's the story? Is it me?'

'Joe,' says Matt, 'these guys are all big action heroes and they don't want to sit down in front of you, mess up some play, and look foolish.'

'But we're only having a bit of fun.'

'That's the movie business, that's the way it is.'

We get down to three handed and I've got most of the cash, but the last thing I want is for them to think that I've taken them down. For me it's been great fun meeting and playing with them, so to finish the night we agree to pool the cash and split it three ways.

Matt's a great guy, so we exchange email addresses and phone numbers to stay in touch. I later get an email from him to say that he'll be in Melbourne for the premiere of *The Bourne Supremacy* at the Rivoli in Camberwell, and he organizes seats for my family and me. There are lots of local celebrities there and when we turn up my kids are ushered in front of them to the best seats in the house, and they're just bursting with pride. Later, we have dinner at Silks at Crown Casino and then we sit down with Matt and a few mates of mine to play a little poker. I'd actually sent emails out to my mates saying, *Would you like to join Matt Damon and me to play some poker tonight?* My phone rang off the hook with acceptances, but one mate, Billy 'The Croc' Argyros, who's an extremely good player and an inductee into the Australian Poker Hall of Fame, misread Matt's surname and didn't turn up. The following day his wife gave him a serve for about half an hour telling him how bloody silly he was. Matt was still jet-lagged from his flight but such is his love of poker and his endurance that we played for a good six hours that night.

Coincidentally, I first became interested in No-Limit Texas Hold 'em after watching the movie *Rounders*, in which Matt starred. He was sitting at the table in his role as Mike McDermott in the first hand I ever saw played. I wonder if our friendship might have been destined.

38

60 Minutes
Landing on the Moon

In early 2007 I'm contacted by Peter Overton, a reporter for the Australian *60 Minutes*, and he says that they want do a story on me. Peter has covered many big stories and isn't without his own 15 minutes of fame, which occurred when he interviewed a feisty Tom Cruise. (Peter asked him a fairly innocuous question about his life post-divorce with Nicole Kidman, and was told by a very pissed off Tom to 'Put his manners back in,' while the interview was beamed around the world.) In the three months that it took Peter to put the story together on me I found him to be a true gentleman and a good guy.

One of the ways I think Peter will properly see what I do is to invite him home for a game of poker with my mates and me. I know he'll want to question them, and I give them a heads-up on what I think he'll ask so they can have their answers ready once the cameras are rolling. I also organize with the dealer to make sure that when we play, Peter is dealt two aces, my very excitable cousin Billy is dealt two kings, and the deck is stacked appropriately. Peter gets his aces and raises, the table folds around to Billy who re-raises, and Peter calls. The flop comes K-7-4, Peter bets and Billy cunningly smooth calls. Fourth street is an eight,

Peter bets, and in a flash Billy is all-in; Peter, who's looking a little confused, calls as the cameras continue to roll. The dealer flicks the river over, and — surprise, surprise — it's an ace and Billy's on his feet screaming that he's been ripped off. I get the exact reaction that I anticipated; Peter thinks he's won on the up-and-up and Billy thinks he's been set up.

Peter then goes around the table and asks my mates what type of bloke I am and what makes me that way. The answers are along the lines of 'Joe's a really great bloke, yeah, Joe's a terrific mate. Joe's a very good poker player,' and I'm thinking, *Come on fellers, you can elaborate a little more than that.* These guys are all smart, articulate and more than capable of giving informed opinions, but there's one thing that's stopping them, which is something I've also witnessed with many other people over the past few years: they're camera shy, and so long as the cameras continue to whir their answers will be stilted and one-dimensional. Fortunately, I've never had a problem with cameras. (In fact, in 2007 I even had a small role in a horror movie starring Jesse Johnson, son of Don, and the lead singer of Australian band Rogue Traders, Natalie Bassingthwaite. The movie is called *Prey* and I act the part of a sleazy hotel manager who plays online poker most of the time.) When the story is finally televised, the only part that's aired from that night is the dealer turning over the river to give Peter the win, and Billy jumping out of his seat and bleating.

The main part of the interview takes place in July 2007 when Peter and the *60 Minutes* crew travel to Las Vegas to watch me play in the 2007 WSOP. I'm standing next to Matt Damon at the Rio where we are attending a red carpet function at which the celebrities get together to play poker for charity, when I say to Peter, 'Do you know this guy?'

'Do I ever,' he responds. 'I believe you play a bit of poker with Joe.'

Matt looks over at me and grins. 'You didn't tell him what happened, did you?'

'Nope, I just said we had some fun. I didn't tell him how you beat me.'

'Good. I mean, I just want to spare you the embarrassment, Joe.'

'What do you think of Joe, the bloke from the suburbs of Melbourne who became World Champion?' Peter asks.

'Poker can bring out the worst in people,' Matt responds, 'but when you see somebody winning with grace, class and dignity, it's nice.'

'This is great, isn't it, all these people here?' I say. 'Wait until my mates in Preston see me on TV.'

The interview then flicks back to a barbecue at my house before we departed for Vegas, where Peter says, 'Here, "Diamond Joe" Hachem is just average Joe.' ('Diamond Joe' is a *60 Minutes* creation. No one has called me that before, or since.)

When Peter interviews Jeanie, she's not as flattering as Matt and when asked what I'm like, she responds, 'He's just Joe to me, he's my husband. I don't see anything, and women jump up on him —"

'No, no, that's not true,' I say, interrupting.

'I look at them, all jumping up and down, going crazy for his autograph, and I think, "Are these people serious?"' She giggles.

'It's only Joe,' I say, laughing.

'It's only Joe, it's not Brad Pitt. Sorry, honey.'

'Now tell me about the barbecue,' says Peter. 'I thought it might be bigger, grander, even gold-plated. Nearly 20 million in the bank. Doesn't that change a person's outlook?'

'No, it hasn't,' Jeanie responds.

'Adulation and fame?'

'None of it, none of it at all,' Jeanie says.

'You're happy with the barbecue on Sunday and a nice bottle of red?'

'The barbecue, the bottle of red, a nice Scotch,' I say. 'You know, that's — you know, it's simple.'

'That's real, that's what's real,' Jeanie agrees.

Later, as we're all sitting in the lounge room, Peter asks 'So, you've won millions playing poker, why bother turning up for a game where you put ten dollars in the pot?'

'Nights like these aren't about winning money,' I say, 'they're about spending time with my mates. They know Joe Hachem pre-"Joe Hachem" so I can just be myself, relax and enjoy.'

Peter narrates: 'Joe's mates not only helped sharpen his poker skills, they were with him in Vegas when he had the big win, a win they're still over the moon about.'

'It's like witnessing the first step on the moon. For us, that's what it's like.' I say.

'Landing on the moon?'

'Yep.'

'Bet you Neil Armstrong wishes he got ten million dollars for walking on the moon.'

'I don't know where that frigging came from!' I say, and burst out laughing. 'Landing on the moon!' The boys are laughing and for months after the interview I have mates taking the piss out of me for that moon comment. I put it down to a momentary brain fade.

Later, Peter asks Jeanie and me what it was like to win the WSOP.

'That was beautiful. That was pretty sweet,' Jeanie says, smiling.

'What was that line you told me yesterday about the bank?' I ask her.

'The bank doesn't own us any more.'

'Actually,' I continue, 'one of the highlights of my life is walking into the bank with a check for my mortgage and saying, "Thank you very much," and seeing the look on the teller's face.'

'What a moment,' Peter says.

'It was,' Jeanie agrees.

'A special moment,' I smile.

Back in Vegas I say to Peter, 'Take a seat, let's have a game.'

'Money, glamor, deal me in,' replies Peter. 'But to get a piece of the action I've got a few things to learn from the master.'

'Being a poker player is like being a spy,' I say. 'You don't want to give away the right information; you want to give away the incorrect information.'

'Give us your poker face if you get a pair of aces,' Peter laughs.

'My poker face is the same, whether I get a pair of aces or a seven and a three. I put my bet out and simply rest, focus on a point at the table, keep my breathing under control, and not give up any information.'

'We play a hand, the rookie and the champ,' Peter narrates. 'I've got a nine and a seven. Joe has a pair of jacks. But on the flop two more sevens for me, and I have three of a kind.'

'Oh, my God!' I exclaim. 'You've just whooped the World Champ, sir. You bluffed me into believing you didn't have anything.'

'Look at that, I just beat the World Champion,' Peter beams.

'I'll just give you my bracelet right now,' I laugh.

'I feel fantastic. How do you feel?'

'Well done. Good.'

'But this week in Vegas,' Peter says, 'Diamond Joe Hachem won't be such a pushover. He's far too determined to prove he can do it all again'.

§

Unfortunately, the 2007 WSOP doesn't go as well as I would've liked. The tournament is so big now that I play on Day 1C, which is the third of four first days, and I manage to survive and finish with $35,300 in chips. I play again on Day 2A and early on I go all-in with A-8 after the flop of A-10-10, and am called by an opponent with A-Q. When my hand doesn't improve on the turn or the river I lose the pot and bust out of the tournament. Ah well, that's poker.

39

Poker After Dark

Poker After Dark is an hour-long television program featuring six professionals playing for a winner-take-all prize of $120,000 that airs early in the mornings, six days a week on NBC. I'm in Vegas in June 2007 preparing for the WSOP when I'm invited to play in my first After Dark Tournament at the South Point Casino in a field comprising Doyle Brunson, Johnny Chan, Jamie Gold, Greg Raymer and Huck Seed. The game is promoted as a match between the old champions — Doyle, Johnny and Huck — against the new champions, Jamie, Greg and me.

Johnny gets a great run of cards and goes on a phenomenal rush, eliminating Greg, Jamie, Huck and Doyle, and it gets down to heads-up between him and me. He didn't get his nickname 'The Orient Express' by playing passively, and in the next four or five hands he continually re-raises me, and I just don't have the cards to do anything about it. In no time at all he has me covered five to one and appears as though he's coasting to his fourth After Dark win, which will give him a 100 percent success rate. I hear Phil Hellmuth talking with commentator and hostess Shana Hiatt, and she asks him if he's played against me much. To break things up I say, 'Why don't you come down to Australia, Phil, and then we can play some poker,' but Johnny is a picture of concentration and not about to get into extra-curricular table talk. He's one of the finest players in the world at playing the man rather than the cards, and he's very adept at picking up weaknesses in his opponents and exploiting them.

I should tell you a little about Phil. He won the Main Event in1989, stopping Johnny Chan from winning three times in a row, and won his 11th bracelet at the 2007 WSOP. He has an ego bigger than life at the poker tables, but away from them he's quite a nice guy. When he's within 30 feet of a poker table and wearing his poker cap and top he turns into a different person; he goes into poker-playing mode and his desire to win transforms into his alter ego, the Poker Brat.

But now back to Johnny and the poker. I'm sure there's not a person in the room who doesn't think that he's about to finish me off — all but one that is. I've played a lot of poker when I've been down to only a few chips and have never understood why others go on tilt and make desperate plays just because they're the short stack. Anyhow, I'm confident that if I get some cards I can peg Johnny's lead back, and then who knows what might happen?

As it turns out, I start to rebuild my stack by chipping away and playing very aggressively, and then we get into a hand where I have 7-8 off-suit. I raise and for once Johnny calls rather than re-raising. We see the flop, which comes 8c-8d-4c, giving me trips. Johnny checks to me and I bet, praying that he raises me all-in, which he soon does. I call and he shows me his flush draw, Kc-7c. I avoid a club and take the lead for the first time since the six of us sat down to play. After that hand I gain momentum and steam-roll Johnny without losing the lead before claiming the upset victory — a prized entry on my CV. Prior to commencing play we agreed to go out to dinner once the game was over, but Johnny is totally pissed off and no longer in the mood for socializing.

Phil, Greg and I decide that we'll still go out to dinner, even if Johnny is steaming. We go to a popular traditional Italian restaurant on the Strip, and Phil and his ego order an expensive bottle of wine to go with our pasta. He's just taken a large mouthful when this guy walks past our table and recognizes Greg. 'Oh, Mr Raymer,' he says. 'Oh my God, I love the way you play,' and then he notices me. 'Mr Hachem, it's such a pleasure to meet you. I'm a big fan and watch you on television all the time,' and with that he walks back to his table. I look over at Greg and burst into laughter knowing what must be going through Phil's mind. He's nearly choking on his pasta and is in semi-shock. When the guy gets back to his table his mates must have told him that Phil Hellmuth is sitting with us, because a minute later he's back at our table, saying, 'I'm sorry, Mr Hellmuth, I just didn't realize it was you. But I do follow your play on television.'

'That's alright,' Phil responds, trying to be humble and accept the apology. But we know better! With that we finish off the wine, stomachs and egos having been fully satisfied.

40

The World is My Poker Table

After the 2007 WSOP I take a few weeks off before eagerly accepting an invitation to play in a major tournament in Sun City, about 115 miles from Johannesburg in South Africa. I've always wanted to visit South Africa and I'm joined by my fantastic manager and friend, Andrew 'Neo' Neophitou, who is also keen to see the sights. Sun City is home to four unbelievable hotels, the Sun City Casino, and 25 acres of tropical plants and palms of every variety, which make up the gardens of the Lost City. There are two Gary Player-designed championship golf courses, one of which has a particularly challenging water hazard on the 13th hole: 38 crocodiles. The resort is surrounded by the Pilanesberg National Park, which is inhabited by all kinds of exotic animals. Seeing these majestic creatures in their natural habitat is a truly humbling experience and makes me realize how insignificant we humans really are in the scheme of things. Since I started my 'travelthon' in 2005, I've not seen anything in the world that even remotely compares with the beauty and grandeur of South Africa.

The tournament is a $3,000 No-Limit Hold 'em buy-in with re-buys and I end up making 14 of them at $1,000 a throw, which probably tells you how I was going. At the end of the re-buy period I finally run hot and bust everyone on my table out of the tournament, regaining all of my chips and then some. Having battled my way back into contention with a lot of concentration, I then get shifted to the feature table and over the next four hours every time I enter a pot I have the second best hand and lose all of my hard-earned chips before reaching the money. I was infuriated with myself for letting another opportunity slip through my fingers, but on the day the cards just didn't fall my way.

The South African people are lovely and very respectful, and I can tell they don't want to cramp my space. They do not pursue me too much for autographs or photos, but they are warm and friendly in a distant way. I sense that they would like to open up, however, their respect for my privacy restrains them. On the last day of the tournament, I'm enjoying a drink on the patio with Neo and a few of the players we've become friendly with — better make that a few drinks — and we're feeling just a little merry. One of the other patrons pulls out his camera, summons up his courage and asks me for a photo, and before you know it there are 40 flashbulbs popping off. Next thing you know there's a full-bore photo shoot going on, the drinks are flowing freely, and I'm having a ball. I'm taking a photo with a lovely young girl, and I look over at her boyfriend and say to him, 'You're a very lucky man, mate,' and he replies, 'She's the best.' The girl then leans over and whispers to me, 'Ask him why he hasn't asked me to marry him yet.' And so, feeling very relaxed and happy, I say, 'Why haven't you proposed? What are you waiting for? She's really lovely and she's not going to wait for ever.' He looks at me and says, 'Joe, if you promise to come and be the MC at our wedding I'll propose right now.'

'Sure, sure, of course I'll come and be your MC,' I babble, surprising myself probably more than anyone else. With that he drops to one knee in front of her, and now there are tears and sniffling coming from everyone. 'Will you marry me, Nicki?' he asks, and she says, 'Oh, yes, I love you, David.' She's crying, their friends are crying and there's champagne corks popping everywhere. Neo jokingly says to me, 'Not only can you win poker tournaments but now you can also get people to propose!'

It turns out that David and Nicki are the 'it' couple of the South African poker community and childhood sweethearts. We exchange email addresses and when I clear the cobwebs from my head the following morning I come to the realization that I've committed myself to returning to South Africa for their wedding. When I get home I discuss it with Jeanie and we think it would be a great place to take the kids in the school holidays next year. As the time drew closer, however, complications arose and PokerStars wanted me to go to Macau. I didn't know how I was going to break the bad news to them, but then, out of the blue, I receive an email from David and Nicki thanking me, but also letting me know that they're going to be having a small intimate wedding and that only direct family will be attending.

❧

In November 2007 I'm excited to be traveling to the first poker tournament ever held in China. This is the start of the Asia Pacific Poker Tour (APPT) sponsored by PokerStars to allow people in our part of the world to play in major tournaments. The historic event is taking place in the former Portuguese enclave of Macau, located 30 miles to the west of Hong Kong, which has undergone a massive transformation in the past few years and is now a very modern city boasting some of the finest hotels and casinos in the world. The venue for this momentous event is the Grand Waldo Hotel and Casino. I've really been looking forward to playing in this event. What could be better than winning the inaugural tournament played in China while at the same time adding an APPT title to my WSOP and WPT titles? There are 352 starters in the Main Event, including WSOP World Champions Mansour Matloubli and Scotty Nyugen. Despite my aspirations, this is not going to be an easy tournament to win.

I play well during the first three days and accumulate chips while keeping my risk very low. The fourth day is altogether something else, though, and I endure one of those periods during which I'm card dead and my stack is being substantially eroded. There are 15 players left, I'm the short stack at my table and I've reached the point where I need to make a stand. I'm in late position when I go all-in pre-flop with K-8, but when my opponent in the big blind calls and turns over A-Q I'm in trouble. I get lucky on the turn with a king and I'm on my way to the final table — one step closer to another title. It's Jeanie's birthday today and I promised her and the kids that I'd make it to the final table, so it's a nice present. Of the nine players on the final table, I think four are very good and have a chance of winning; the others have done really well to make it but I doubt that one of them is going to walk away with the prize.

I'm nervous and jittery before we sit down at the final table, which is a good sign because it means I'm alert and sharp. Dinh Le, a Vietnamese resident of England, is the overwhelming chip leader and one of those who I think can win; I'm in sixth place with a stack slightly less than the average, and Englishman Simon

Randall is the short stack. Soon, Simon goes all-in against online qualifier and rookie Sangkyoun Kim from South Korea. Simon's looking good with A-Q against Sangkyoun's K-10, but when Sangkyoun hits a king on the flop and another on the turn it's the end for the Englishman.

Unfortunately for me, my cards don't improve from the previous day, and I'm eagerly awaiting a big pair. As if on cue, I look down at my hole cards and see two aces staring at me. Sangkyoun raises to $60,000, I pop it up another $90,000 knowing that he can't fold, and he looks at me and says, 'How come you didn't go all-in?' I look down at my chip stack of $34,000 and reply, 'This is taxi money so I can get home.' The whole idea is to get him to put all his chips in the pot, and he thinks for about a minute before he puts me all-in turning over A-Q — beautiful! The pot is $422,000, I'm a 92 percent favorite to win, and when I drag this pot in I'm going to be snapping at the heels of the leaders. Sangkyoun looks sick, and as I leave the table to go and sit with Jeanie and Tony I say, 'He's going to need an absolute miracle.' The flop comes K-J-5, and I laugh, 'Oh no, now he's got four outs.' My odds have dropped to 82 percent and I can feel that dreaded sinking feeling deep in the pit of my stomach. Sure enough, the turn card is a ten, and I'm now a 33 to one underdog; I need a queen on the river, and only a queen, to split the pot. The river is a four and I'm on my way home. I'm stunned and totally gutted — winning this inaugural tournament meant an awful lot to me. Daniel Negreanu doing the commentary describes it as 'about as bad a beat as you can get'.

Dinh Le goes on to win and my nemesis, Sangkyoun Kim, finishes third, which, given his poker background, is a remarkable achievement in his first live tournament.

❧

A long year is about to come to an end in December when I play in the APPT Grand Final at Star City in Sydney, which is won by one of the rising young stars in Australian poker, Grant Levy, who becomes the first Australian to win a million-dollar tournament prize on home soil.

A late change on the APPT schedule is the addition of the PokerStars Asia Pacific Poker Tournament of Champions, which features fellow Team PokerStars pros Chris Moneymaker, Greg Raymer, Isabelle Mercier and my good friend Scotty Nguyen, plus four of the season's APPT winners: Brett Parise (Manila), Ziv Bachar (Seoul), Grant Levy (Sydney) and Eric Assadourian, who won the high-roller event in Macau. The APPT Grand Final winner, Grant Levy, has done well to front up to this event just 12 hours after taking out the title with little or no sleep since. I'm glad that Eric is on the table; he's a young gun, and we have something of a connection because he won the Melbourne Championship back in 2006, where I came third. At that time he was arrogant and abrasive but since then he's matured into a fine young man. We became good friends at the high-roller event when he was feeling sick and just couldn't do anything right. I said to him during one of the breaks, 'Just be yourself, mate. Play your own game and don't worry about anything else.' He later told me that those few words uplifted him and he went on to win. He's a fine player, and we have a lot of fun when we play together.

This tournament gives me the chance to play against some good friends, who also all happen to be world-class players, and if things turn out well for me there will be a $50,000 first prize heading to the Shane Warne Foundation. We also have a $5,000 side bet between us that will see the winner take all. These events always challenge me, and I like to raise my game to a different level because you can be sure at a table like this that there'll be no erratic or crazy play. People say these sorts of tournaments are about bragging rights but really, for the pros, it's just another day at the office. Early in play the blinds are $500/$500 and Chris limps in, I raise to $2,000 with 10h-4h, and Grant and Greg call. It's back to Chris and he takes only a few seconds to call. The flop comes 9h-Qh-3h and I think, *How good is this?* I've flopped a flush. Greg and Chris check to me, I make it $5,000, and Grant on the button raises another $12,000. Greg folds and in an instant Chris goes all-in, I call, Grant folds and Chris shows me Ad-Qh. I'm a 74 percent favourite to win, but any heart on the turn or the river will beat me. I stand up and shout, 'Come on Shane Warne Foundation. One time baby,' and the dealer turns over the four of clubs on the turn. The river is the two of clubs, I drag in a huge pot of $218,500 and Chris who's looking shell shocked, is eliminated. The real story of this hand only comes out later when it's revealed that Grant's mucked what would have been the winning hand — a jack high flush.

Soon after Eric raises to $1,500, I call from the big blind with 10s-8d but the flop doesn't help me, so I check and he bets $1,500. There's a lot of banter and I say, "Is that how we're gonna play?" as I muck my cards and Eric shows me trip kings. "I can read your cards even before you even know your cards," I say.

"Come on," he scoffs, and I respond, "That fake bet you used, I invented that while you were still in diapers actually."

Immediately after the dinner break I lead out for $45,000 with As-9d and Brett pushes his remaining chips all-in. I take no time in calling and he shows me Ah-8s and I have him dominated. The flop comes Ad-8d-2h and Brett now how has two pair and is an overwhelming favourite to take the pot down. The turn is the Qh and now I have only three outs, all nines and am going to need a miracle on the river. The dealer flicks over the river, and I look down and see the beautiful nine of hearts, and Brett is eliminated. I'm playing well, and also being helped with a very good run of cards.

The table gets down to three of us with Scotty having $55,000 in chips, Greg, $74,000, and I have a huge $771,000 chip stack. The next hand Scotty goes all-in pre-flop with A-8, Greg gets out of the way, and when I call and turn over a pair of aces Scotty just can't believe it. Even I'm cringing about the remarkable run of cards that's been coming my way. Scotty looks down at his cards and says, 'This is a dead man's hand,' and I respond with, 'If you double up here I couldn't be happier for you.' The flop comes 10-2-10, the turn card's a four and I embrace Scotty and say, 'Thank you, man.' We hear him do an interview with Paul Khoury shortly after: 'Don't worry baby,' he says, 'I'll be back, and maybe I'll play Joe or the Fossilman.' He pauses to laugh, then continues with, 'But I don't like how he looks at me with those snake eyes,' just loud enough for Greg, who's also laughing, to hear.

Greg says to me, 'The poker gods in Australia must be different to the ones back in the States, Joe, because here they're on your side.' Almost as if on cue I peek at my cards and see A-K, and Daniel Negreanu, who's doing the commentary, is totally nonplussed: 'I'm in shock about how many great hands Joe Hachem's getting. He's going to go all-in.' Greg has Qs-Js which is not a bad hand in heads-up and he calls. The flop comes 8h-8c-8s, which is not much help to Greg, and he says, 'How about a nine of spades on the turn? I'm looking for outs.' Unfortunately for him it's a king of diamonds. I finally get to win a major title on home soil and take home a beautiful trophy. More importantly, the kids who are the beneficiaries of the Shane Warne Foundation get $50,000, which gives me an enormous amount of satisfaction.

41

A Hole in My Heart

In 2006 Uncle Vince's wife, Amne, has a medical check up and they find spots on her lungs, which they suspect is lung cancer. For the next 18 months Uncle Vince nurses Amne, doing everything possible to make her comfortable. During this time they hardly miss a weekend barbecue, and while the last thing we want to do is burden them, we want to keep Uncle Vince company and help lift Amne's spirits by showing how much we love her. As soon as I knew the extent of her metastasis I realize there was little possibility of her beating this dreadful cancer, but my Mum and uncles didn't want to accept the futility of her condition and would say, 'She's looking better, I think she's improving,' all the time praying for a miracle. They always held the hope that somehow she'd manage to beat the cancer.

In September 2007 I'm overseas when I get the phone call that I knew was inevitable, and now Uncle Vince is left by himself to raise Dib. I was heartbroken at the passing of Amne and devastated for my uncle. I just can't fathom the reason why this wonderful man has been plagued with so much bad luck.

I can see him fading away and he's terribly depressed. I say to him, 'Uncle, you have to pull yourself together, you have to look after Dib or they'll come and take him away from you.' He rambles on about the US dollar and whether it's up or down, and I realize he is worried about me, concerned the currency fluctuations are eroding my winnings. During this grim time he never asks for anything but instead keeps lecturing me about looking after Mum and my family. What he doesn't understand is that no matter how long I live *I'll* never be able to repay *him* for his kindness, love and guidance.

I'm becoming increasingly stressed about him and since Amne's passing he seems to have lost the will to live. When I raise my concerns he comes out with his famous line, 'I am steel, don't worry about me,' and flexes his arms above his head in the pose of a weightlifter even though by this stage he's sickly skinny and weighs no more than 120 pounds.

He deteriorates further and, despite our insistence, he refuses to let his brother Dib take him to see a doctor. For all his courage and fearlessness Uncle Vince has always been wary of doctors and scared of even a small injection. On Sunday, he instead asks Dib to take him to the chemist where he buys some over-the-counter cough medicine, and tells everyone not to worry about him. The following morning he gets his son ready to go to school and the driver comes to pick Dib up. He usually goes with the driver to school, but on this day Uncle Vince tells him, 'I'm not feeling well this morning. Do you mind dropping Dib off?' and as he closes the front door his lungs collapse, he falls to the floor and he's unable to breathe. I lose my uncle, my father figure, my mentor and my best friend just eight months after he lost his wife. He was only 57 years old.

I've been back from overseas for seven days and this is one of the few times I haven't been to visit him after an international trip. I'm shattered and sick to the core when I hear the shocking news. I feel like I've been robbed; he should have lived for at least another 20 years. I know I'll never be able to complete my mission with him — I'll never be able to pay the massive debt of gratitude I owe him.

Poor Dib doesn't know whether he's coming or going. His autism is so severe that he needs full-time help, and while I wrestle with the thought of adopting him and bringing him into my home, I just can't do it. The responsibility is too much. I decide that Dib is far better off being cared for by professionals who are expert in helping those with chronic autism, and I do what I can financially.

The day I deliver the eulogy is one of the saddest of my life. 'I am who I am today thanks to Khaule Mansour (Uncle Vince). He has been in my life for 42 years and will be there forever, whether he is on Earth or in Heaven. He practically raised Tony and me, but that was only the tip of the iceberg. He loved all his nephews, nieces and cousins with unwavering loyalty. He considered it his mission in life to ensure that all those he loved were okay and doing well. He never ever worried about what was best for him. Never!

'My earliest memory of Khaule Mansour was when I was about five years old, and he punished me for taking an orange from the fruit shop. He made me kneel in the corner for what seemed like hours, making sure I learned my lesson. I did. The many lessons he taught us cost nothing, but in actual fact they were priceless.

'The history of Khaoule Mansour's barbecues goes back to when we lived in Northcote 25 years ago. Every afternoon at about 4pm the barbecue would be lit, then again at 11pm, and usually yet again at 5am. We would come home from night-clubbing only to find Mansour awaiting our arrival before lighting the barbecue and cooking up a feast. The stories are too many to tell here but let it be known that our 70-foot-long wooden fence was eventually sacrificed in the pursuit of the eternal barbecue.'

When Vince passed away on 15 May 2008 he left me with a hole in my heart that will never be filled, and I'm not ashamed to say that I have cried myself to sleep on many nights since that shocking day. The pain and hurt is still raw, and there is never a day when I do not think of him.

42

Ask Your Boss for a Raise

In March 2008 I'm at the Deerfoot Inn and Casino in Calgary, Alberta, Canada to play in the Canadian No-Limit Hold 'em Heads-Up Main Event. There are 64 starters who've each paid $5,000 to enter and the first prize is $100,000. This is one of those rare times when being well known and having a prominent profile doesn't help. I win my first two rounds but in the round of 16 I have to start playing at 1am to fit in with the tournament's television commitments, and while I manage to win and reach the quarter finals, my match doesn't finish until 6.30am and I'm totally stuffed. At noon on the same day I'm back at the table, eyes hanging out of my head, and this is one of the very few times that I can't remember any details of the game; however, I do know I was beaten, finishing in sixth place. I really enjoy the heads-up format and the tournament organizers have done a fine job in promoting and managing the tournament. Huck Seed, who has placed highly in many recent heads-up tournaments, is a deserving winner.

From Calgary I travel down to San Jose to contest the Bay 101 Casino Shooting Star WPT No-Limit Texas Hold 'em Championship. The Bay 101 Shooting Star is a bounty event, which is unique, the only one of its type on the WPT circuit. There are 376 starters and each table has a professional player ('shooting star') who's the bounty. Any player to knock out a bounty gets a $5,000 on-the-spot cash reward and a printed T-shirt inscribed with 'I knocked out Joe Hachem (or whoever the bounty might be) from the Bay 101.'

I'm with Antonio, Phil Laak and Jennifer Tilly, and we grab a cab to the casino. The driver is friendly and talkative and says to me, 'Man, you've gotta get into that poker. You can make a lotta money out of it.'

'Really,' I say. 'Tell me about it.'

'You can play online and you can play tournaments. These guys are always making stacks playing tournaments. Don't go wasting your time playing that casino rubbish, just stick to poker.'

'But I've gotta get the money to do it. How can I do that?'

'When you get home ask your boss for a raise and whatever that raise is, save it for a few months until you've built up a healthy balance, then go and play poker with that. You don't want to be playing with your real money because that's for your life.'

'That's real good advice,' I say, turning to the others in the back. 'When I get back home I'm gonna tell the manager of Starbucks that he has to give me a raise.'

This goes on for about 15 minutes and we're nearing the casino when I say, 'Okay guys, I've got $100 left. I think I should go straight to the poker tables.'

'No!' The driver shouts. 'Don't do that. Save it. Put it away, it's not for today. Go home and get your raise and then come back and play.'

It was so funny — the others even videotaped it — but we never let on to the driver.

This tournament is great fun and I have an absolute ball participating. The casino is packed with the maddest fans I've ever run across, but I say this in the nicest way. They're just so keen and enthusiastic — they literally stalk you in the hallways for a photo or an autograph — and they're also the friendliest and warmest. I can't think of another place where I've been made to feel so welcome.

For the first three days I play very well and build my stack in a steady, controlled manner, never once putting my tournament life at risk. By the start of the fourth day we're down to 20 playing on four tables of five, and I'm about to get into a huge hand against Brandon Cantu, who's already got the scalps of Bill Edler, John Juanda and Phil Laak hanging off his belt. Tournament Director Matt Savage is standing at the table, microphone in hand, television camera next to him, giving a blow-by-blow description of the play. It's just me and Cantu left in the hand, small blind versus big blind, and he's called my pre-flop raise. This is not only tense, hard-fought poker but theater at its absolute best. Matt barks, 'The flop is 9c-6d-5d and Joe Hachem from the small blind bets $20,000, and Brandon Cantu calls from the big blind.' I think Brandon's made a few wild plays and I've been waiting for my chance to trap him. When he calls it's exactly what I thought he'd do. I'm guessing he's got nothing and he'll make his play on the turn by going all-in. Matt continues, 'The turn card is the two of spades, Hachem bets $40,000 and Cantu raises to $150,000.'

I didn't expect that raise, and now I start to second-guess myself — maybe he's got a hand, maybe he's trapping me. I start to go over all the hands he could have from a small straight to a big pair, but in the end the best I can come up with is that he's bluffing and trying to take the pot away from me. I'm sure I've got him. On the other hand, I'm really enjoying this tournament and I'll still have $170,000 if I muck my hand, so I ask myself, *Are you ready to leave?* I'm not, but if I go all-in and win the pot I'll be the chip leader, and another WPT title and the million dollar first prize will beckon — sure it's fun but there's also an awful lot at stake. Decisions, decisions … I know he's pot-committed and will almost certainly call if I move all-in. Nearly four minutes elapses before I finally decide what I'm going to do, and Matt shouts excitedly into his microphone, 'Hachem's all-in!'

Brandon looks as though he's just lost the lottery and throws his hands up in the air saying, 'How much is it?' and the dealer makes an exact count. A moment later Matt yells, 'Cantu calls! Hachem has K-9 for top pair of nines and Cantu has A-6 for a pair of sixes.' My read has been spot on, and I'm a 90 percent favorite to double up and take this monster pot down, but Brandon still has five outs — with any ace or six on the river I'll be sent packing. As is my custom, I walk away from the table and then I hear Matt yell those dreaded words, 'Oh, the river's the ace of diamonds,' and there's a shocked moan from the crowd. I say, 'No, no,' and hold my head in disbelief. I become Brandon's fourth bounty, and a tournament official counts him out $5,000 in cash at the table and gives him another T-shirt. I finish 20th, and as I stand to leave the fans give me a warm round of applause — but my fun in San Jose for 2008 is over. Outwardly, I'm totally calm but I'm so pissed off that you could light cigars off my ear lobes. I walk a few laps around the casino, regain my composure, and return to the table to shake everyone's hand and wish them well.

The only two shooting stars left in the tournament are Jennifer Harman and J. C. Tran, but Brandon Cantu is like a one-man demolition team and wins the next 17 hands, adding the bounty of J. C. to his list on the way to a crushing and well-earned victory.

I take the opportunity to spend some quality time with Antonio and we drive to San Fran where I have one of the best Vietnamese meals of my life, a noodle and rice dish that only costs $10. We also go on a hike across the Golden Gate Bridge — the only way to get a proper perspective of its height and immensity. The views of the bay, the surroundings and Alcatraz are breathtaking, truly making it a day to remember.

After visiting San Fran I can now understand why Mark Twain once said, 'The coldest winter I ever spent was a summer in San Francisco.'

43

Monte Carlo
Releasing the Tension

The European Poker Tour Grand Final, the richest tournament in Europe, takes place in April 2008 at the spectacular Monte Carlo Bay Hotel, which overlooks the Mediterranean Sea and has the beautiful hills of Monte Carlo as a backdrop. There are 842 entrants who have each paid €10,000 for the honor of taking a seat, an investment that will yield €2,020,000 for the winner. Most of the great poker players in the world have entered, including former World Champions and my PokerStars team-mates, Chris Moneymaker and Greg Raymer.

John Duthie launched the televised European Poker Tour in association with PokerStars in 2004 and his brainchild has grown to be Europe's richest poker circuit. John is a well known director of television dramas and a very good poker player in his own right. He won the 2000 Poker Million on television, earning £1 million in doing so, and helped promote the game in the United Kingdom and Europe. He also made the final table of the $3,000 No-Limit Hold 'em event at the 2005 WSOP. This unique man has mixed his entrepreneurial skills with his passion for poker to come up with the EPT, the most prestigious circuit in Europe.

My planning for the event isn't too smart in that I travel for 30 hours to get to Monte Carlo and then have only one day to get over the jet lag and time differences before I'm at the tables playing for more than 12 hours a day. If you could go to bed straight after playing and immediately fall asleep this wouldn't be a problem, but I don't know any professional player who can do this. As a result, I'm tired on the first day, but don't really notice it as I've got gallons of adrenalin pumping through my veins. However, it will eventually catch up with me.

The casino is packed with spectators, friends and relatives, and I get off to a flying start. By midway through Day Three I'm one of the five chip leaders, and there's a real buzz in the room from those who are supporting me and members of my PokerStars team are talking about me adding the EPT Main Event to my CV. I knew stamina and endurance would go a long way towards winning an event like this, but sometimes there are more important priorities in life. In my case, it's my family, and the focus of my travel planning is to always ensure I'm away from home for the least possible amount of time as opposed to making sure I'm fully rested.

Tightness and tension are gripping the tables and you can actually feel the hostility in the air as we near the elimination of the bubble, who'll be out in 81st place. Compounding this tension is the media mass and it seems that there is a reporter, camera man or photographer for each of the 82 remaining players. I've been in this situation many times before and know that once the bubble is eliminated there'll be an outpouring of relief, but that's still a little way off. I get into a huge hand against a young Hungarian, Peter Traply: the community cards are A-6-J-A-3 and I bet €80,000 chips into Peter on the river. He thinks for only a few seconds before calling and showing me A-10. I calmly tap the table and say, 'Nice call, Peter,' as I muck my hand and he drags in a monster pot of €200,000 chips. Then, out of nowhere, this large, well-fed guy who hasn't said a word the whole time we've been playing asks if he can see my cards. I tell him I don't have to show them as the winning hand has already been shown, the dealer agrees, and proceeds to muck them. The guy looks over at me as I'm standing to stretch my legs and says, 'Are you trying to angle shoot or something? Don't be such an asshole.' I can't quite remember the exact words but he also accuses me of being rude to the dealers. For those of you who don't know, the difference between an angle shooter and a cheat is only a matter of degrees, and no one's going to call me a cheat and get away with it. The Aussie 'don't take shit from anyone' mentality and the Lebanese blood combine, and I'm at boiling point when I lunge across the table and give him a withering verbal serve. Fortunately, the EPT doesn't have an f-bomb penalty, but if they did, I wouldn't have been playing for about two days. I don't notice it but players at every table in the casino are on their feet craning their necks to see what's going on — they sure don't need to strain their ears. Antonio rushes over from an adjoining table and jumps on my back and pins my arms to my sides as he drags me away from the table. I swing my head around to see who it is, and Antonio's got a huge grin on his face as if to say, *What are you doing, you donkey?* I feel other arms on me but I'm still struggling to get back to the table to tell him a few more home truths. Security personnel position themselves between me and the table, and after a few more minutes I come to my senses and realize my actions are inappropriate. This guy is never going to amount to anything and I shouldn't have let him get under my skin. I decide it's time to go for a walk, get some fresh air and calm down.

I haven't discussed this little fracas in public since it occurred, but many have said that if Antonio hadn't jumped in I would've decked the guy. That's not true. I was angry, but there's no way I was ever going to throw the first punch. To be honest, in the heat of the moment I would have loved the opportunity to retaliate. I'm a great believer in saying 'please' and 'thank you' to everyone, irrespective of their station in life, and I'm unfailingly courteous to dealers, even when they accidentally muck aces on me. Everyone deserves unconditional respect until they do something to lose that respect, and I expect the same in return. I'm never going to subserviently take crap from anyone. I've got a healthy ego and a lot of pride. I don't think I'm any better than anyone else, but don't let anyone think they're better than me. In retrospect, I should have conveyed the same message I sent to this guy with a little less emotion — alright, a lot less emotion.

That evening over a cold beer, Antonio says to me, with a huge smile on his face, 'You know, all you did today was give that loser his 15 minutes of fame.'

'Yeah.'

'You donkey.'

'It sure released a lot of tension from the room,' I say, grinning.

'Yeah.' Antonio laughs, rolling his eyes to the ceiling.

The following morning I talk to one of the reporters whose photographer has managed to capture me in full flight the prior day. I have to say that they're very, very ugly photos — so ugly they make me laugh and I ask him to email copies to me.

Later in the day I'm on a table with Robin Keston bemoaning the fact that I haven't had a pair for ages, and in a flash he's taking the piss out of me. 'You sound like my wife,' he says. 'You're going to whine yourself to the final table.'

'It's the only thing I can do to keep myself awake,' I say, laughing, but I'm totally spent, and I can feel the exhaustion overtaking me. Robin's a Pom, so he probably knows an awful lot about whining, but he's also a good bloke who gets on well with us Aussies because he has a great sense of humor.

We've already been at it for more than 12 hours and I feel totally stuffed, but know we won't finish until we have a final table. I've been bleeding chips for the past five hours and the cards have turned cold on me. I have 10-6 and when the flop comes 10-4-3 I'm all-in; Isaac Baron, a talented young Californian player, calls in an instant, showing me J-10 and I'm in big trouble. The turn card is a five, which provides me with a glimmer of hope, and eight more outs. I now need a two, six or seven if I'm to survive. There's been a million times when I would have loved the river to be an ace, but when the dealer turns one over I'm busted out in 11th place. I am so disappointed once again, another major title has slipped through my fingers, but all I can do is get up and get ready for the next battle.

🐃

I'm back in Vegas for the WSOP in June 2008 where I finish 35th and in the money in the Pot-Limit Omaha Hi/Lo or Better, and 23rd in the H.O.R.S.E. I'm the bubble, or close to the bubble, in another seven tournaments but there's no cigar. By the time I get to the Main Event I'm annoyed that I haven't been able to get anything going. My cards are cold, but I hang in there and make it through the first day hoping things will improve the next day. They don't, I'm card dead, and am eliminated before the day is out. It's been a very frustrating series for me.

I return to Vegas just before Christmas to play in the Five Diamond at the Bellagio, and as I didn't play in 2007, I consider that I'm defending the title I won in 2006. There are 497 players who each paid $15,000 to enter, the first prize is $1,538,730, and the top 100 players will make it to the money. It's late afternoon on the third day, I'm struggling and need to build my stack or get out. I haven't had a big hand for ages when I look down at my hole cards and a beautiful pair of kings is smiling up at me. The blinds are $2,000/$4,000 and the antes $500. I raise to $10,000 from early position, a player in late position calls, and the button, Robert Mizrachi, raises to $40,000. In a heartbeat I'm all-in, the caller folds and Robert calls, turning over Ad-Kd. When the caller mucks his cards he accidentally flips them over and we see A-J, and I think, *Great, there are only two aces in the deck to help Robert.* As seems to often be the way in this situation, the first card in the flop is an ace, and it's *arrivederci* for me. I finish 106th, just six out of the money. I'm not worried about the money and I walk away from the table thinking, *I played well, but it just wasn't my day.*

44

The Aussie Millions
A Love–Hate Relationship

On 14 January 2009, Crown Casino puts on a magnificent welcoming party at Breezes restaurant for players in the Aussie Millions. It's more than a welcoming party, though: it's a celebration of the Australian Poker Hall of Fame and the induction of inaugural inductees.

Breezes is packed to the rafters, the waiters and waitresses are making sure that no one goes hungry, the drinks are flowing freely, and there's a great band who are belting out *We Can Be Heroes*. Crown has also organized for snake handlers to be in attendance and there are snakes, a crocodile and large lizards on display. It's a fabulous atmosphere, everyone is enjoying themselves and the night is a credit to Crown.

The Hall of Fame is the brainchild of Maurie 'The Master' Pears, the former head of PokerNetwork and a player, ambassador and promoter of poker in Australia for more than forty years. His stated aim is a long-time desire to honor and set in stone those poker players, casinos and promoters who've done so much to bring the game to the standard of excellence that it is today. The Poker Hall of Fame in the USA was established in 1979 and since then some 33 players have been inducted. Now, with the help and support of the Crown Casino, Poker Network and Bluff Australasia, we have our own Australian Poker Hall of Fame. In Maurie's words, 'More than 25 years have passed since the first hands of tournament poker were dealt in an Australian casino, so it's long overdue for us to induct "the best of the best" and honor their achievements.'

Jonno Pittock and former triple world boxing champion Jeff Fenech make the inductions to Billy 'The Croc' Argyros, Gary Benson, Antanas 'Tony G' Gouga, Mel Judah, Jeff Lisandro, Lee Nelson and yours truly.

The last-minute surprise inductee is Maurie Pears himself, and no one is more deserving of the honor than Maurie who's the doyen of poker Down Under. In talking about poker in Australia, he says, 'We've come to the second-largest poker game in the world, the Aussie Millions, and its about time we had our own Hall of Fame to celebrate our own champions.'

I become the recipient of a great honor when I'm also inducted as the inaugural Legend in the Australian Poker Hall of Fame. Jonno Pittock tells a warming story about the buzz that went around the Crown Poker Room at the time of my victory in 2005. 'You could've cut the air with a knife when I announced over the PA system that Joe had won the Main Event. It was like we'd all won it.'

In my speech, I say, 'I just happened to be the guy in the right place at the right time. Some of the guys who are my fellow inductees have been developing the game and been in the game a lot longer than what I have and I feel honored to be with them. I'm just happy to be the guy who won at the right time and, you know, kicked off the boom.'

The Aussie Millions main event played at Crown has never

been won by a local and at the launch of the 2009 tournament I throw down the challenge to my compatriots and say, 'I think it's about time an Aussie took home the title. Come on, get your acts together.' There are 681 starters and first prize is AU$2 million, which is a far cry from 74 entries and total prize money of AU$74,000, as it was when the tournament was first played in 1998 under the name 'Australasian Poker Championship'. It's now the richest tournament in the Southern Hemisphere and a number of international professionals have traveled Down Under to contest it including Scotty Nguyen, Chris Ferguson and Erik Seidel, to name just a few. Quite simply, it is one of the best tournaments in the world, and I've watched it grow like a small child from humble beginnings to the world-class event that it is today. Australia is a long way from the rest of the world and initially the pros and international players only came Down Under for the novelty or a 'one off' travel experience. Now they say, 'We can't wait to come back next year, we love Australia, everyone in Melbourne is so friendly and the tournament and its management are great.' When I hear comments like this my chest fills with pride, and they add to the burning hunger within me to win my national tournament.

The venue, Crown Casino, cannot be surpassed anywhere in the world and has something for everyone, including small-stakes poker games for novices to very high stakes games for the more experienced players. Add a brilliantly planned poker room that has 65 world-class tables, run so professionally by Jonno Pittock and his crew, and you have a haven for poker players. And then there's the luxurious accommodation, friendly staff, fine restaurants, a ten-pin bowling alley, fashion boutiques, movie theatres and the famous VIP room, all of which make for an unforgettable experience.

I have a love–hate relationship with the Aussie Millions — I love it, and it hates me. I've never made the final table but nearly every time I've played it I've got into a zone, and felt bullet-proof and invincible only to crash out shortly thereafter. Over the years I've had more than my fair share of bad beats, and the one time I got close, I played one hand badly and that was the end of me.

In 2007, I'm coming off winning the Five Diamond and going deep in the Bahamas. I'm playing some of my best poker when the tournament gets underway. Again I've got ahead of myself and it doesn't matter how well I'm playing, once this tournament starts it has its own special way of belting me around. True to form, by the end of the first day I'm severely short-stacked with only $4,000 in chips, and I've had to battle, scrimp and save to still be alive at the close of play. I'm battered and bruised but continue to fight and claw my way back into the tournament, and not only make it to the fourth day, but start to see some daylight. The blinds are $6,000/$12,000 and I have $240,000 in chips in front of me when I make it $35,000 with A-10; it folds around to the small blind, who pops it up to $80,000. I call for $45,000 deciding I'm going to go with my hand if I have any piece of the flop. The flop comes K-10-8 and my opponent, who I've never seen before and who I don't have a read on, puts me all-in for $160,000. Shit! Somehow I convince myself that he has me dead with A-K or perhaps aces or kings, and I fold. This is a dreadful play and if I was going to fold after flopping the ten what was I ever doing playing the hand in the first place? This play began my demise and I just couldn't win a hand after it. I am eventually knocked out in 23rd place.

In 2006, I go all-in with A-K and when my opponent, who has me covered, turns over K-Q. I'm a raging hot favorite to double up. Incredibly, he hits a diamond on the river for a four-card flush and I'm busted out in the bubble.

Last year I made a great start and at the end of the first day. I'm in the top-ten chip leaders along with Phil Ivey and Andy Black. I then get into a big hand against Peter Ling, who gets the better of me with a pair of aces when I've got queens and I lose $40,000 in chips. We then get moved to the television table and in one of the early hands, Peter raises from under the gun, I call from the button with 3c-5c and Phil Ivey calls from the small blind. The flop comes 7-3-3 with two spades, Phil checks, Peter bets $15,000 and I make it $40,000. Phil folds, and Peter spends a long time thinking about it before putting me all-in with 6-6. When he sees my trips he looks very seedy. The turn is the jack of spades and I glance over at his cards, see the six of spades, and think, *Don't do it to me again. Please don't do it to me again. Not another four-card flush.* Almost as if preordained, the dealer flips over the two of spades and my 2008 tournament is over. I can still spit the dummy with the best of them (in private) but in public I pride myself on my composure. This is just too much, though, and I slam my fist into the table, curse Crown, curse my cards and I'm outta there, leaving only expletives behind. It's only when I cool down that I find out that the cameras weren't rolling for my little performance and I breathe a massive sigh of relief.

My desire to be the first Aussie to win the Aussie Millions is overwhelming, and while many locals have made the final table over the years, none has won it. In fact, I can think of nothing more important than winning my national championship, especially when it's being held in what I see as my own backyard. How great would it be for me to claim it in 2009? I can't help wondering if it's just waiting for me to be the Aussie who finally breaks through and wins it. I've always thought that if and when I make it to the final table, I'll definitely take it down.

I make it through to the third day when I look down to see Qs-Qc, and the small blind raises to $5,700 pre-flop. I go all-in from the big blind for $35,000. He calls and turns over Ah-8h, and I'm a 68 percent favorite to win, but when the flop comes Ac-7s-5s, I'm a massive underdog. The turn card is the nine of spades and my odds improve slightly. I can win with a queen or any spade, but it's not to be, and when the river's a six of clubs, that's the end of my tournament for 2009. It's been another disappointing Aussie Millions for me but when former chef and IT expert Stewart Scott dominates the tournament to become the first Australian winner, it's some consolation. Maybe someone higher up was listening to my speech when I threw the gauntlet down to my fellow Aussies. Congratulations Stewart, well done, and let's hope your win opens the floodgates for more local winners.

I'll never be the first Australian to win the Aussie Millions but I'm no less determined to add it to my CV. Perhaps in 2010 it'll return some of the love I've given to it over the years.

45

Warney

I first met Shane Warne early in 2007. To those readers in the U.S. who haven't heard of him, he's the Michael Jordan of world cricket, a living legend in Australia and all cricketing nations. Until his recent retirement, large crowds flocked to sporting arenas around the globe just to see him play. In fact, many believe him to be the greatest cricketer ever to have played the game. Off the field he's larger than life, with a mop of blonde hair, a perpetually cheeky grin, and is commonly known in Australia by his nickname, 'Warney'. The only thing that's bigger than Shane's sporting reputation and achievements is his heart. He's kind, generous and has that critical quality that's so important to me: loyalty to his mates through thick and thin.

Like many sportsmen around the world he's a compulsive poker fan, and since retiring from cricket he's been playing in tournaments at home in Australia and internationally. In fact, we've played in a number of the same tournaments in Australia, the UK and the US. Shane is not one to do things by half measures.

We hit it off instantly and I discover that he founded and is chairman of the Shane Warne Foundation, a charity that supports seriously ill and underprivileged children and teenagers in Australia. I couldn't have met Shane at a better time, because just then I was looking for a charity or worthy cause that I could actively help and support. When he invited me to join the foundation as one of only two patrons (the other patron is Russell Crowe) I was thrilled and couldn't say yes quickly enough. Poker is so much like life and sometimes you can get a bad beat through no fault of your own. With the Shane Warne Foundation we try to even the score for those children in need.

We bounce a few ideas off each other about how we're going to raise some badly needed funds and eventually come up with the Joe Hachem & Shane Warne Annual Poker Tournament, a $1,000 buy-in with unlimited re-buys and a $25,000 first prize. With the generous help of Crown and other sponsors, the inaugural event is held on 30 November 2007. It's not just a poker night, though, and we auction off some great 'money can't buy' items, including a 'walk-on role' in Hugh Jackman's latest movie, *Wolverine*

Each of the six players at the final table is guaranteed $5,000, but there's a twist: Shane and I join the table to keep the finalists honest. It's a marvelous night attended by Russell Crowe and other local celebrities, and we end up raising $250,000 for the Shane Warne Foundation. My involvement with this fine organization gives me the opportunity that I've been looking for to give something back to the community.

In 2008, Wild Turkey sponsors the Joe Hachem & Shane Warne Charity Poker Event, and we get a huge number of celebrities supporting it including Tony G, Billy 'The Croc' Argyros, Jeff Fenech, Kevin Muscat, Brian McFadden and numerous current and former star Australian Rules footballers. It is such a success that we take bookings for 200 guests for next year's event before the night is over, which is fantastic considering that at the inaugural tournament the previous year we limited the number of entrants to 120. I have no doubt that this extremely worthwhile event has cemented its place on Melbourne's celebrity calendar, and it's something that Shane and I take a lot of pride in.

46

7 February 2009
Black Saturday

As I'm finishing the *Pass the Sugar* manuscript, my beautiful home state of Victoria is struck by the worst and most horrific tragedy in its history.

On 20 January 2009 the mercury climbs to 105 degrees (40.5°C), followed by three unbearable days from the 28th to the 30th of January where maximum temperatures hover between 110 (43.5°C) and 113 degrees (45.1°C). Railway lines buckle, the power systems break down causing black-outs across thousands of houses, and many senior citizens lose their lives, unable to cope with the extreme heat. The state is as dry as tinder; lawns that were green only a few weeks earlier are parched yellow, and golf courses look like arid deserts. There are outbreaks of fire in the country and the Country Fire Authority is hard-pressed to contain them.

Drought conditions have existed for years and it hasn't rained in the five weeks leading up to Saturday, 7 February. Weather warnings for that day are scary and the forecast is for severe temperatures, northerly winds and extreme fire danger. There is a total fire ban across the state but before the day is over it will become an inferno with temperatures soaring to an all-time record of nearly 116 degrees (46.4°C). Over 170 men, women and children lose their lives that day, 2000 homes are destroyed, and a million native animals die. The small and beautiful town of Marysville is decimated by fireballs, and the radiant heat is so oppressive that buildings literally explode before the flames. It's a tragedy on a massive scale accompanied by incredible acts of heroism. Seasoned fire fighters later say that they have often seen fires fly up the sides of mountains, but never before have they seen them hurtle down the other side with the same fury. In the aftermath of Black Saturday the police launch investigations into many fires that they say were deliberately lit.

A few days after Black Saturday I travel to the regional Victorian towns of Whittlesea and Kinglake with Shane Warne and some Australian Rules football stars to provide whatever moral support we can. Kinglake is the worst-affected area with more than 1,000 houses being lost. It's eerie to see mile after mile of trees completely burnt out: the once-splendid, fully-leafed trees are now no more than black match sticks protruding from the ash-covered ground.

There are 7000 Victorians without roofs over their heads and the Red Cross springs into action, launching a Bushfire Appeal. Politicians, sports people and average Aussies get behind it and dig deep into their pockets. Media personality Eddie Maguire and TV network Channel Nine support the appeal with a telethon where, along with a number of Australians, I help man the phones. Aussies give generously and donations are even received from residents in Townsville, some 1650 miles away in North Queensland, which is remarkable, as it's coping with its own crippling flood disaster. More than $300 million dollars is raised, an incredible response for a country with a population of only 20 million.

Michelle Stott, marketing manager for PokerStars in Australia, and I are anxious to make some tangible contribution to the bushfire relief effort so we set up an online tournament in which I will play. Of the $32 entry free, $16 goes into the pool and the other $16 goes to the appeal, which PokerStars very generously agree to match dollar for dollar. In our anxiety to do something for the fire victims we have rushed the tournament, and while we get 452 starters and raise nearly $15,000, many people log on while I'm playing and tell me how disappointed they are that they didn't know about it, so we are planning another event. I'm knocked out of my tournament in 24th place, but I'm not concerned in the slightest. I've really enjoyed myself and there's been a lot of banter during the afternoon. More importantly, we've raised some badly needed money for the bushfire appeal. It's times like these that I'm grateful to be able to put my celebrity status to good use.

47

Mentoring the Next Poker Star

One of my ultimate goals is to bring poker into good stead, make sure it has a good reputation and to grow it in Australia and internationally. I work on this on an ongoing basis but it's not just confined to poker played in casinos and online. I'd like to see it played in more homes. It's such a social game where, when you're playing with your mates, you can put in as little as $20 and sit around eating pizza, drinking beer and having fun in the knowledge that no one's going to lose their shirt or get upset.

From a professional perspective I'm looking to promote poker as a game or, as I prefer to describe it, a sport, where we get major sponsorship onboard and a professional tour. I also enjoy public speaking, holding seminars, and providing advice on websites, all with the intent of making poker more popular and mainstream.

When Lee Nelson, the 2006 Aussie Millions Champion, approached me to collaborate with him in setting up World Poker Seminars, I was more than happy to get involved. It's Lee's brain-child and its purpose is to educate and teach all levels of poker players in Australasia and Asia the finer points and strategies of the game. I've been teaching right from my early university days when I used to lecture nurses about the mechanics of our bodies, so it's only a small jump to teaching the mechanics of poker. Our inaugural seminar is held at the APPT SkyCity Festival of Poker in Auckland in October 2008. It runs for nearly 12 hours and, in addition to Lee and me, poker professionals Tony Dunst, Tysen Streib and Dennis Waterman make presentations, coach one-on-one and answer questions. We get great participation from the attendees and the feedback at the close is all positive.

The success of our initial seminar has motivated me to consider reactivating CardAcademy.com, a site I helped found and in which I was heavily involved up until late 2007.

Three years ago I was in Barcelona chewing the fat with Emad when I came up with the bones of an idea that I know will give poker a huge boost in Australia if I can get it off the ground. I refine my thoughts and then begin approaching television stations with the concept for a show that would center around finding Australia's next poker star. *The Apprentice* and *Big Brother meet poker* best describes the show's broad outline. I'll take eleven carefully selected applicants on a poker journey with me, and each week one will be eliminated until we're left with a winner who'll get to experience first-hand, life on the world poker circuit while being tutored and counseled one-on-one by me. The television stations seem very interested but at the time they're not convinced that the public is ready for this type of show. Michelle and PokerStars are great supporters of the concept and generously decide to sponsor the show. This is the catalyst for getting it off the ground and we enter into a contract with Channel Ten.

People may not believe it, but playing poker imitates life. Often you find yourself on an out-of-control rollercoaster where the highs are exhilarating and unbelievable, while the lows are so deep they take you to places that you didn't know existed. One of the qualities I hope to ingrain in the rookie is the means by which he or she can tame that wild rollercoaster, because this is fundamental to an elite poker player's success.

My goal is to produce a show of excellence that will be entertaining for viewers and rewarding for contestants. After that, I'd like to host a show with Shane Warne in which we invite celebrities to play poker with all of the proceeds going to charity. Poker is so popular in Australia now that I'm sure a show like this would attract viewers, be successful, and help the underprivileged in our community.

Time has flown since that heady Saturday morning at the Horseshoe where my life changed forever with that beautiful 6h-5d-4d flop. Poker has been so good to me and there's hardly a day that goes by when I don't think how lucky I am. By the same token, the demands on my time are never-ending, and striking a balance between family, friends and poker can sometimes prove taxing. We always tend to think that our neighbors' fields are greener and I know that many aspire to and envy my post-2005 WSOP lifestyle. I'm certainly not complaining, but aspirants should be aware that I work incredibly hard promoting the sport of poker and that one of the downsides of success is an almost complete lack of privacy. Achieving the success that I have had is one thing, but maintaining it takes a lot more work. My priorities have never changed in life: my family comes first. I want my tombstone to read, *Joe Hachem was a great husband and father*; this is far more important to me than any success I might enjoy on the green felt. But that is not to say that I wouldn't like to be even more successful at the poker tables. In fact, I recently had a dream about the all-time money winners and my name was at the top of the list with $13,683,000. After my Letterman dream on the way to Los Angeles I'm hardly likely to ignore this one, and only time will tell if it, too, will come true.

I have so many goals still to achieve — winning the Aussie Millions and another bracelet at the 2009 WSOP are on my radar — but my major project this year is to unearth and mentor the next poker star from Down Under.

I hope you enjoyed my story as much as I have enjoyed living it. Next time you drag in a big pot, remember to yell out "Pass the Sugar!"

My Seven Golden Rules:

1. Family is forever, everything else comes and goes.

2. Be disciplined enough to throw away a bad hand quickly.

3. Manage your bankroll. Bad money management is the number one reason people go broke.

4. Listen to your gut, it's almost always right.

5. Get back up and fight on regardless of how many times you get knocked down. That's what separates champions from chumps.

6. Be patient enough to wait for the good hands, disciplined enough to play your position and courageous enough to follow your convictions.

7. When the rabbit has the gun ... run.

Afterword

Peter Ralph

In July, 2008 I was contacted by my publisher, David Tenenbaum, and asked if I'd like to help Joe Hachem write his autobiography. I write business themed suspense fiction, and I just didn't think I had the level of poker expertise to be of any help, so I declined. When I told my eldest son, Peter, what I'd done, he said, 'Are you mad, Dad, don't you know how big this guy is?' I, of course, knew who Joe was, I think every Aussie did, and the television footage of him wrapping himself up in the Australian flag is an enduring image.

Six weeks went by and David phones me again, and asks me if I'd like to meet Joe at Crown Casino. David has given him one of my novels, he's read and enjoyed it, and thinks I might be okay. When we meet he's charming and very easy to like, but I also let him know of my reservations. He's tells me not to worry, that he'll handle anything to do with the finer points of poker, and his confidence rubs off on me and I become quite keen to get involved. I phone David later that day to ask him how long it'll be before we'll know whether Joe needs me to help. He says something like, 'You're in, if he hadn't liked you he would've told you then and there.' Later that day, to provide me with some background, he sends me notes on playing poker that Joe has written, and they're very impressive.

As a prelude to our first meeting about the book I decide to do some research about Joe on Google and when I type his name in I get more than 225,000 hits. Far out! During that first meeting he gives me a quick lesson on the skill element of Hold 'em when he says, 'Pete, if we played a hand now you could beat me, and you may even get lucky over fifteen minutes and if you got really really lucky you might even be ahead after half an hour. However if we played for four hours I'd own your house, your car and all of your bank accounts.' If given the opportunity to play against him I think I'll pass.

He also needs to be in control — of everything! He's out in the kitchen after he's put his house on the market, and he says to the agent, 'Have we got a plan?'

'Yes, we've got a plan?'

We leave Jeanie with the agent and go into the study near the front door. As Jeanie's showing him out, Joes looks up and says, 'You have a plan?'

'Yes, I have a plan.'

'Good.'

I see Jeanie take a quick glance over at Joe and start to slip away, but she's too late. 'What's the plan, hon?' All this took place in less than two minutes.

We're on a tight deadline and he is regularly overseas so in lieu of face to face we have Skype sessions, but I can always hear the keyboard going while we're talking and know exactly what he's doing — playing online poker on PokerStars. When I'm at his home he sits in front of a large screen regularly playing three tournaments at once while talking to me and taking phone numerous calls.

When we struggle over a word he'll say 'Come on Pete, help me,' or worse, 'Have you got it, genius?' This is a monumental misuse of the word, genius, and invariably he comes up with the word himself anyway. One day I ask him if he uses a Thesaurus when he writes, and he grins at me like I've asked the most absurd question before responding, 'I don't have the patience, Pete, and besides if I can't think of the word it doesn't exist.' I laugh every time I think about this outrageous comment. The fact is that Joe's articulate and a natural writer … the only reason he needed any help was because of his poker commitments. There was just no way for him to find the time to take on the task by himself. He's also a natural on television and it's difficult to believe that he had no training when he did his first ever television interview on the Jay Leno Show.

Some of the chapters and hands are easy, but the first hand Joe plays against Scott Lazar takes four sessions before he's happy we've got it right — this for one paragraph. The chapters about Elei and Uncle Vince are really tough, and Joe becomes very emotional and choked up as we struggle to get the words on paper.

My youngest son, Ben, is one of Joe's biggest fans and when he's playing on PokerStars he always has a separate screen open on Joe, so he can see how he's playing. When the Bushfire Appeal tournament's on he's determined to make it deep enough into the tournament to be on a table with Joe and sends him a message, 'Take it easy on me, Joe, I'm Peter Ralph's son,' and gets the response, 'Now I'm more determined than ever to bust you.'

Joe has an idyllic and enviable home life but his business/ poker playing life is something else. He gets more than a hundred emails every day, numerous phone calls, attends many meetings, has online and live poker commitments, and works extremely hard. If there's a downside to being famous it's the complete loss of privacy. It's fortunate that he loves poker and likes people and someone asking for an autograph will never experience that legendary temper no matter how stressed he is — with these people he is always warm and genuinely likes making them feel better about themselves.

Meeting and getting to know Joe over the past nine months has been both a pleasure and great experience, but I think I'll stick to the money markets rather than becoming a 'rabbit' on the poker tables. Yes I knew Joe had won the 2005 World Championship and the $7.5m back in 2005 — what I didn't know was how big that achievement really was.

Joe is one of only four poker players in the world to ever win the WSOP Main Event and a World Poker Tour Title, but he is totally without airs or pretence. He doesn't differentiate between the car park attendant and his corporate connections — everyone is treated the same — with cordiality, humility and good grace.

Any errors, oversights or mistakes are mine, and were probably made when Joe was taking down a big pot online.

Bibliography

Brunson, Doyle. *Super/System*. B&G, Las Vegas, 1979.

Cloutier, T.J & McEvoy, Tom. *Championship No-Limit & Pot-Limit Hold'Em*. Cardoza Publishing, New York, 2004.

Harrington, Dan & Robertie, Bill. *Harrington on Hold'em*. Two Plus Two Publishing LLC, Nevada, 2004

McManus, James. *Positively Fifth Street*. Farrar, Strauss & Giroux, New York, 2003.